Colin McEvedy

# The New Penguin Atlas of Ancient History

*Maps devised by the author and drawn by David Woodroffe*

PENGUIN BOOKS

Title-page illustration: a silver coin minted *c.* 500 BC at Acragas, a Greek colony in Sicily
(Artist: David Woodroffe)

Also by Colin McEvedy

*The New Penguin Atlas of Medieval History*
*The Penguin Atlas of Modern History*
*The New Penguin Atlas of Recent History*
*The Penguin Atlas of African History*

PENGUIN BOOKS

Published by the Penguin Group
Penguin Books Ltd, 80 Strand, London WC2R 0RL, England
Penguin Group (USA) Inc., 375 Hudson Street, New York, New York 10014, USA
Penguin Group (Canada), 10 Alcorn Avenue, Toronto, Ontario, Canada M4V 3B2
(a division of Pearson Penguin Canada Inc.)
Penguin Ireland, 25 St Stephen's Green, Dublin 2, Ireland
(a division of Penguin Books Ltd)
Penguin Group (Australia), 250 Camberwell Road,
Camberwell, Victoria 3124, Australia (a division of Pearson Australia Group Pty Ltd)
Penguin Books India Pvt Ltd, 11 Community Centre,
Panchsheel Park, New Delhi – 110 017, India
Penguin Group (NZ), cnr Airborne and Rosedale Roads, Albany,
Auckland 1310, New Zealand (a division of Pearson New Zealand Ltd)
Penguin Books (South Africa) (Pty) Ltd, 24 Sturdee Avenue,
Rosebank 2196, South Africa

Penguin Books Ltd, Registered Offices: 80 Strand, London WC2R 0RL, England

www.penguin.com

First published 1967
Second edition 2002
15  14  13  12  11

Copyright © Colin McEvedy, 1967, 2002
All rights reserved

The moral right of the author has been asserted

Typseset in 'TheAntiqua B'
Manufactured in China by South China Printing Co. Ltd

ISBN : 978-0140-51348-6

*Contents*

# Introduction

This atlas has the same general aims as the companion volume on Medieval History already published as a Penguin: the thesis behind it is that there is a valid unit of study in the area comprised by Europe, the southern coast of the Mediterranean and the Near East. Accordingly, the geographical framework is held constant and the changes of people and state are projected on this background in a series of diagrams of constant scale. The book is, I hope, sufficiently well ordered to be useful as a work of reference, but its primary purpose is to present as a coherent story the origin and evolution of the historic cultures of Europe and the Near East up to the fourth century AD.

These cultures form a single interacting system because they were isolated from the rest of the world. The isolation was not complete – there were gaps in the geographical barriers that ringed them round – but in any given generation only a tiny minority will have journeyed in or out of the area. For all practical purposes this part of the human race – and it is an important part, never less than a third of the world's population – worked out its destiny without reference to, or contributions by, any other part of the globe.

The geographical elements that boxed in the Europe–Near East community are the Arctic Ocean in the north, the Atlantic Ocean in the west, and the Sahara Desert and Arabian Sea in the south. On the eastern side there are no absolute boundaries: in the northern part we have the Ural Mountains, the traditional boundary of Europe, and in the south the various mountain ranges that separate India from the rest of Asia, but both are permeable, and between them there is a wide open gap through which people could and did move freely. So we need to look at this side of the box – and also a fuzzy area at the eastern end of the Sahara – in rather more detail.

Take the African section first. Here we have a clear case of leakage in the shape of the Nile, which runs right across the Sahara and is inhabited, though sometimes very sparsely, along its entire length. For much of our period the Saharan stretch is the seat of the Kingdom of Kush, clearly an appendage of the Ancient Near East and, as such, demanding inclusion in it. Our boundary therefore dips south of the Sahara at this point and follows the Blue Nile into the Abyssinian massif. From there it runs round to the Arabian Sea, reaching the coast some distance south of Cape Gardafui. The question we have to face is whether there was any movement from the south into Kush, Abyssinia or Somalia. This seems unlikely because the population pressure was all the other way. We know that Nilo-Saharan

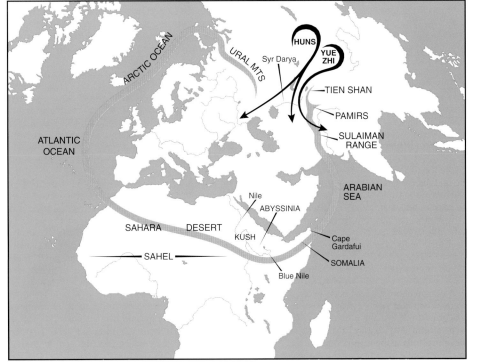

**Fig. 1** *The boundaries of the Europe-Near East area*
There were only two intrusions into the area during the period covered by the Atlas, both by nomadic peoples using the Central Asian gap. The Yuezhi moved in during the second century BC, then out again, into India, during the second century AD. The Huns arrived from the Altai region in the fourth century AD.

5

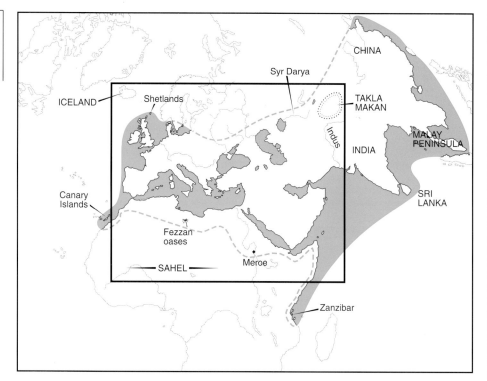

**Fig. 2** *The base map used in the Atlas (black rectangle) and, in blue, the world as known to the classical geographer Claudius Ptolemy*

which is reassuring as it was here that Alexander the Great founded Alexandria Eschate ('Alexandria the Furthest', modern Chojend) and turned his army round. Here, it was reckoned, civilization ended and another world began.

Now we have defined the Europe–Near East area, we can set about making an efficient base map for it. We don't want any more of the surrounding oceans than is necessary and we don't need the far north where nothing ever happens. What we do want is the Mediterranean and Near East arranged on the map's horizontal axis. The best way of bringing this about is to use a conical projection, as in Figs. 1 and 2. This brings the long axis of the Mediterranean, and a prolongation of this line running to the head of the Persian Gulf, up to the horizontal. It also means that we get interesting glimpses into the worlds adjacent to our own. We can see the topmost part of sub-Saharan Africa, the Sahel, the southern shore of the great sand sea. We can see the nearest part of India, the Indus Valley. And we get a good view of the sector of the steppe beyond the Syr Darya, plus all of its desert annexe, the Takla Makan. There is little that we don't need, Iceland being the obvious example: it was unknown and uninhabited during our period. The sole disadvantage of the projection is that it puts a bit of a spin on the cardinal points. They are near enough normal in the left hand part of the map but they rotate in an anti-clockwise direction the further you go to the right. By the time you have reached the right hand margin, east is pointing to 2 o'clock instead of 3.

The next stage is to get the history on to the base map. For this we need a coherent system of representing the different peoples and nations involved. There is only one classifying system that meets our needs, the linguistic tree developed over the last hundred years or more, which puts the different ethno-linguistic groups into meaningful clusters. As far as our map is concerned there are nine of these, with a tenth appearing right at the end of our period, in the fourth century AD. The nine

and Cushitic peoples spread out into the Sahel and down the Somali coast: there is no evidence of any reflux movement. So this sector of our boundary, which at first sight looked a bit dodgy, comes good.

The eastern side of the box can't be closed as securely. The ancient and correspondingly eroded Urals are not a significant barrier, and though the mountains along the north-west frontier of India are new and formidable, there are many ways through them. Exemplifying that is the fact that the native peoples living either side of these ranges were the same: Uralians in the case of the Urals, Elamo-Dravidians in the case of the Indian mountains. Subsequently, as people settled down, Iran and India did develop different identities, suggesting that for agricultural societies the barrier between the two was more effective. The same cannot be said for the Urals. The saving grace here is that the role of the Uralians in early European history is so passive, and their numbers so few, that whether they moved back and forth through their mountains matters not at all. The Uralian zone was politically inert and it is unimportant where we draw our line across it.

This brings us to the final section, the Central Asian gap. There is no barrier to movement here, and once techniques had been evolved for living in this semi-arid region, people were free to come and go as they liked. Whatever line we draw is going to be arbitrary so we may as well take the shortest, from the Urals to the Pamirs. For much of its length this line parallels the Syr Darya, the ancient Jaxartes, are put in their geographical homelands in Fig. 3, dated (somewhat earlier than most linguists would approve of) at 6000 BC. At the top is the Uralic group of which Finnic and Magyar (Hungarian) are the best known today, though it is also still spoken by some of the peoples in the original homeland area. Below Uralic comes Indo-European, the progenitor of nearly all the other European languages, and of Farsi (Persian) and Hindi too. To the west and south of Indo-European is a somewhat hypothetical West Mediterranean group. The sole surviving member is Basque, known in classical times as Iberian, and to make a group out of it you have to add in Etruscan. As we can't understand the

Etruscan language this may seem over-bold, but it is generally conceded that if it was Indo-European we should be able to – Etruscan inscriptions are relatively numerous, they are in a straightforward, fully deciphered alphabetic script, and there are even a few bilinguals – and if it has any relatives at all Basque is the best bet. Sceptics should consider the way similar problems with the Caucasian group have been sorted out. Not so long ago Caucasian was a purely geographical construct, consisting of several dozen apparently unrelated languages. Now these have all been put in one or other of two genetically related groups, South Caucasian (Kartvelian), of which the best known representative is Georgian,

and North Caucasian, of which the most familiar at the moment is probably Chechen. The map anticipates the day when these two are united to form the single unit that their proximity demands. Recent work is also responsible for the next group, Elamo-Dravidian, a splendid creation which links the Elamite language, the earliest we know of in Iran, via the Brahui tongue still spoken in Baluchistan (western Pakistan) to the Dravidian languages of South India. This allows us to fill in a useful-sized segment of our map, and tells us what sort of people the Indo-Europeans were replacing as they moved east and south-east into Iran and India. The sixth group, Afro-Asiatic, is long established (it used to be known as Hamito-Semitic) and has an uncontested homeland spreading out from Arabia across North Africa and the western side of the Red Sea. The seventh, Nilo-Saharan, is perhaps not entirely kosher, but as it is marginal to our interest, this needn't concern us too much. The eighth, Niger-Congo, the stem for many of the languages of sub-Saharan Africa, is entirely outside our concern, and the ninth, Sumerian, stands in isolation as intriguing (does it relate to one of the Caucasian groups, or to Elamo-Dravidian, or is it genuinely *sui generis*?) as it is splendid (because the Sumerians were the inventors of the world's first script). The intruders of the fourth century AD are the Huns, members of the Altaic (Central Asian) group represented today by the Turks and Mongols.

The next map (fig. 4) shows the way the shadings and other conventions used in the Atlas relate to this ethno-linguistic classification. Three groups – the West Mediterranean, Caucasian and Sumerian – are missing because they are left unshaded throughout. Four have simple shadings which are not developed further: Uralic (a light tint), Elamo-Dravidian (a 'rainfall' shading), Nilo-Saharan (vertically banded) and Niger-Congo (a dark tint). One, Altaic, has a border of black circles. The Afro-Asiatics have an oblique cross-hatch with a wide mesh: when this stock splits into its African and Asiatic components the Asiatic element (Semitic) keeps the wide mesh, but the African elements (Berber, Egyptian and Cushitic) are given a closer web. Finally, the

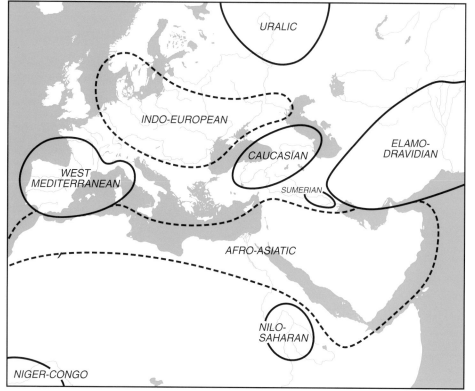

**Fig. 3** *Language groups, 6000 BC*

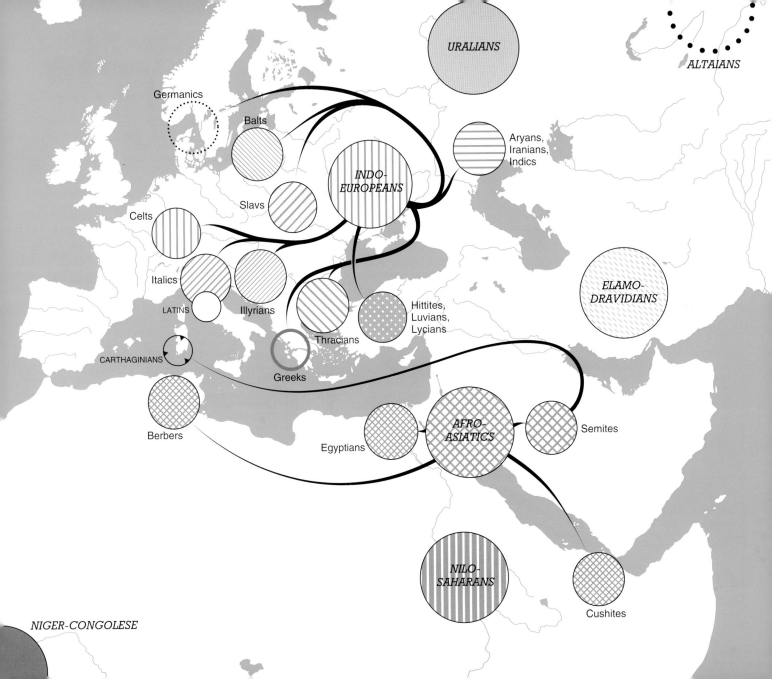

URALIANS

ALTAIANS

Germanics

Balts

Aryans,
Iranians,
Indics

INDO-
EUROPEANS

Slavs

ELAMO-
DRAVIDIANS

Celts

Italics

Illyrians

LATINS

Thracians

Hittites,
Luvians,
Lycians

CARTHAGINIANS

Greeks

Berbers

Egyptians

AFRO-
ASIATICS

Semites

NILO-
SAHARANS

Cushites

NIGER-CONGOLESE

**Fig. 4** *Key to the shadings used in the Atlas*

*Introduction*

Indo-Europeans start off vertically lined, which is simple enough, but go on to generate what must seem, at least at first sight, a bewildering variety of patterns. This kaleidoscope is caused by the need to distinguish between ten different offshoots of the original Indo-European stem. Among them only the Celts retain the original vertical lines, the Germanics get a border of dots, the Aryans are horizontally lined, the Hittites vertically cross-hatched, and the Greeks given a grey border. The Italics, Illyrians and Slavs are diagonally shaded, as are the Balts and Thracians, though in the opposite direction: the individual distinctions are made by varying the closeness of the shading. There is no visual logic to any of this, and to understand how the various languages relate to each other you will need to refer to Fig. 5 which shows how Indo-European evolved during the period of interest to us. The final point to note about Fig. 4 is the way that the Latins and Carthaginians have been singled out for special treatment. When the Latins emerge as a distinct entity within the Italic bloc (on map 415 BC) they lose their Italic shading, and the top Latins, the Romans, are consequently unshaded from start to finish. Similar special status is awarded to the Carthaginians (maps 515–192 BC): they get a barbed border instead of the cross-hatch that, as Semites, they rightfully deserve. The reason in both cases is the need for clarity: sticking to the linguistically correct shadings would overload the maps and make them very difficult to read.

The assumption underlying all this – that ethnic and linguistic identities go hand in hand – was anathema to linguists of the old school, and isn't all that popular today. However it is clear that, as regards our period at least, both are aspects of the same process, differentiation as a consequence of geographical isolation. Given enough time any isolated population can be relied on to generate its own language, its own lifestyle, and, indeed, its own political system. The trick, then, is to identify the geographical areas that have acted as nurses to the nations of antiquity. In some cases this is easy. Afro-Asiatic, for example, covers Africa north of the Sahara, plus Arabia. It divides into languages specific to North Africa east of the Nile valley (Berber), the Nile valley (Egyptian), the western

coast of the Red Sea (Cushitic), and Arabia (Semitic). In the case of Indo-European, however, there has been great debate about the position and extent of its original homeland, and no consensus has been reached as yet as to when the individual languages established their identity.

The arguments about the position of the original homeland (*Heimat* in the largely German literature) are probably drawing to a conclusion now. Leaving apart the dottier proposals (Anatolia, Armenia, even, would you believe, Egypt) the suggested homelands either fall within the vertically shaded zone shown on Fig. 4 or within an eastward extension of this reaching a bit further into Turkestan. A few have plumped for an area corresponding to the entire shaded zone. In favour of this last idea is the fact that there are no river names other than Indo-European ones within this area. Also in favour is the recently demonstrated linkage between Elamite and Dravidian, for the *Heimat* of this new Elamo-Dravidian group is at least 3,000 km across. We already know that the Afro-Asiatic group measured 5,000 km east to west. It seems extremely unlikely that a group as successful as Indo-European had a smaller homeland than these two. We can pretty safely go with the wide angle vision, i.e. the vertically shaded area, spanning some 2,500 km, on Fig. 4.

The matter of chronology is more contentious. The assumption in Fig. 3 is that all these language groups were in being, and in their respective homelands, by 6000 BC. This would not be acceptable to the general run of archaeologists, who traditionally look to neolithic or later movements to explain how this map, or their version of it, came about. But it can't be said that any of the connections they have made has won general acceptance, and there's something more to this than just the tendency of academics to nitpick each other's ideas. Just as journalists always imagine that the crux of the action is wherever they happen to be at the time, so archaeologists look for answers in the places where they have the most evidence. And the many, multiply subdivided cultures of Europe's Neolithic and Bronze Ages have provided just the grist they need for their mills. Specific cultures have been suggested as primordially Indo-European (ignoring     9

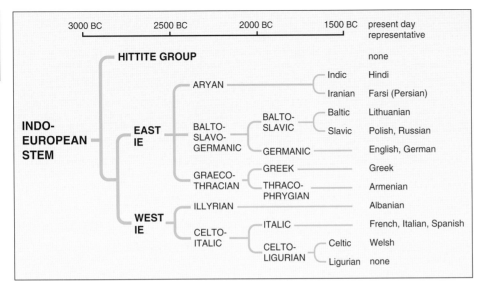

Fig. 5 *Development of the Indo-European language tree, 3000–1500 BC*

As for the subdivisions of Indo-European, the basic requirement is that they should make geographical sense, that each linguistic group should have its environmental niche, or *ecosphere*. We have seen how this is clearly the case with the Afro-Asiatic languages, North Africa generating Berber, the Nile Valley Egyptian, the Red Sea littoral Cushitic, and Arabia and the Levant Semitic. And we know of many later instances where exactly the same thing is true of Indo-European languages, perhaps the best documented being the development of Spanish, French, and Italian from Latin in the early medieval period. But how do we make the very first splits in the Indo-European tree? The view adopted here is that there was a three-way division in the early third millennium BC, with the eastern half of the existing *Heimat* developing distinguishing characteristics of its own, and a southern (Hittite) group being created by a migration from the original homeland area into Anatolia (Fig. 5 and map 2750 BC in the Atlas). The identity of the southern group will have been immediately fortified by the population bottleneck imposed by the Bosporus and Dardanelles. The area beyond this constriction, Western Anatolia, subsequently became the ecosphere of the Hittite peoples – the Luvians and the Hittites proper.

The next stage is the break-up of the Eastern phylum. The essential division is a three-way split into Balto-Slavo-Germanic (in Eastern Europe and Scandinavia), Graeco-Thracian (in the East Balkans and on the Russian steppe), and Aryan (in the steppe lands north of the Caspian and Aral seas). Then three becomes five as Germanic splits off from Balto-Slavic and Greek from Thracian. These developments are charted on map 2250 BC. From a cartographic point of view the most interesting of this new crop are Germanic and Greek, because both achieved their identity within ecospheres of a special 'littoral' type. The distinguishing feature of littoral ecospheres is that most places within them are on or near the sea: they can be defined by a simple topographical exercise that relies on this fact, and this has been done for the Greek case in Figs. 6.1–6.3.

the fact that there is a very poor – some would say non-existent – correlation between linguistic and archaeological boundaries): evidence of migration in the necessary directions has been found in the excavated material (an even more dodgy proposition). I too, though no archaeologist, must own up to similar sins in my youth. It is now clear, to me at least, that this whole endeavour has been fruitless, not just because it is a game without rules, but because we have all been looking in the wrong place. My current version of the truth is that West Mediterranean and Indo-European homelands were formed during the ninth millennium BC, at the upper palaeolithic/mesolithic boundary, when Europe was repopulated at the end of the last glaciation.

There are a couple of things to be said in favour of this scenario. One is its economy. Once the initial formulation is conceded there is no problem about subsequent developments, many of which take place *in situ*. Another derives from the overall chronology of man's social evolution. It is a commonplace to say that life is speeding up all the

time, that lifestyles that lasted for centuries in the medieval period, and for a generation or more in early modern times, now turn over every decade. Now look back along this exponentially rising curve to the period of concern to us, first of all to Pharaonic Egypt which had a material culture that hardly budged in 2,500 years, then, before that, to the upper palaeolithic era, when cave-painters kept the same conventions for 20,000 years, and then to the lower palaeolithic where 300,000 years could and did pass without discernible change of any sort. In this context it seems fair to say that Fig. 3, which most archaeologists would be prepared to accept is a reasonable reconstruction of the situation in 3000 BC, is more likely to apply to 6000 BC than some quite different formulation. This means that the *LBK*-folk, spotlighted as the pioneer Indo-European group in the first edition of this atlas, are unlikely to have been responsible for establishing the Indo-Europeans as the core population of Central Europe; the chances are that they merely represent a current within an already widespread Indo-European stratum.[1]

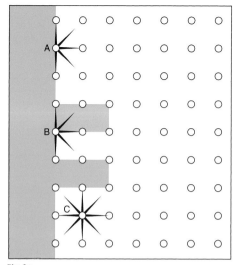

Fig. 6.1

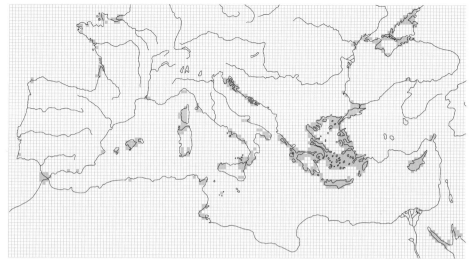

Fig. 6.2

## Fig. 6 *The Aegean ecosphere*

6.1 provides the theoretical basis for the concept, showing the relationships within a group of equally spaced communities on straight and indented coastlines. On the straight stretch of coast community A relates to only two coastal communities as against three inland. On the indented stretch all five of B's relationships are with coastal communities. It therefore rates as a member of a littoral community whereas A, though equally on the sea, does not. Most interesting is C which, with five coastal neighbours as against three inland, gets incorporated in the littoral sphere even though it is out of sight of the sea.

6.2 applies this analysis to the Mediterranean, taking each square of the grid that contains a bit of coastline and counting it as part of a littoral community if a majority of its neighbours are littoral too. Sea squares don't count, but inland squares are added to the total if their neighbours are predominantly littoral (as with C in 6.1).

6.3 shows the relative size of the various littoral communities of the Mediterranean-Black Sea area, taking ten squares as the minimum needed for a place on the histogram. The Aegean far outranks the rest: the fact that it has been the only one to generate a new language – the best the rest have ever done is dialects – supports the conclusion that this is the only one worth calling an ecosphere. The others are mainly interesting for the way that the four nearest to the Aegean provided lodgement for the Greeks when they began to expand beyond the Aegean.

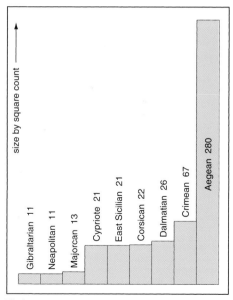

Fig. 6.3

As can be seen from Fig. 6.2, the ecosphere boundary includes the rim of the Aegean and Sea of Marmara (Propontis) as well as the peninsula and islands of Greece proper. In fact it took the Greeks, who started out as a purely peninsular people, a considerable time to fill out this new environment – the islands were settled in the late Bronze Age, but the east coast only in the early Iron Age and the north shore and Sea of Marmara not till the classical period. Indeed the process was still incomplete when the Greeks began spilling over into adjacent areas that had the same littoral nature – Cyprus in the east, the Crimea in the north-east, and Sicily and southern Italy to the west.[2]

Ethno-linguistic prehistory is a relatively new subject and it should be no surprise that views about it differ, often fundamentally. Classical Greece and Rome, on the other hand, have been studied forever, and one would have expected that by now the broad outlines would be firmly established. Not so. There are two important areas where the picture currently presented is completely, gloriously, 180° wrong. The first concerns the political structure of peninsular Greece. Classical Greece – the Greece of the sixth to fourth centuries BC – was divided into a great many independent states, some of moderate size, many very small. It is customary to refer to these as city states. The vast majority of them were nothing of the sort. The largest (Sparta, Aetolia, Thessaly) had no urban centres at all, while the smallest were equally rural, consisting of no more than a single village and its surrounding lands. There were a few federated states, for example Boeotia (a dozen little towns, headed up by Thebes) or Achaea (another dozen, but with equal standing). Finally there were the genuine city states, with small towns at their centres where the citizens congregated for business or pleasure. Most of them are to be found within a short arc of territory in central Greece stretching from Athens via Corinth to Argos.

All this seems a million miles away from the usual picture of Greece as akin to Renaissance Italy where twenty cities jostled each other on a chessboard extending over the entire north of the peninsula. How can the political vocabulary and the social reality have drifted so far apart? The simplest answer is that nearly all books about classical Greece turn out to be books about Athens. If there are any doubts about initial generalizations they are quickly left behind in the rush to extol the institutions, procedures, achievements and glories of this misleading paradigm, at once a city, a city state, and the capital of an empire. But what if we lift our eyes from Athens for a moment, move a bit to the left and look at its much more representative neighbour Megara (Fig. 7). This was a small state (Greek *polis*), the majority of whose citizens certainly lived in the countryside (*agros*), but which had built itself a dignified little town (*asty*) as its seat of government. But the fact that they had a perfectly good word for an urban centre in *asty* didn't stop the Greeks using the word *polis* for both Megara state and Megara town, as they did for both Athens state and Athens city. So, if you choose to translate *polis* as city, which Athens-oriented classical historians do, you end up describing all the states of peninsular Greece as cities, or, in an attempt to make some sense out of the term, city states. Most of them – at least 90 per cent – were not.[3]

Of course you could argue that anyone who knows anything about the subject understands all this, and there is no real harm in the muddle. Alas, even this isn't true. Debates on the population figures likely to apply to Greek towns, surely an important topic, typically founder at an early stage because of a failure to distinguish between citizenship figures for the *polis* (all that the Greeks were interested in) and residence in the *asty*. A good example is the way Diodorus' statement that Alexandria had 300,000 'free people' has been used to support population

**Fig. 7** *Megara: polis, agros and asty*

Megara is a good example of a run-of-the-mill Greek city state of the classical period. Its economy was entirely rural and for most of its citizens a visit to Megara town would have been a rare outing.

The overall population figure is based on Megara's 3,000-strong contribution to the Greek army at the battle of Plataea (assuming this was half of the adult male population and multiplying by 4): it is in line with the carrying capacity of the 470 km² *agros*. The population figure for Megara town is derived from a comparison with the *asty* of Athens, which had about 7,000 inhabitants on the eve of the Persian wars, before any special factors had kicked in. The area of Attica (the *agros* of the Athenian *polis*) was five times larger than the Megarid (the *agros* of Megara), so 3,000 for Megara town is more likely to be an over-estimate than an under-estimate.

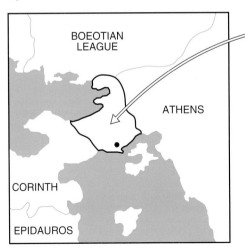

BOEOTIAN LEAGUE

ATHENS

CORINTH

EPIDAUROS

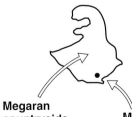

**THE STATE (*polis*) OF MEGARA**
population 24,000

**Megaran countryside (*agros*)**
population 21,000

**Megara town (*asty*)**
population 3,000

estimates for the city ranging up to and even beyond the million mark. In fact Diodorus' figure, if it is based on anything at all, must derive from the citizen roll, which was, in effect, a register of all the Greeks in Egypt. (Greeks had to be citizens of somewhere and there were only two alternatives to Alexandria, a tiny settlement at Naucratis and a somewhat more substantial colony at Ptolemais.) It is of no relevance to the population of Alexandria town.

This brings us to the second blind spot in current thinking. Classical scholars are absolutely wedded to the idea that ancient Rome had a population of a million or more. Historical demographers have told them that this cannot be so, it flies in the face of what we know of the size of cities in the ancient world, it makes no sense at all, but the academic consensus remains rock solid. It is almost as though admitting to a lower figure would somehow diminish the standing of classical studies. This is not sensible and we will have none of it: the atlas uses a ballpark figure of 250,000.[4]

Of course, these blind spots are minor blemishes on what is a vast and noble edifice: no one is going to question the integrity of the building as a whole or of the practices of the army of scholars who maintain it. But when we move next door, when we leave history for prehistory, we enter a less impressive structure. This is not entirely the prehistorian's fault. The materials at his disposal are of uncertain strength, and it is often unclear whether they will bear the weight of the hypotheses they are asked to carry. People react to problems of this sort in different ways. Some build to large safety factors, searching around for extra material to shore up their walls. Others respond more neurotically, erecting many-storeyed, extremely perilous structures, decked out with advertisements in a special archaeologist-speak that goes like this:

| | |
|---|---|
| *Major new civilization* | a particularly disappointing dig |
| *History will have to be rewritten* | confirms an existing footnote in the standard work on the subject |
| *A great city* | a few hovels, maybe a village |
| *The Venice of its day* | any site that has produced a few articles from somewhere else |
| *Earliest known* | undated |

This hyperbolic language can perhaps be excused on the grounds that the archaeologist has to finance his digs, and no one is going to be enthusiastic about funding the confirmation of a footnote. Much harder to bear is the muddle and confusion that archaeologists are prepared to tolerate in their terminology. Neolithic, for example, normally a descriptive term limited to food producing communities, is sometimes used chronologically, to refer to hunter-gatherers living in neolithic times, e.g. the 'middle neolithic' Pit-Comb ware culture of north-east Europe. Bronze Age is another term that doesn't necessarily mean what it says: Aegean Early Bronze 1 has no bronze at all. It's not that more precise descriptions are lacking, there is actually a superfluity of them – either subneolithic or ceramic mesolithic would do for the Pit-Comb ware people, and eneolithic or chalcolithic for Aegean Early Bronze 1 – but nobody seems interested in tidying things up. Worse than that, there is a reflex in favour of the status quo. When Flinders Petrie, an eminent Egyptologist if ever there was one, pointed out that Middle Egyptian Bronze Age implements were actually copper, you might expect his observations to cause something of a a rethink. Not a bit of it: the official view is still that his remarks, though technically correct, are, in some wider sense, unhelpful, even confusing. That's a tale from a fair while ago, but how about this, from the standard work on the Aegean Bronze Age published in the 1990s: 'For the sake of simplicity vessels which might be of copper or bronze are referred to as "bronze" throughout'. Wow!

There seems to be a measure of intellectual catching up to be done here. Some habits of thought – for example the convention that the Director of a dig has exclusive rights when it comes to saying what it means – have a certain old world charm. But others seem merely blinkered. It is good that schol-

ars pore over their king lists and try to work out regnal dates, but shouldn't some of them be exploring other approaches? It seems absurd that pharaonic Egypt, which has bequeathed us vast quantities of wood in the form of boats, beams and statues, has fewer radio-carbon dates than any comparable old world culture, and no dendrochronology at all.

The lack of scientific discipline is felt in other fields than the purely technical. Prehistorians far too often succumb to fashions in interpretation, rushing from one side to another of the argument in a way that endangers common sense. One recent example of this is the ban that has been proclaimed on migration. At one time all prehistoric people were on their way to somewhere else: now none of them are moving at all. So far from invading India, the Aryans were there from the start: even the Sea Peoples turn out to have been simple stay-at-homes. Think pink, think static. Of course, the wheel will turn and the Aryans and Sea Peoples resume their traditional (undoubtedly correct) aggressions, but there is a lack of balance about this sort of thing which is to no one's credit.

So much for historians and prehistorians. What about the authors and editors of historical atlases? Are they subject to human weakness too? Alas, to a degree, the answer has to be yes. They have a tendency to work to fuzzy dates: maps showing 'Europe around 1160' or 'in the late twelfth century', or even 'in the age of the Crusades' are all too common. There is a general failure to sort the data presented. Place-name entries use the same style for towns and trading posts, for major castles and minor monasteries, for battlefields and treaty sites. In the earlier periods insecurities in the data are concealed rather than signposted. Finally, there is the question of the appropriate pictorial means of representing the historical information. That the line of Hadrian's wall represents the Roman frontier of Britain might seem self-evident, but for much of its life there were outpost forts up to 30 km in advance of it. Do we put them in or leave them out? As far as this Atlas is concerned, the small scale of the base map usually solves this type of problem, but there are still questions of presentation, as, for example, with the Roman frontier in North Africa. Do we give it the fussy detail it had in reality? **13**

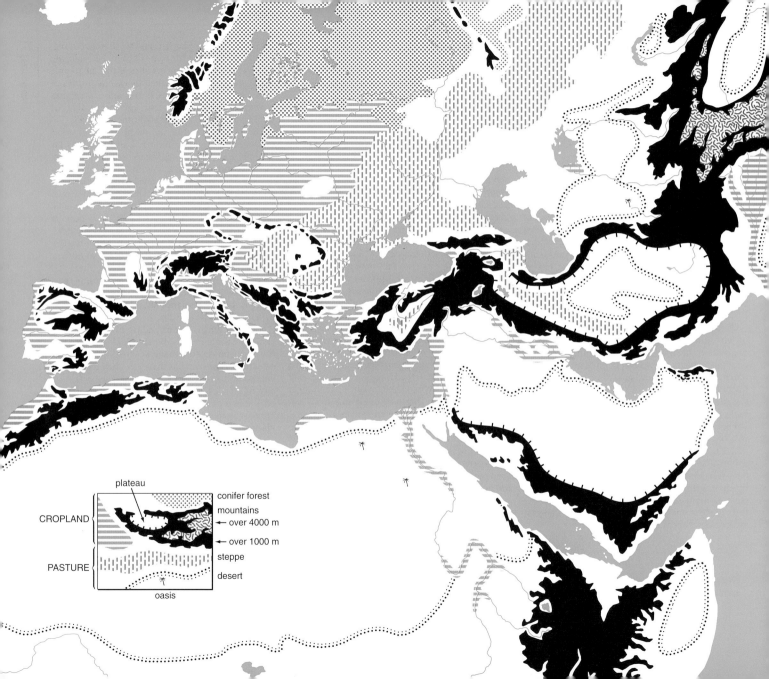

plateau

CROPLAND

PASTURE

conifer forest
mountains
← over 4000 m
← over 1000 m
steppe
desert

oasis

## Fig. 8 *The physical geography of the Europe-Near East area*
*(If you lose your way in the course of this survey, pick up the names from the index maps A and B at the back of the book.)*

The mountain ranges of Europe are too well known to require detailed comment. Starting on the left we have the various sierras of the Iberian peninsula, topped off by the Pyrenees, which provide a natural frontier between Spain and France. Southern France leads us to the Alps, which put a similar cap on the Italian peninsula. Within Italy the Apennines form a curving spine which divides the country into three compartments: the Po valley in the north, Etruria-Latium-Campania along the Mediterranean shin, and Apulia, the heel, in the south. The line terminates in the toe (modern Calabria), making it too lumpy to be of much use to anyone. Beyond Italy is the Balkan chain, of which Greece is the half submerged southern end: its jagged coastline was created as the sea flooded into its valleys. Across the Aegean, Anatolia has a similarly complicated western littoral, a rolling central plateau, and a mountainous east culminating in the Armenian knot, centred to the north of Lake Van. North of the Armenian knot is the Caucasus range, the traditional dividing line between Europe and Asia in this part of the world.

Further east the names are less familiar. East of Armenia is the Iranian Plateau, defined on its western side by the Zagros Mountains, overlooking Mesopotamia (Iraq), and on the east by the Sulaiman and associated ranges that separate Iran from India. Moving up from the northern end of the Sulaimans, we meet the tip of the 4,000 metre high Central Asian massif. The southern border of this, facing India, is formed by the Himalaya, the northern border by the Kun Lun Shan, and the tip is the Hindu Kush. To the left of the Hindu Kush are the Pamirs, and north and east of them the Tien Shan (Celestial Mountains). The oval area enclosed by the Tien Shan, the Pamirs and the Kun Lun Shan is the Tarim basin.

The list of deserts is dominated by Africa's Sahara, forming the southern border of our region. Next come the deserts of the Arabian peninsula, the Nafud in the north and the Rub al-Khali ('Empty Quarter') in the south. Then the Great Salt Desert (Dasht e-lut) of the Iranian Plateau. Then, moving up the right hand side of the map,

we reach the Central Asian desert zone, divided by the Oxus into the Kara Kum and Kizil Kum (Black and Red Deserts, respectively south and north of the Oxus). Finally there's the Takla Makan, the desert occupying much of the basin of the Tarim.

Productive land comes in two grades: good enough for animal husbandry only, and good enough for agriculture of all types. In the first category are the scrub on the fringes of the desert, the hills at the foot of the mountain ranges and, at the level of technology prevailing in the ancient world, the grasslands of the Eurasian steppe. Much of Western Europe and scattered parts of the Near East attain the second level. Within the Near East we have to recognize a sub-division of the arable into rainfall-dependent and irrigation-dependent lands. Egypt is the classic example of the second type: the country only exists because of the Nile, which turns an area of the Sahara, where rainfall ranges from zero to pitiful, into a ribbon of cropland topped off by a superbly fertile delta. The other major irrigated zones are southern Mesopotamia, which depends on the Tigris and Euphrates to water its fields, and the Indus valley. The famous Fertile Crescent, the arch of land running from Palestine up through Syria and then down through Mesopotamia, is actually a composite zone, its agriculture sustained by rainfall in its western half and irrigation in the east, while the roof of the arch is predominantly pastoral.

For fun I've put in three oases: Siwa and Dakhla a bit to the west of the Egyptian Nile because they mark the limits of Egyptian influence in this direction, and up in the Kara Kum, Marv, the point where one of the smaller rivers running off the Hindu Kush gives up the ghost and sinks into the sand. At the lower edge of the map note the semi-desert strip known as the Sahel, the southern shore of the vast Saharan sand sea, and, split by the Red Sea, the Abyssinian and Arabian mountain ranges which attract enough rainfall to make life possible in areas that would otherwise be annexed to the Saharan and Arabian deserts.

Or do we give it a pleasantly flowing form indicating that Roman rule, in principal, extended as far south as the edge of the Sahara? Of course we go for the second option – taking the first would imply that the frontier was more active and of more concern to the Roman government than it actually was. The simplification is allowable, not just on the basis of clarity, but of emphasis. If this sounds like special pleading (which it is), then the full confession is as follows. The Atlas selects the data – and hypotheses – needed to tell the story of the origins and development of the classical civilizations of Europe and the Near East. It illustrates the necessary facts and hypotheses in a series of diagrams. Given the scale of the events it deals with, and the small compass within which they have to be fitted, the picture can only be approximate. But if it is, in every sense of the word, a partial history, it does make intermittent attempts at honesty. The more hypothetical constructions are signalled by the use of italics, as, for example, archaeological cultures (in italics in both maps and text), and language groups (maps only). Where facts are disputed or lacking, there is a section at the back of the book (*Notes*, pp. 118–19) which – sometimes – describes the way the difficulty has been dealt with. And the dates of the maps are meant to be binding, though they can only be so within the limits of current understanding: this means a leeway of up to 100 years either side at 2750 BC, 50 years at 1575 BC, 25 years at 980 BC, and a year or so from 670 BC on.[5]

With too many facts competing for too little space every historical cartographer has to develop rules for what gets in and what doesn't. One way of keeping control of the flood of data is to have special maps devoted to special topics, and the Atlas makes frequent use of this option. These specialized maps – on the spread of literacy, the evolution of towns and trade routes, the growth of population and, right at the end, the progress of Christianity – allow the main sequence to concentrate on the political narrative. Another way of reducing clutter is to banish place-names to index maps at the back of the Atlas (pp. 123 and 125). The original edition of the Atlas was pretty fanatical about this: a name on the maps in the main sequence, for example, meant that the community concerned was in some sense a **15** player in the political game. This time round I have been a bit more relaxed, and if its nature is clear, it helps the story along and there is room for it, I've allowed the odd place name to slip in in small type. (When this isn't the case locate the item by picking up the letter/number combination from the index, and then using the index map.) The quest for clarity has also meant that major physical features such as mountains and deserts are excluded. As these determine much of the story, and are an element that ought to be taken aboard before rather than after reading the Atlas, Fig. 8 displays, and its caption rehearses, the more important features.

My love affair with ancient history goes back a very long way, to schoolboy readings of Gibbon and Herodotus, and unasked for essays presented to surprised teachers. Many people and many institutions have encouraged and aided my note-taking, nitpicking and niggling since then, and many friends, relatives and professionals helped me translate my enthusiasms into map form. To all of them I am intensely grateful. Hopefully none of them will mind me singling out for special mention my brother, Brian McEvedy, who combined medicine with Egyptology, my secretary of many years, Sandra Cook, my cartographer, David Woodroffe, Alan Glover, my first editor at Penguin Books, and, specifically for this book, Andrew Sherratt of the Ashmolean Museum, Oxford, who actually read the whole thing *twice* and saved me from many a solecism.

## Notes

1. Don't be frightened by the names archaeologists give to their cultures. Most of them are simply the names of the sites where the culture's characteristic artefacts were first excavated. The rest are taken from the objects themselves, as with *bell beaker*, a pottery drinking vessel that has the shape of an upturned bell. German can make this look difficult, but it isn't really: *LBK* is simply an acronym for *Linienbandkeramik*, meaning pottery decorated with bands made up of parallel lines.

2. The core of the Germanic *Heimat* is the Danish archipelago. It also takes in the various adjacent littoral zones in Norway and Sweden, as well as the present-day Dutch and German coasts as far as Zeeland in the west and Rugen in the east. However, the largest of all the northern littoral ecospheres, the area corresponding to the medieval earldom of Orkney, lay beyond the Germanics' reach during antiquity.

3. The fit between classical Greek colonies and the city state concept is much better because, of necessity, each colony started out as a single, defensible settlement. Some failed to grow much, and ended up as purely rural communities, but most developed urban characteristics and qualify – so long as they remained free – for the title of city state. Hellenistic colonies, on the other hand, were never sovereign, and no matter how grand they became, were not cities in the original Greek sense of the term. They did, however, add yet another layer of meaning to the word *polis*, for as they developed into administrative centres, i.e. county towns, it became usual to refer to the county as a city. A. H. M. Jones' great work *The Cities of the Eastern Roman Provinces* is actually a book about the counties into which the Eastern Empire was divided, not about cities at all.

4. Calculations of ancient Rome's population depend on four bits of information. The first is the result of a survey of the city's housing taken in Constantine's day. It gives the number of houses as 1,790, and the number of apartments as 46,000. On the basis of ten persons to a house and four to an apartment, this yields a population figure of 1,790 x 10 + 46,000 x 4 = 201,900. The second is the number of people who got a free wheat ration from the state. When the rosters were monitored properly, as they were by Julius Caesar and Augustus, they totalled 150,000 and 'a few more than 200,000' respectively. The third is the census of AD 1526, when 45,178 people lived in the 220 hectares of the *abitato*, the inhabited quarter of the city. Applied to the walled area of ancient Rome (1380 ha.) this yields a population figure of 283,000. However, something of the order of a third of the classical city was public space of one sort or another (gardens, temples, baths) which brings us back to 200,000 again. Finally, there is the size of the city when it did reach the million mark in AD 1931. At 6,780 ha. it was bigger than ancient Rome by a factor of 4.9, suggesting a population of 204,000 for the classical city.

The million men deal with this data in some pretty contorted ways. First they say that apartment (*insula*) is really an apartment block, which enables them to use any multiplier they fancy. This is not allowable. The minimum ground floor space of an apartment block is of the order of 300 m² (0.03 ha.): 46,000 of them would occupy the entire area within the Aurelian walls, leaving no space for streets between them, let alone the city's grander houses and the gardens and public buildings that figure so prominently among the city's amenities. As to the 200,000 or so who got the wheat ration, the million men say that they were adult males and need a multiplier of 4, plus a bit more for slaves. This won't do either: the only named recipient we know of is a woman, and reliefs on the Arch of Constantine show that the queues for imperial handouts included women and children (even infants). As to slaves, there must have been very few in Rome, because giving them their liberty made them eligible for the handout too: masters will surely have opted to be served by freedmen at the state's expense rather than by slaves maintained out of their own pockets. It may sound surprising but there were even cases of non-Romans voluntarily entering into slavery so they could be set free and thus, as Roman citizens, qualify for the dole. So 200,000 it is, as Augustus said, and indeed who ever heard of a dictator who put a smaller figure on his largesse than he needed to. If he had fed a million Romans he would have said so.

5. The Mesopotamian and Egyptian king lists, typically quoted with exact dates for each reign, are really floating chronologies, with no certainly fixed points before the Assyrian period. They can (sometimes) tell you how long a king reigned, but not exactly when.

In the case of the Assyrians it is worth noting that present-day Assyriologists have stuck to the system used by the compilers of their king lists, in which each monarch is assumed to have completed the year in which he died, e.g. Tiglath-Pilesar III 744–722, Sargon II 721–705. This turns Sargon's deportation of the ten tribes in 722 into an event of his predecessor's reign, an unnecessary if scholarly way of generating errors. In the Atlas the regnal dates follow normal, as opposed to Assyriological, practice.

# The Atlas

During the Pleistocene era – the last two million years or so – the earth's climate alternated between periods of intense cold (Ice Ages or glaciations) and spells of better weather (often better than today). The split wasn't even, the warm phases being shorter than the cold: in fact the final warm interval, the Eemian interglacial, only lasted about 15,000 years. At its end, roughly 130,000 years ago, the cold returned with a vengeance, and things stayed bad or worse until about 18,000 BC. Throughout this time an icecap a mile or more thick covered the whole of Scandinavia and in the really cold spells – the glacial maxima, of which one was in progress at the date of this map – the icecap grew even larger, lapping over into Germany and Russia, and extending across the North Sea to link up with a smaller cap in the British Isles. The amount of water locked up in this vast structure – and in its even vaster North American cousin – reduced the sea level by more than 100 metres. The presence of the icecap (and its Alpine satellite), the lowered sea level and the enhanced pack-ice in the north Atlantic make this a pretty odd-looking map.[1]

Man had been present in Europe for at least half a million years by this time, originally in the form of *Homo erectus*, then, from some time around the start of the last Ice Age, as something reasonably close to modern man, *Homo sapiens*. This European population slowly developed specific anatomical traits that make its skeletal remains easily recognizable: heavy brows, protruding teeth and a squarer, more chunky overall build. The first example to be recognized as a significant find turned up in a quarry at Neanderthal, in Germany, in 1856 (19 on the map); hence the term Neanderthal man. The initial consensus was that this was a distinct, and distinctly sub-human, species, *Homo neanderthalensis*. In line with this view reconstruction drawings portrayed him as a shaggy creature, clearly prone to aggressive outbursts. Subsequently anthropologists softened the image. It was pointed out that no one knew how hairy Neanderthal man was, that his physique represented an adaptation to glacial conditions, and that his brain was every bit as big as modern man's. He was eventually reclassified as *Homo sapiens neanderthalensis* (i.e. a variety of modern man) and a new set of drawings was pre-

pared which presented him as someone you could reasonably share a park bench with. Recently the pendulum has swung back again. Neanderthal man's voice box is simpler than ours, suggesting that his speech was restricted and that, given the close connection between speech and thought, maybe his ideas were too. The reconstruction artists have responded by putting back some of the hair, and the anthropologists have begun referring to him as *Homo neanderthalensis* again. The new view fits with the fact that when truly modern men arrived in Europe, which they did not long after the date of the map, they appear to have had no truck with the Neanderthalers. The poor woolly things were gradually pushed into backwaters and eventually, after some 10,000 years of co-existence, into extinction.[2]

The arrival of modern man in Europe creates an important dividing line in the palaeolithic (Old Stone Age). Neanderthal man had used a fairly simple range of stone tools, termed *Mousterian* after the site where the industry was first defined (9 on the map). Modern man brought with him a much richer tradition of toolmaking, the *Aurignacian*. The change is conventionally taken to mark the transition from the middle palaeolithic to the upper palaeolithic (upper being the more recent looking at it from the excavator's point of view). The Neanderthals did their best to keep up, producing their own version of *Aurignacian*. As you might expect, this *Chatelperronian* industry is a bit hamfisted. Geographically it is restricted to western Europe, though Neanderthals seem to have lasted at least as long in the east as they did in the west.

1. The Mediterranean, though shrunken, is still recognizable, as is the equally reduced Black Sea. The relationship between the two has changed, however, because the Mediterranean has fallen below the level of the Bosporus shelf, which means that the Black Sea has joined the Caspian and Aral as a third inland sea. The other two are larger than they are today because the cold weather has reduced evaporation: as a result the Aral is overflowing into the Caspian, and the Caspian into the Black Sea. This increased freshwater input has helped flush out the salt water from the Black Sea.

Nearly all the geologists who work on this, the final ice age agree on one thing: it began with a W. For North Americans it's the Wisconsin glaciation, to north Europeans it's the Weichsel, and for the Swiss, who practically invented the subject, it's the Wurm. For the Russians, alas, it's the Valdez.

2. The numbered sites are: 1 and 2 Gibraltar (Forbes Quarry and Devil's Tower); 3 Zafarraya; 4 Banyolas; 5–11 La Ferrassie, Combe-Grenal, Regourdou, La Chapelle-aux-Saintes, Le Moustier, Roc de Marsal, Pech de la Azé; 12 La Quina; 13 St Cesaire; 14 Chatelperron; 15 Arcy-sur-Cure; 16 Abri Moula; 17 Hortus; 18 Spy; 19 Neanderthal; 20 Monte Circeo (Grotta Guattari); 21 Tata; 22 Krapina; 23 Vindija; 24 Kiik Koba; 25 Dederiyeh; 26 Amud; 27 Zuttiyeh; 28 Tabun; 29 Kebara; 30 Shanidar; 31 Mezmaiskaya; 32 Teshik-Tash.

40,000 BC

1—32 finds of
Neanderthal man

Homo sapiens skull
(for comparison only)

The upper palaeolithic lasted from 40,000 to 9500 BC. The basic way of life was essentially the same as in the middle palaeolithic, consisting of small family-based bands of hunter–gatherers picking their way around the landscape from spring to fall, and holing up in caves each winter, but the sites are more numerous and the artefacts more varied. The improvement was cumulative: in the initial, Aurignacian phase (40,000–18,000 BC) the tool-kit was limited to hand-held or simply hafted stone blades; in the next stage, the Solutrean (18,000–4000 BC) the workmanship visibly improves; in the final phase, the Magdalenian (14,000–8500 BC), bone-tipped spears and worked antler harpoons make their appearance, plus, right at the end of the period, the first bows and arrows. Upper palaeolithic man also produced the first representational art: female figurines referred to, perhaps overgenerously, as Venuses, and cave-paintings featuring the animals that were important to him – bison, deer, horse, mammoth, rhino, cave bear and lion. The paintings, which show astonishing confidence, are hidden deep in the caves, and can only have been executed, or viewed, in artificial light. There is no technical problem about this – lamps that used animal fat as a fuel are common finds in the caves – but the paintings' apparently perverse situation has encouraged archaeologists to a lot of free-wheeling thought about magic and ritual. A couple of points are worth making in this context. One is that their situation may not be all that perverse: what we see may be the sole survivors of a range of mostly open air paintings – in rock shelters and cave-mouths – that have long since weathered away. Another is that comparable paintings of more recent date – as, for example, those produced by the native Australians – don't seem to have been the site of any organized activity. Considering that upper palaeolithic man didn't have that much to do in the winter, it seems unnecessary to read too much into his tendency to explore and decorate the recesses of his dwelling places.

In the eastern part of Europe, on the Russian steppe, there were no caves to retreat to in the winter, and upper palaeolithic man had to face the risk of freezing to death or come up with a new idea. Around the date of this map he found the new idea: houses constructed from mammoth bones. Skulls, tusks and long bones from up to one hundred mammoths were needed to build one of these structures, the same animals presumably supplying the skin needed to make them weatherproof. The state of the mammoth bones used is variable which suggests that many of them had been scavenged, rather than hunted. This is not in itself surprising but it provides ammunition for those who think that upper palaeolithic man didn't hunt mammoths at all, merely helped himself to the remains of dead ones. This links up with questions about the decline in mammoth numbers that set in around this time. Did man the hunter play a significant role in this? Or was it simply due to global warming?

There is no doubt that, by the date of this map, the world was less cold than it had been. After a long period in which the Ice Age had been unrelenting (there was only a slight amelioration between the maximum in 40,000 BC and the final low in 18,000 BC) temperatures had begun to edge up – slowly, unevenly but significantly. As a result the Scandinavian ice-cap contracted, losing contact with its British counterpart and exposing 'North Sea Land'. The sea level rose from –120 to –70 metres. And the vegetation zones shifted northward, diminishing the habitat for which the Ice Age fauna had evolved. This imposed particular strains on the larger non-ruminant herbivores. The mammoths responded by getting smaller and fewer, which suggests that they were on the way out without any assistance from the hunting lobby. All the same, the likelihood must be that man accelerated the process. Bands of upper palaeolithic hunters certainly followed the mammoth herds as they retreated northward: it was this move that led to the discovery of the Bering land bridge and, circa 12,000 BC, the colonization of North America. And in North America the coincidence of mammoth (and mastodon) remains and upper palaeolithic weaponry, leaves little doubt that the first Americans arrived with all the skills necessary for killing elephant.

*Key to cave paintings:*

1 La Covaciella; 2 Altamira; 3 El Castillo; 4 Le Portel; 5 Niaux; 6 Rouffignac; 7 Lascaux; 8 Cougnac; 9 Chauvet; 10 Cosquer.

Radiocarbon dates from these sites are spread across the entire upper palaeolithic from the early Aurignacian (Chauvet, dated to 30,000 BC) to the middle Magdalenian (Le Portel, dated 10,000 BC).

*Key to mammoth bone houses:*

1 Mezin; 2 Dobranichevka; 3 Gontsy; 4 Mezhirich.

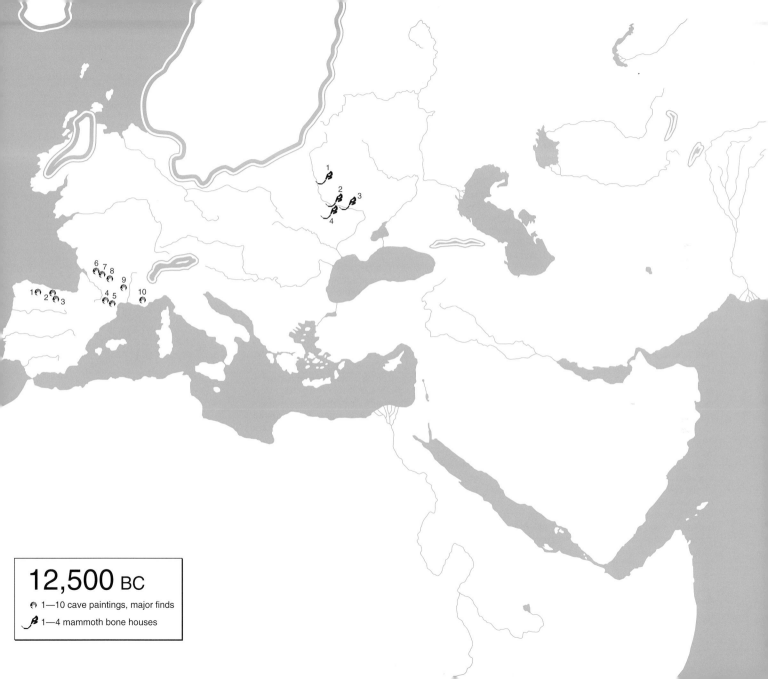

12,500 BC

🐚 1—10 cave paintings, major finds

🦣 1—4 mammoth bone houses

The retreat of the ice went in fits and starts, with the most important pause coming in 11,000–9500 BC when a renewed spell of cold weather stabilized the Scandinavian ice-cap in the position shown on the map. To the south of the ice-cap the Baltic makes its first appearance: it began life as an inland sea fed by meltwater from the cap; subsequently salt water flooded in from the North Sea creating a new permutation known as the Yoldia Sea. The connection between North Sea and Yoldia Sea ran across central Sweden, which might seem surprising considering that the sea level was still 50 metres below today's level. But the weight of the ice-cap had depressed this whole region, and though the land did begin to rise up again once the ice had gone, it did so very slowly. It wasn't until some time after the date of this map – probably about 8600 BC – that the link was severed and another freshwater version of the Baltic, the Ancylus Lake, took the place of the Yoldia Sea.

There were now no mammoths or rhinos in Europe: more to the point the reindeer, which had been the favoured prey of the Magdalenians, had vanished from the plains. The upper palaeolithic way of life was preserved by a few bands of hunters who followed the reindeer herds as they retreated northward: the assumption here is that these were the ancestors of today's Lapps. The rest of Europe passed into a new cultural phase, the mesolithic (Middle Stone Age). The mesolithic world is sometimes called impoverished because it lacked the art of the upper palaeolithic and the glamour of the bison chase, but though large quarry had become relatively scarce, and mesolithic man, to make ends meet, spent much of his time hunting the inglorious snail and the frankly sessile nut, his tool-kit contained some important new items, wooden saws with rows of small geometrically chipped flints for teeth for example. As a result he was better at making things. Bows and arrows become more common; the boat, in the form of the dug-out canoe, makes its first appearance. The canoes were sufficiently seaworthy to take mesolithic man to Cyprus, where he found (and promptly slaughtered) an interesting miniaturized megafauna of pygmy hippos and dwarf elephants.

As suggested in the introduction, the likelihood is that the major language groups were already in existence by this time. Of the seven that concern us we can place the West Mediterraneans in Spain and the Indo-Europeans in Central Europe and on the Russian steppe: both these groups will have expanded into the area left vacant by the Lapps, with the Indo-Europeans benefiting more than the West Mediterraneans. To the north-east of the Indo-Europeans we can place the Uralians, spread either side of the Ural mountains, to the south-east the Caucasians, with their centre of gravity south of the Caucasus range. That leaves the Elamo-Dravidians in Iran and north-west India, the Afro-Asiatics in north Africa and Arabia, and the Nilo-Saharans straddling the middle Nile. Just inside the map, but outside the proper focus of this atlas, is the northernmost portion of the Niger-Congolese stock of West Africa.[1]

None of these groups was very numerous. Something over 50,000 would be a fair guess for the populations of the largest, the Indo-Europeans and Afro-Asiatics, while the Nilo-Saharans and Uralians probably numbered less than 10,000. Figures of this order were all that a hunter–gatherer life-style could sustain. But if the food base could be increased, so could numbers, and by the date of this map the inhabitants of some parts of the Near East – specifically Palestine, Syria and the lands overlooking Mesopotamia – had taken the first step down this road: they were supplementing the standard mesolithic fare with wild wheat. Sickles made on the microlithic saw principle and stone mortars and pestles demonstrate no more than this, and the term proto-agricultural is perhaps unjustifiably teleological, but the planting of the crop, the final advance needed to carry man out of the mesolithic, food-gathering phase, and into the agriculture of the neolithic, was indeed close at hand.[2]

The wedge protruding in from the right hand border of the map, which is a constant feature from now on, represents the core of the Central Asian massif.

1. The area allocated to the Indo-Europeans coincides with the European distribution of the horse, confirming an association that linguists have postulated for the earliest stages of Indo-European evolution. The horses were small, but bigger than the equids native to the Near East, the onager and the donkey, or ass. They are represented today by the species known as Przewalski's horse (*E. przewalski*) as distinct from the much enlarged contemporary domestic horse (*E. caballus*) and the onagers and donkeys (*E. hemionus* and *E. africanus*).

The Lapps can be assumed to have had a language of their own at this time, but we know nothing of its nature: by the time they appear in the historical record, around AD 1000, they have become Finnish speakers. This doesn't put their distinctiveness in doubt: anthropologists discerned this long ago, and it has been amply confirmed by genetic studies.

2. The best known culture of this intermediate type is the Natufian of Palestine, represented by the left-hand limb of the proto-agricultural arc, but the fact that it is the best known doesn't necessarily mean that it was the pace-setter; it may simply reflect the fact that archaeologists have put more effort into Palestine than anywhere else.

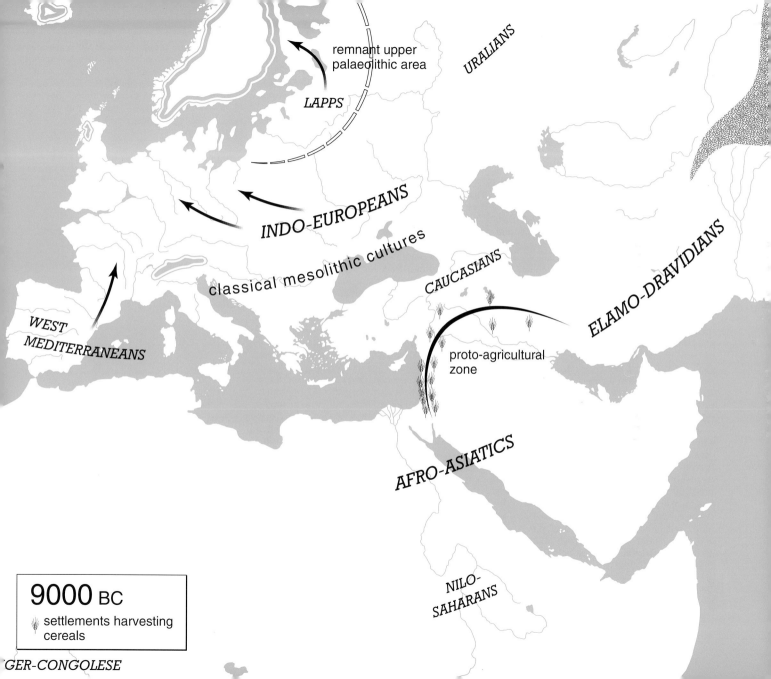

remnant upper
palaeolithic area

*LAPPS*

*URALIANS*

*INDO-EUROPEANS*

classical mesolithic cultures

*CAUCASIANS*

*ELAMO-DRAVIDIANS*

proto-agricultural
zone

*WEST
MEDITERRANEANS*

*AFRO-ASIATICS*

9000 BC

settlements harvesting
cereals

*NILO-
SAHARANS*

*GER-CONGOLESE*

By the late sixth millennium BC the last Ice Age was effectively over. The Scandinavian and Alpine ice-caps had melted away leaving behind only a scattering of individual glaciers, none large enough to show on a map of this scale. Sea levels were within 10 metres of present day values, sufficient to sever the connection between the British Isles and the European continent and to submerge all of 'North Sea Land' bar a few patches like the Dogger and Norfolk banks. It was also enough to raise the Mediterranean above the Bosporan shelf, as a result of which salt water flooded into the Black Sea (c. 5650 BC), enlarging it to its present dimensions. Meanwhile the Baltic completed another stage in its evolution when, around 6500 BC, the general rise in sea level created the present day set of links with the North Sea. Termed the Littorina Sea by geologists, this version was a bit bigger than the Baltic we are familiar with because the region still bore the imprint of the Scandinavian ice cap. It quietly morphed towards its present outline as the land recovered (a process that still has some way to go).

On the human scale the prime event of this era is the invention of agriculture, the so-called 'neolithic revolution'. In reality the multiple skills involved in farming took a long time to develop, and the neolithic was more evolutionary than revolutionary at its original focus in the Near East. This is hardly something to be surprised about because the Near Eastern pioneers were doing three entirely different things – learning to plant and harvest grasses such as wheat and barley, domesticating a wide range of animals including sheep, goats, pigs and cattle, and developing a range of permanent containers, first in stone, then in pottery. These technologies were created in the Fertile Crescent (Palestine, Syria and Iraq) and the lands flanking it on the north-west (Anatolia) and north-east (Iran). Roughly speaking cereal culture was mastered in the course of the ninth millennium, domestication of sheep, goats and pigs in the eighth, and domestication of cattle in the seventh, with the first pottery appearing towards the end of the period. The earliest farming groups to spread beyond the Near East did so before the invention of pottery: remains of these aceramic (pre-pottery) neolithic communities have been found on Cyprus and in northern Greece as well as in the Indus Valley to the east. The major push into Europe came later, when fully neolithic farming groups spread through the northern Balkans (*Karanovo*, *Starčevo*, and *Körös-Criş* cultures) and then across Central Europe (the *Linienbandkeramik*, 'Linear banded ware', conventionally abbreviated to *LBK* by German archaeologists). By this time, the sixth millennium BC, the Near Eastern communities had raised their game by learning to smelt copper, an achievement that makes them formally chalcolithic (copper and stone using).[1]

While the *LBK*-folk were spreading across central Europe, other pioneers were bringing the neolithic revolution to the continent's Mediterranean coast. Their hallmark is a pottery decorated with impressed designs: they got to France ahead of the *LBK*-folk and had reached the Atlantic coast, via the valley of the Garonne, by the date of this map. In the north of Europe the pre-existing *Ertebølle* population learnt some neolithic technology (pottery, polished stone tools) from their *LBK* neighbours, but otherwise continued in their food-gathering way of life (in their case principally as fishermen). This compromise, which archaeologists term subneolithic, was also adopted by the inhabitants of the Pontic steppe. Elsewhere – in Spain, the British Isles, northern Scandinavia and most of European Russia – the living patterns remained purely mesolithic, as they did in all North Africa outside the Nile valley. The lower, Egyptian part of the Nile was the setting for a neolithic culture, if not a very long established one: the middle (Sudanese) Nile was subneolithic. It is interesting that Egypt, for so long regarded as the site of man's emergence from barbarism, turns out to have been a laggard by Near Eastern standards, experiencing the farming revolution little, if at all, earlier than Europe.

Looming as large on the map as the cultures and technologies defined by the archaeologist are the ethno-linguistic groups discussed in the Introduction and introduced on the previous map. All bar three – the Lapps, West Mediterraneans and Caucasians – are now given distinctive shadings. The Uralians are tinted, the Indo-Europeans vertically lined, the Afro-Asiatics crosshatched, the Elamo-Dravidians given a 'rainfall' pattern, and Nilo-Saharans vertical bars. The fraction of the Niger-Congolese group visible in the bottom left-hand corner is given a dark tint. The Indo-European shading will evolve in the complicated manner summarized in the Introduction: the other ethno-linguistic groups keep their shadings – or lack of them – for the rest of the atlas. On this map they indicate the likely range of each group in the sixth millennium BC.

1. Copper ores are typically brightly coloured, and the smelting temperature is low: the technology, in this preliminary phase, was used mainly for beads and bangles, and didn't have much effect on lifestyles.

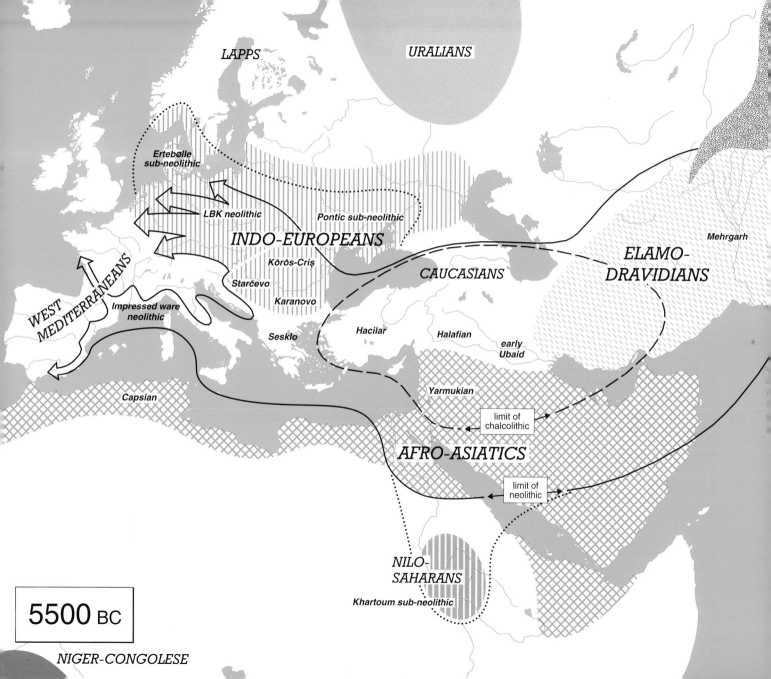

LAPPS

URALIANS

Ertebølle
sub-neolithic

LBK neolithic

Pontic sub-neolithic

INDO-EUROPEANS

Körös-Criş

Starčevo

CAUCASIANS

ELAMO-
DRAVIDIANS

Mehrgarh

WEST
MEDITERRANEANS

Impressed ware
neolithic

Karanovo

Sesklo

Hacilar

Halafian

early
Ubaid

Capsian

Yarmukian

limit of
chalcolithic

AFRO-ASIATICS

limit of
neolithic

NILO-
SAHARANS

Khartoum sub-neolithic

5500 BC

NIGER-CONGOLESE

The most important feature of this map is the appearance of a proto-urban culture in Mesopotamia. By using the annual flood of the Tigris and Euphrates to irrigate their crops, the *Ubaid* folk gradually built up a much denser network of settlements than had been achieved before. This quantitative change became the basis for qualitative advance when the populations of some of the individual villages rose to the 1,000 mark, for this is the level at which settlements begin to acquire some of the characteristics – public buildings, occupational specialization – that we associate with urban life. And towns duly made their appearance in the early fourth millennium BC, when the *Ubaid* culture gave way to the *Uruk*. It was a giant step forward.[1]

Meanwhile, in the course of the fifth millennium BC, the farming revolution completed its conquest of western Europe. *LBK*-derived cultures were responsible for the incorporation of Scandinavia and Britain into the neolithic world, Scandinavia becoming a province of the German *TRB* culture (the acronym stands for *Trichterbecher*, meaning 'funnel beaker'), while Britain's *Windmill Hill* culture is seen as an offshoot of the Rhineland's *Michelsberg*. In Britain's case the implication is that this marks the island's incorporation in the Indo-European zone, which brings us to the vexed question of non-Indo-Europeans here and elsewhere in Western Europe. There is no doubt about the existence of non-Indo-Europeans in the southern half of this region: the ancestors of the present-day Basques, the Iberians, originally held all of Spain plus the quarter of France south of the Loire and west of the Rhône. And in Italy there were the Etruscans, the assumed aborigines of the entire peninsula. These two provide the underpinning for the West Mediterranean group as shown on the map. Whether other members of this group provided the basal population of north west France and the British Isles is moot. The only evidence is the survival of a few non-Indo-European sounding place names, and philologists are always changing their minds about this sort of thing.[2]

At the other end of Europe there were now chalcolithic farming communities along the banks of the great Russian rivers. Despite claims to the contrary there is no evidence that the Dnieper-Don group, the *Sredni Stog* folk, had domesticated the horse, which remained an animal to be hunted and eaten, rather than corralled and ridden, until well into the third millennium. In the Near East the donkey was domesticated in the course of the fourth millennium, but probably only near its end.

An important ethno-linguistic development to note on this map is the division of the African half of the Afro-Asiatic phylum into three components, each with its own ecosphere: Berber (on the North African littoral), Egyptian (in the lower Nile valley), and Cushite (in the Eritrean-Ethiopian sector of the Horn of Africa). The Arabian half of the phylum can now be identified as Semitic, with Arabia as its ecosphere.

One people who do not appear on the map are the megalith-builders, who once occupied a great deal of space in archaeological texts. In the original version of the story the megalith-builders were Egyptians who sailed westward and taught the neolithic people of Atlantic Europe how to use large, undressed stones (megaliths) to construct communal tombs. The tombs certainly exist but they are much older than any equivalent Egyptian building: in Brittany, for example, they date back to the mid-fifth millennium BC, whereas the first Egyptian stone-built tombs (which, incidentally, used dressed stones) only date to the early third millennium. Nor can they be said to represent the West Mediterranean, as opposed to the Indo-European, component in the neolithic development of the region because they eventually spread to the Scandinavian littoral, way beyond any likely migration by Westerners. It seems that a fashion for communal burial tombs spread through the coastal peoples of western Europe not long after they first adopted a settled way of life: there is no ethnic pattern to it, and though it could represent a system of beliefs – a 'megalithic religion' – if it does, we have no way of recovering this.

None of which has stopped enthusiasts sailing soggy papyrus boats into the Atlantic.

1. Because there is no suggestion that this cultural change implies any change in the nature of the population, we can be confident that both the *Ubaid* folk and their *Uruk* successors were Sumerians, the people occupying this area when the historical record opens. Unfortunately the equation is not all that revealing: Sumerian is a unique language, with no known connection (so far) to any other, living or dead.

Irrigation was first practised along the northern fringe of the Mesopotamian plain, where people of the *Hassuna* culture were damming and diverting streams in the early sixth millennium. The *Ubaid/Uruk* achievement, utilizing major rivers, was on a quite different scale.

2. The map assumes that it was around this time that the Uralians spread westward, confining the Lapps to Scandinavia.

LAPPS

URALIANS

limit of
neolithic

Pit/Comb ware
sub-neolithic

Khvalynsk

limit of
chalcolithic

Windmill
Hill

TRB

Michelsberg

North
Caspian

Sredni Stog

Passage
Grave

Chassey

Tripoyle

INDO-EUROPEANS

ELAMO-
DRAVIDIANS

CAUCASIANS

Lagozza

Vinča

Gumelnitsa

WEST MEDITERRANEANS

Almerian

Diana

Proto-urban

BERBERS

SEMITES

EGYPTIANS

Nagada

NILO-
SAHARANS

CUSHITES

4000 BC

In the interval between this map and the last – more specifically in the period 3500–3250 BC – man learnt to write. The business of accumulating knowledge, the key to our species' success, could now begin. Details of how the first scripts evolved and spread will be found two maps further on: here all we need to note is that by 2750 BC the inhabitants of the Fertile Crescent, and the flanking lands of Egypt and Iran, had the capacity to keep records, and hence move from prehistory to history. As regards Mesopotamia, where the Sumerians invented the first script of all, the dividends for the historian are not very impressive. All we know is that the land was divided into a couple of dozen 'city-states' whose priest-kings contended for an overall supremacy that was rarely retained by any of them for long. The best-remembered of these early rulers is Gilgamesh of Uruk (c. 2650), who in later centuries became the hero of a famous tale of love, death and the search for immortality. In the real world his achievement was to win the suzerainty of Sumer for Uruk by defeating Agga of Kish, the previous holder of the title. Gilgamesh is said to have reigned for 126 years, which gives some idea of the problems Sumerologists have in constructing a believable chronology for the period. At least it's an improvement on the 1,000 years or more allocated to his immediate predecessors.[1]

Egypt's king lists are a little more helpful. They begin with Menes, King of Upper Egypt (the up-river, i.e. southern part of the country), who, around 3000 BC, conquered Lower Egypt (the Delta), politically uniting the country. Subsequently, as first Pharaoh of the first dynasty, he ruled this entire stretch of the Nile valley from Memphis, the capital he founded at the junction of the 'Two Lands' (Upper and Lower Egypt). This amply justifies Egypt's claim to be the world's oldest state. However nothing significant is recorded of his successors until the advent of the third dynasty's King Djoser (c. 2630–2610). Djoser decided that the relatively simple tombs constructed for earlier pharaohs wouldn't do for him, and he ordered his vizier Imhotep to build something bigger and better. Imhotep obliged with a six-storey step pyramid 60 metres high, erected at Saqqara, on the desert escarpment overlooking Memphis. Little did he know what he had started.

For the remainder of the literate area we have no history at all. The Elamites, the inhabitants of the part of the Iranian plateau facing Sumer, have left only store-keeper's accounts, and even these haven't been deciphered as yet. Syria had a scattering of city states (of which Ebla is the best known) with nomadic tribes in between. Palestine seems to have been a scaled down version of Syria.

In Europe we can now recognize a division of the Indo-Europeans into three separate sub-stocks. First to break off from the main stem was the proto-Hittite group, which moved from the Balkans to Anatolia: a date for this migration of around 2750 BC gives the Hittite languages, which are all rather similar, an appropriate amount of time to differentiate before they enter the historical record early in the next millennium. Subsequent to the departure of the Hittites a split took place between West and East Indo-European speakers, with the dividing line between the two running from just to the left of Denmark down to the middle Danube. Each of these three groups – West, East and Hittite – now sports its own shading. Note that the Tocharians, an Indo-European tribe that has wandered off into central Asia, are given the western shading. The apparent paradox of a western language in an eastern position caused considerable flutter in the philological dovecote when the literary remains of Tocharian first came to light in the nineteenth century, but all it means is that the Tocharians must have become isolated before the East Indo-European group had developed its distinguishing characteristics.

By this time the use of copper had spread right across Europe, changing the formal description of the communities there from neolithic to chalcolithic. Some became so adept at making copper tools that the term 'Copper Age' is not inappropriate. This is certainly the case as regards the Mediterranean world from Spain through to the Aegean. Even the humble Iceman – an Alpine shepherd frozen into a glacier around 3000 BC – had a copper axe to go with his flint knife. But the Near East and southeastern Europe had gone one better: they were now in the Bronze Age. Bronze is an alloy of 90 per cent copper and 10 per cent tin or arsenic: it makes stronger and sharper weapons and tools than pure copper; it is also easier to cast. The technology had

been a long time in the making. The initial step was the introduction of arsenic bronzes in the fourth millennium: the first tin bronzes followed in the early third millennium; maturity was not reached till later in the third millennium when tin bronze became the sole type. At the date of this map arsenic bronze was still the commoner form.[2]

On the bottom edge of the map note the spread of Nilo-Saharan and Cushitic pastoralists westward through the Sahel towards the Niger bend. This *Leiterband* movement completes the advance of the neolithic as far as our map is concerned: there were still hunter–gatherers in the far north where no other way of life was possible, but we no longer need to demarcate the neolithic area and the line doing so has been dropped.

1. Although the historic land of Sumer was restricted to lower (down-river, southern) Mesopotamia, recent excavations at the northern site of Nagar have produced tablets exactly the same as the earliest discovered in the south. This would seem to prove what some have long suspected, that in the protohistoric period (late fourth millennium) the Sumerians were running all of Mesopotamia. When they lost the northern half is unknown: it can't have been much later than the date of this map: on the other hand the fact that the somewhat later Eblaite (West Semitic) archive has a considerable Sumerian leavening suggests that it can't have been a lot earlier.

2. The invention of arsenic bronze seems to have taken place in the Anatolian-Caucasian area. Because it involved smelting copper and arsenic ores together the product was highly variable: the smiths probably learnt to pick out the more useful samples by eye – arsenic bronze has a silvery tint. Tin bronzes are first found in Mesopotamia in Early Dynastic levels (from 3000 BC). As Mesopotamia has no tin deposits the suggestion is that the discovery was made in the Afghan massif, which does. Tin bronze improved on its arsenic-based predecessor in two ways: the alloying process could be controlled more easily (because tin was available as a metal) and the alloy itself was superior as regards strength and ease of casting. Also, it didn't kill you while you were making it.

Egypt remained ignorant of bronze: pure copper artefacts are the rule there until well into the second millennium.

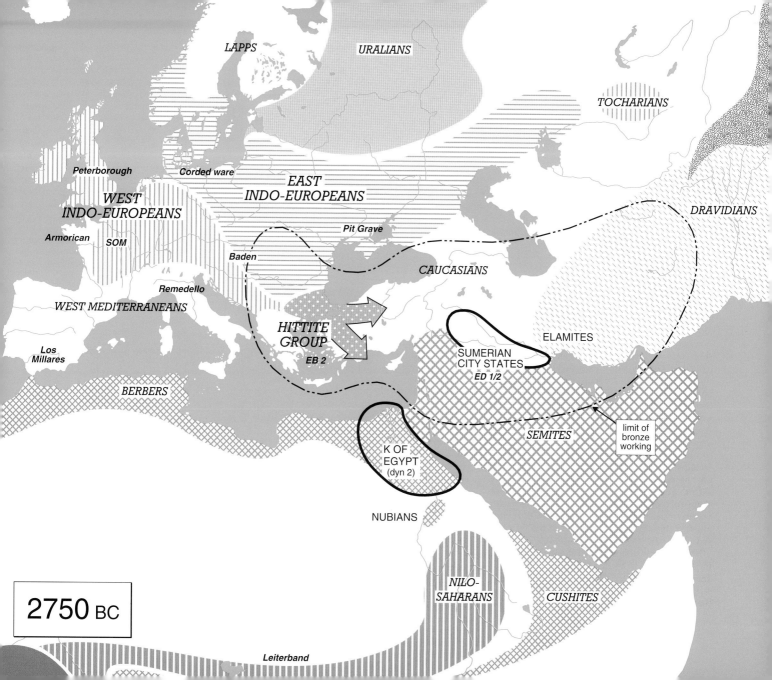

LAPPS

URALIANS

TOCHARIANS

Peterborough

Corded ware

EAST
INDO-EUROPEANS

DRAVIDIANS

WEST
INDO-EUROPEANS

Armorican   SOM

Pit Grave

Baden

CAUCASIANS

Remedello

WEST MEDITERRANEANS

HITTITE
GROUP

EB 2

SUMERIAN
CITY STATES

ED 1/2

ELAMITES

Los
Millares

BERBERS

limit of
bronze
working

K OF
EGYPT
(dyn 2)

SEMITES

NUBIANS

**2750** BC

NILO-
SAHARANS

CUSHITES

Leiterband

In the twenty-third century BC Sargon of Akkad created the first in what was to be a long sequence of Mesopotamian empires. His background is interesting, partly because he is the first to claim to have been found floating in a Moses basket, more cogently because he was a Semite, not a Sumerian. Semitic pastoralists had probably been present in Sumer from its beginnings: by Sargon's day they had entirely replaced the Sumerians in the northern third of Mesopotamia, and were beginning to do so in the middle third, the land of Akkad. Sargon, despite its humble origins, proved able to seize power in the important city-state of Kish, and then win the primacy of Sumer from its current holder, Lugalzagesi of Uruk. Subsequently he led a series of expeditions beyond Mesopotamia – to Mari, on the upper Euphrates, to Ebla in Syria, to the 'Cedar Mountain' in this region, and to Purushkanda, unlocated but thought to lie beyond the Taurus, on the Anatolian plateau. His grandson Naram-Sin was to add Susa, the capital of nearer Elam, to an Empire that already stretched from the Upper Sea (the Mediterranean) to the Lower (the Persian Gulf).[1]

In Egypt this was the pyramid age. Pharaoh Snofru, founder of the fourth dynasty (c. 2575–2465), built no less than three, progressively modifying Djoser's design until he had achieved something near the classic pyramid shape, and, in the case of two of them, heights of over 100 metres. His successor Cheops took the process to its logical conclusion, sharpening the angle and increasing the base. With a height of 147 metres his Great Pyramid at Giza became the tallest structure ever raised by man, a record it was to hold for more than 4,000 years. Cheops was followed by Khephren, who came close with a 143.5 metre monster: Mycerinus, builder of the last of the three Giza pyramids, was content with a comparative tiddler of 65.5 metres. Similar figures satisfied the subsequent pharaohs of the fifth and sixth dynasties (together c. 2465–2150).[2]

History's third literate civilization appeared in the Indus Valley in the later third millennium. We know very little about it because we can't read its script, and even if we could we'd probably be little the wiser: the surviving inscriptions are nearly all on seals and are unlikely to yield anything much beyond the names of their owners.

We can now take our development of the Indo-European family tree a stage further by splitting the Western sub-family into two and the Eastern initially into three, and then into five. The Western pair are Celto-Italic and Illyrian. The initial three-way division of the Easterners is into Germanics and Balto-Slavics in the north, Greeks and Thracians in the south-west, and Aryans in the east. The reason why the Germanics then split off from the Balto-Slavics is plain to see: the Germanic *Heimat*, the Scandinavian archipelago, is a littoral ecosphere that could hardly stand in sharper contrast to the Balto-Slavic world with its simple shoreline and continental focus. Much the same formulation applies to the Greeks and Thracians. Around the date of this map, the Greeks established their separate identity by moving into the peninsula they have occupied ever since: the original Graeco-Thracian *Heimat*, extending from the Axios to the Don, subsequently became the preserve of the Thracians. Beyond the Don lay the relatively harsh lands that sustained the as yet undivided Aryan stock.

Still undetermined is the nature of the Minoans, the predecessors of the Greeks in the islands of the Greek archipelago, and probably of the mainland too. The smart money is on them being an off-shoot of the Hittite group, but as their (much later) writings are as yet undeciphered there's no certainty about this – they may not even be Indo-Europeans.[3]

Archaeology isn't a great deal of help as regards these developments in the Indo-European ethno-linguistic tree, and, indeed, there is no reason why it should be. It can, however, give important indications of how the Indo-European zone was doing as a whole. The main feature is the *bellbeaker* radiation, a westward advance dated to the period 2550–2250 that can reasonably be thought of as bringing about the Indo-Europeanization of the Mediterranean coast of France and introducing the first Indo-European elements into Spain, as well as completing – if this had not already been achieved – the Indo-European domination of the British Isles. The rather earlier expansion of the *corded ware* group of cultures (2750–2250) is similarly equated with Indo-European expansion in the north-east. The *Fatyanovo* culture of the upper Volga marks the limit of this advance, which put previously Uralian territory in the hands of proto-Balts.[4]

1. Sargon was probably not the first Mesopotamian ruler to march beyond the region's natural boundaries: Lugalzagesi is said to have campaigned as far as the Upper Sea.

Also worth noting is the general nature of the contest for supremacy in Lower Mesopotamia. Although, as far as this map and its predecessor are concerned, only Kish and Uruk were in the ring, there were other players in the years between – Adab, Lagash, Umma and Ur.

2. The Great Pyramid's record was first exceeded by the 148-metre spire added to Rouen cathedral in AD 1876.

3. Minoan is an invented term, derived from the legendary King Minos of Crete (who in real life was probably a Greek). The Greeks called their predecessors in the peninsula Pelasgians, but spoilt the sense of the word by also applying it to pre-Dorian Greeks.

4. The most famous of Europe's prehistoric monuments, Stonehenge in the south of England, was all but completed during the *bell beaker* period. There had been a henge structure (a circular ditch with a circle of upright timbers inside) on the site since the beginning of the third millennium. This was transformed into the elaborate stone structure still visible today in 2600–2300 BC.

Note that the bronze-working line now includes the Indus valley in the east, and southern Italy in the west. Using Afghan tin Indus valley smiths produced tin-bronze from the start: lacking any such source the Italians were restricted to arsenic-bronze.

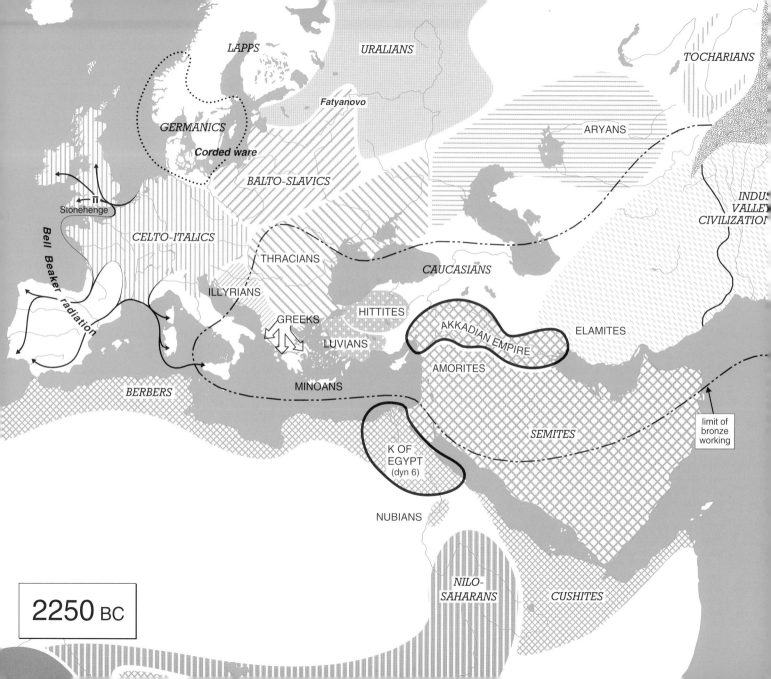

LAPPS

URALIANS

TOCHARIANS

*Fatyanovo*

GERMANICS

**Corded ware**

ARYANS

BALTO-SLAVICS

INDUS
VALLEY
CIVILIZATION

CELTO-ITALICS

Stonehenge

Bell Beaker radiation

THRACIANS

CAUCASIANS

ILLYRIANS

GREEKS

HITTITES

AKKADIAN EMPIRE

ELAMITES

LUVIANS

AMORITES

BERBERS

MINOANS

SEMITES

limit of
bronze
working

K OF
EGYPT
(dyn 6)

NUBIANS

NILO-
SAHARANS

CUSHITES

**2250 BC**

The Near Eastern peoples who pioneered the neolithic way of life also took it to more sophisticated levels than were attained elsewhere. A good example of this is their development of tokens, standardized clay shapes that could be used as pledges. A disc, for example, stood for a sheep; six discs, placed in a container and sealed with the owner's seal, served as a pledge to deliver six sheep to the holder at some appropriate date in the future. Tokens of many different sorts have been found at sites all over the Near East from Palestine to the Iranian plateau: the earliest seem to be as old as the neolithic itself.

In the mid-fourth millennium BC, attention shifted from the token to the container. Breaking the seal to check the contents was something that could only be done once, so it seemed sensible to indicate the contents on the outside. This was done by pressing a sample token onto the clay envelope while it was still wet: six disc-shaped depressions on the outside made it unnecessary to look inside. In fact, it made the tokens superfluous. By the late fourth millennium tokens and containers had been replaced by solid clay tablets, each of which was capable of recording multiple transactions. The extra jump that helped create this 'protoliterate' system was the separation of object and numeral. Instead of writing six sheep as disc-disc-disc-disc-disc-disc, and three cows as triangle-triangle-triangle, the tablets used disc and triangle as headings and recorded the numbers beside them:

Disc OOOOOO
Triangle OOO.

Separate versions of this system evolved in Mesopotamia (proto-Sumerian) and Iran (proto-Elamite): in both cases the headings were drawn on the clay using the sharp end of the stylus, and the numbers impressed using the blunt end.

The final step needed to turn the protoliterate notation into a fully fledged script was taken by the Sumerians around 3000 BC, when they started using the logograms (sheep and cow) as phonograms (sheep and cow as sounds, i.e. as syllables within battleSHEEP and MosCOW). This sort of script is called a logosyllabary, because it contains both logographic (whole word) and syllabic ele-ments. Such scripts can be ambiguous (maybe a MosCOW is a sort of cow?), so the Sumerians added a series of unpronounced signs called determinatives, which showed what class of object was meant (e.g. TOWN MosCOW). At the same time, they speeded up the process of writing by building up the drawings from a series of impressed marks – impressing clay is quicker and neater than trying to draw on it. Because they used a stylus with a triangular cross-section the marks were 'cuneiform' (meaning wedge-shaped). This cuneiform script proved a winner. By the date of the map it was being used to write several other languages besides Sumerian, specifically Akkadian (the language of the Semitic peoples of Mesopotamia), Hurrian (the southernmost of the Caucasian languages), Eblaite (a variant of Amorite, the Semitic language spoken in the western half of the Fertile Crescent) and Elamite. The Elamites developed a true script too, Linear Elamite, but this proved no match for cuneiform and seems only to have been used for a few decades, around 2100 BC. Cuneiform, by contrast, was to go from strength to strength.

Another writing system that was to have a relatively short life was the Indus Valley script. The language of this is thought to be Dravidian, though as no one has managed to decipher the script there can be no certainty about this. More confidently we can say that it was a logosyllabary because it has 200 or so signs, too many for a more advanced system. It developed no earlier than the mid-third millennium BC and lasted only as long as the Indus Valley civilization, i.e. to about 1800–1600 BC. Its appearance suggests that it followed an Elamite model which must indeed be the case given the geography.

That brings us to the Egyptian hieroglyphic script, almost as old as cuneiform, even more impressive, and equally long-lived. It appears in the early third millennium BC and its structure – a logosyllabary with unpronounced determinatives – betrays its Mesopotamian inspiration. However, the Egyptians had been using emblems to identify rulers and tribes since 3000 BC and they drew on this pictographic tradition for their hieroglyphs. As a result their script looks totally different from cuneiform. The pictographs it employs were in fact too elaborate for everyday use so it soon split into two variants: hieroglyphic, reserved for formal inscriptions, and hieratic, a cursive form written with a stylus on clay or with brush and ink on stone, pottery or papyrus.[1]

1. Hieroglyphic simply means 'priestly writing' and indicates the supposed religious monopoly of literacy in ancient Egypt. By (etymologically incorrect) analogy, any form of writing which has a high pictorial content is apt to be called hieroglyphic, as, for example, the later, and quite differently structured, Luvian hieroglyphic. As far as structure is concerned the unique feature of Egyptian hieroglyphic is that the signs are purely consonantal – vowels are not scored at all. Ths wldnt wrk wll n nglsh, but is a practical system for Afro-Asiatic languages where consonants matter much more than vowels.

PROTO-SUMERIAN

PROTO-ELAMITE

INDUS VALLEY GLYPHS

EGYPTIAN HIEROGLYPHIC

HIERATIC

CUNEIFORM

LINEAR ELAMITE

Literacy in
**2250** BC

literate area unshaded

Until the end of the last Ice Age, man was a rare animal. When the weather was at its worst there were probably no more than 100,000 humans of one sort or another in the area covered by the map – a density of less than one individual per 200 km² of habitable land. Numbers will have risen as the ice retreated, but only at an inchingly slow rate: 250,000 people would be a reasonable guess for 9000 BC, the eve of the neolithic revolution. This was the event that forever changed the demographic scene, for population increased rapidly wherever farming was introduced, and, as farming itself improved, a rising curve became the order of the day. Numbers will have reached a million by the date of our fourth map (5500 BC), and doubled every millennium thereafter. By 2250 BC we are looking at a population of 10 million (out of a global total of 25 million). Man had become ubiquitous.

Well, not quite. There were areas – the Sahara is the obvious example – where humans were effectively absent, and others – most obviously in the far north – where they were still leading an Ice Age life at Ice Age densities. Then too there were lands where farming was a recent introduction and people still comparatively thin on the ground. The 70,000 or so inhabitants of Britain, for instance, will have been scarcely visible in what was, at this time, an almost completely untamed environment. People will have been easier to find in somewhere like France, which had ten times the population, but even there there will have been large gaps between the inhabited areas. For contiguous settlements we have to turn to the Near East where irrigating agriculture both required and sustained much denser populations. The valleys of the Nile, the Tigris and Euphrates, and the Indus each contained populations of the same order of magnitude as France – say 750,000 people – but within a much smaller orbit. This proved enough to set the wheels of civilization in motion.

One result of the greater density of population in these parts of the Near East was an increase in settlement size. West Europeans typically lived in scattered homesteads, whereas the East European or Near Easterner was, as often as not, a villager. In the course of the third millennium BC the Mesopotamians took this distinction a stage further: the most prosperous of their villages – perhaps as many as two dozen of them – grew into towns. These towns, which we can think of as having populations in the 3,000–6,000 range, became the nuclei of 'city-states', county-sized units that were to be the building blocks of Early Mesopotamian history. The map shows the dozen of most importance in the late third millennium, those we can guess had populations of 5,000 or more, plus Agade, the residence Sargon built for himself after establishing his hegemony over Mesopotamia, though this was probably a palace, not a town.

How far down this road did the other river valley civilizations go? In the case of Egypt the answer is no distance at all. In its Old Kingdom phase (dynasties 1 to 6, c. 3000–2150) the country was run from the Pharaoh's palace, which moved about from reign to reign but was generally to be found within a day's walk of the Temple of Ptah at Memphis. But neither palace nor temple will have ranked as a town, nor do we know of anywhere else in Egypt that did. The Indus Valley civilization, on the other hand, has produced two sites that appear to have urban dimensions (i.e. areas in the 20–50 ha. range), Mohenjo Daro and Harappa. What this means in political terms is difficult to say: they could be the northern and southern capitals of a single state, or two independent centres, or the sole surviving elements of a Mesopotamian-type patchwork of 'city-states'.

To what extent were the three Near Eastern civilizations in touch with each other? The somewhat surprising answer is that there seems to have been significant contact between Mesopotamia and the Indus valley, but no sustained traffic between Mesopotamia and Egypt.[1] This probably has to do with the lack of any native sources of copper in both Mesopotamia and the Indus Valley. We know that the Mesopotamians obtained much of their copper from Magan (generally conceded to be Oman, in southeast Arabia) via Dilmun (probably Bahrain). In Magan they could well have met up with merchants from the Indus, who had a trading post at Sutkagen Dor, on the coast opposite Oman. The source of the tin used in the Near East is more mysterious. There are no deposits in Mesopotamia or its borderlands, and all one can say is that the source lay to the east, probably in the streams running off the mountains of Afghanistan. There is no prob-

lem about the distances involved in this trade. Lapis lazuli is found at Mesopotamian sites from the late fourth millennium BC on, and the only place where this semi-precious stone occurs – in Badakshan, in north-east Afghanistan – is at least as far away as the likely sources of tin. At this date the lapis (and tin) probably got to Mesopotamia via the sea route from the Indus valley: there's a Harappan outpost at Shortugai on the upper Oxus, only a short distance downstream from the lapis mountain, and with such long distances involved, sailing down the Indus and up the Persian Gulf will surely have been quicker than the land route across Iran. The same applies to the connection between Egypt and the Levant; once the maritime link with Byblos was established what overland traffic there was is likely to have fallen off sharply.

1. The fact that there was no sustained traffic between Egypt and Mesopotamia does not mean that there was no contact at all. As already noted Mesopotamia provided the inspiration for Egypt's hieroglyphic script, and the same can be said for Djoser's step pyramid, which clearly mimics Mesopotamia's ziggurats (brick step pyramids, topped off with a temple). As far as the Levant is concerned there is no doubt about the contact with Egypt: articles inscribed with the names of Old Kingdom pharaohs have turned up at both Byblos and Ebla. This said, the complete absence of bronze artefacts in Old Kingdom Egypt suggests that the trade route between the two was a pretty tenuous affair.

SILVER

Nagar

Ebla

Mari

Agade

SILVER

LAPIS

Shortugai +

Harappa

TIN?

Mohenjo
Daro

Sutkagen Dor +

Susa

1 Sippar
2 Eshnunna

COPPER

Bahrain +

Byblos +

Memphis □

GOLD

Towns and trade routes in
## 2250 BC

- ◆ town
- + trading post
- □ royal residence

key to Mesopotamian towns
1 Sippar
2 Eshnunna
3 Kish
4 Adab
5 Umma
6 Lagash
7 Isin
8 Shuruppak
9 Uruk
10 Ur

At the end of dynasty 6 the Egyptian king list goes to pieces. After ascribing a reign of ninety-nine years to the dynasty's final pharaoh, Pepy II, it has a downright goofy dynasty 7 ('Seventy pharaohs in seventy days') followed by an obscure dynasty 8 (twenty-seven unnamed pharaohs ruling 146 years). The general assumption among Egyptologists is that the central authority nose-dived during this period, which is thought to have covered most of the twenty-first century BC. Subsequently two distinct kingdoms appeared, one centred on Heracleopolis (dynasties 9 and 10) the other on Thebes (dynasty 11). Around 2040 BC the Theban prince Mentuhotpe I overcame the Heracleopolitans, bringing to a close the 'First Intermediate Period' and inaugurating the 'Middle Kingdom' (middle in time; it comes between the Old Kingdom and the New or Empire). The Middle Kingdom was to prove itself every bit the equal of the Old: the writ of Pharaoh – at this juncture Amenemhet III of the twelfth dynasty – ran unchallenged throughout the Two Lands.

Mesopotamia had similar ups and downs. Sargon's successors maintained his empire for something over a century, then, shortly after 2200 BC, the Guti, barbarians from the Zagros, overran Akkad and put an end to both empire and dynasty. Order was restored by Sumerian rulers, first a king of Uruk who expelled the Guti, then the kings of Ur's third dynasty, who created an empire almost as extensive as Sargon's. This Sumerian Indian summer lasted till near the end of the twenty-first century BC, when it was terminated by an Elamite army that put Ur to the sack. For the next two and a half centuries (twentieth to mid-eighteenth) Mesopotamia reverts to its traditional pattern of competing city states. This time the names are all Semitic: the Sumerians, who had named the land, given it its gods and its place at the start of history, have been buried by a new wave of immigrants.

The newcomers were the Amorites, nomads who had been hanging round the western border of Mesopotamia since Sargon's day. Ethnically, they were no different from the more settled Semites of Palestine and Syria, so the patchwork of Amorite city-states, with nomadic tribes of the same stock roaming their fringes, now extended across the entire Fertile Crescent. Making their first appear-

ances in the new Mesopotamian city list are two names that were to become increasingly prominent as the centuries passed: Assur on the upper Tigris, and Babylon just south of the Mesopotamian waist. Assur at this stage was far from being the ferociously military state that it later became: if it was remarkable for anything it was for long-distance trading. The discovery of the archives of an Assyrian merchant community in the Anatolian town of Kanesh has given us an important insight into the way this activity was managed. Regular donkey caravans brought tin and textiles from Assur to Kanesh, where all three – tin, textiles and donkeys – were exchanged for silver: subsequently couriers took the silver to Assur. Another archive, this time from the Royal Palace at Mari, indicates that the tin came from Elam via Eshnunna. Mari sent its supply on to various towns in Syria and Palestine, and, via the seaport of Ugarit, to Crete. The Kanesh and Mari documents testify to the vigour and stability of the Near Eastern trading network in the nineteenth century BC: they also afford us a glimpse of the political situation in Anatolia (where the first steps were being taken to create a unitary Hittite Kingdom), though not, alas, in Iran or Crete. Iran is generally thought to have been experiencing an influx of Aryan tribes at this time (horses make their first appearance there during this period): Crete was evolving the sophisticated Palace-centred society that represents the high water mark of the Minoan culture.[1]

Of the various peoples making their first appearance on this map, the Hurrians are the southernmost of the Caucasians, and the Lycians the southernmost of the Luvians: both are mentioned in contemporary Near Eastern texts. Lacking this sort of documentary base, but surely in existence by this time, are the Italics, who can hardly have separated from the Celto-Italic stem any later than this. Their departure enables us to re-label the main stock Celto-Ligurian. Note that an area is left clear in the centre of Arabia in this and succeeding maps to indicate the low population levels of the interior. Also that, as their shadings are now well established, the Berber, Cushite, Semitic and Nilo-Saharan stocks are no longer labelled. Likewise the Lapps and Uralians.

Western Europe has now entered the Bronze Age, thanks to the discovery of the tin deposits of Cornwall, in the south-western corner of Britain. This enables us to drop the 'Bronze line' from the map. But, whereas this is Europe's Early Bronze Age, it is the Middle Bronze Age as far as the Aegean and Near East are concerned. In the Aegean the classification is further complicated by the archaeologists' use of geographical as well as temporal subdivisions: it is the Middle Helladic in the Greek peninsula, Middle Cycladic in the islands and Middle Minoan in Crete.[2]

1. This era in Mesopotamian history is known as the Isin-Larsa period, after the two most important competitors for overall hegemony, Isin (Semitic but not Amorite) and Larsa (Amorite). The competition ended in Isin's overthrow, shortly after the date of this map.

2. Neither copper nor bronze technology crossed the Sahara or travelled further up the Nile than the Sudd marshes. Black Africa was to remain at a neolithic level till its Iron Age began around 500 BC.

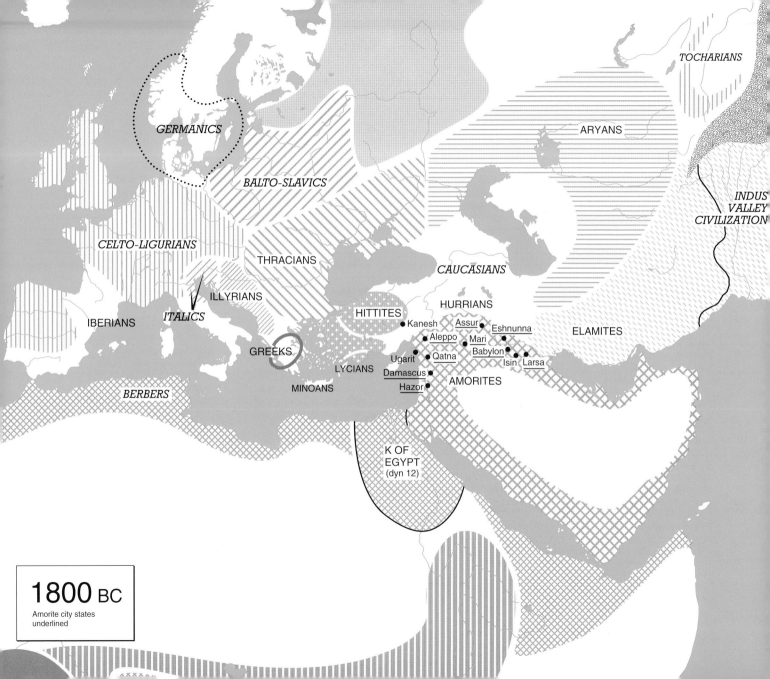

TOCHARIANS

GERMANICS

BALTO-SLAVICS

ARYANS

INDUS
VALLEY
CIVILIZATION

CELTO-LIGURIANS

THRACIANS

CAUCASIANS

IBERIANS

ILLYRIANS

HURRIANS

ITALICS

HITTITES

Kanesh

Assur

Eshnunna

ELAMITES

GREEKS

Aleppo

Mari

Babylon

LYCIANS

Ugarit

Qatna

Isin

Larsa

BERBERS

MINOANS

Damascus

AMORITES

Hazor

K OF
EGYPT
(dyn 12)

**1800 BC**

Amorite city states
underlined

Towards the end of the eighteenth century an Amorite ruler, Hammurabi of Babylon, brought all Mesopotamia under his sway. Today Hammurabi is mainly remembered for his 'Eye for an Eye' law code, but a more important legacy was his promotion of Babylon, which subsequently became the accepted capital of the region. Not that this was obvious at the time, for within forty years of his death his kingdom had been reduced to little more than the city itself. First Isin broke away, as the 'Kingdom of the Sea-Land'. Then Assyria recovered its independence. To add to Babylon's woes, the Kassites of the central Zagros began moving into central Mesopotamia. However the final blow came from a totally unexpected direction. Around 1595, Mursilis I, second king of the newly created Hittite monarchy, led his forces south of the Taurus, took Aleppo, the strongest of the Syrian principalities, and then marched down the Euphrates and captured Babylon. Its sack was the high point of the Hittite Old Kingdom, which drew back into Anatolia on Mursilis' death. Mesopotamia subsequently split four ways, with the Hurrians dominant in the north-west, the Assyrians in the north-east (hidden behind the Mitanni arrow), a Kassite dynasty ensconced in Babylon, and the Kings of the Sea Land ruling the south.

Egypt was in a similar state of division, largely because of the invasion of the Hyksos. The Hyksos – the term is traditionally translated as 'Shepherd Kings' – were Semites from Palestine, who set up a kingdom based at Avaris in the eastern corner of the Delta. It's not unreasonable to see their movement as the last in the Amorite series. When they entered the country (around 1700 BC) the Middle Kingdom was in the hands of the rapidly weakening thirteenth dynasty, which had allowed the Delta Princes of Xois (constituting dynasty 14) to make their fief independent, and Nubia to recover its freedom. The Hyksos, who contribute dynasties 15 and 16 to the king list, made themselves the dominating force in the Nile valley. They did not, however, occupy Upper Egypt, which was ruled by a native line of Princes (dynasty 17) established at Thebes.[1]

If, for Egypt and Mesopotamia, this was a time of foreign domination, the outward forms of their already ancient civilizations were respected and soon adopted by their conquerors. The inhabitants of the Indus Valley were not so fortunate, for their civilization was utterly destroyed by the Aryans who, around the date of this map, invaded the subcontinent. As a culture it had never quite measured up to the other two, which perhaps accounts for the totality of its eclipse. Whereas many of the monuments and much of the lore of Egypt and Mesopotamia survived their decline, the culture of the Indus Valley left only the faintest of memories behind.

In the Rig-veda, the Aryans who invaded India have left us a fairly straightforward picture of themselves as a warrior folk using horse-drawn chariots. The chariot was a new bit of military hardware, which it is safe to presume was an Aryan invention: the Aryans had the horses, and lots of the flat, hard, open space needed to get people thinking about how to go faster. The key to the design was the spoked wheel: this made the chariot the wonder weapon of the age, and as such it played a major role in the various movements that, as we have seen, brought grief to the settled communities of the Near East during this period. The Aryans seem to have provided leadership as well as chariots for at least some of these aggressions. The Kassites were (probably) an Elamite people but their aristocracy may have been Aryan – they certainly worshipped some Aryan-sounding gods. For sure the Hurrians of north Mesopotamia, though Caucasians, owed their organization into a kingdom to an Aryan clan, the Mitanni. But that's probably as far as one can take this idea: nobody now thinks that the Hyksos, who introduced the chariot to Egypt, were Aryans, and the Hittites seem to have simply taken the technology from the Mitanni (a Mitannian training manual has been found at the Hittite capital Hattusas). From Anatolia it passed to the Greeks who, lacking the terrain needed for chariot warfare, used it for parade purposes. Where the Aryans come in again is in the chariot's spread eastward to China, where it appears in Shang tombs of the thirteenth century BC. At a later date we find Aryan tribes strung across the Asian steppe all the way to Gansu, China's north-western border province, and it's not unreasonable to put the beginnings of this eastward spread back to this era.[2]

In western Europe note the Italic expansion across central Italy, bypassing the non-Indo-European people of Etruria (modern Tuscany). Also the beginning of the split between the mainstream Celts (of northern France, the Rhine and the upper Danube) and the Ligurians (of southern France and the north-eastern corner of Italy). There is no accepted term for the Celto-Ligurian related peoples of the Iberian peninsula, now occupying as much territory as the natives, the non-Indo-European Iberians.

A contemporary event that has attracted a lot of attention is the eruption of Thera, the volcanic Aegean island now known as Santorini. This was certainly a catastrophic event, ten times as powerful as the more famous eruption of Vesuvius in AD 79 (and thirty times as powerful as that of Mt. St Helens in 1980). It undoubtedly destroyed the Minoan settlement on the island, and the *tsunami* (tidal wave) it caused will have been responsible for many more deaths in the coastal communities of neighbouring islands and along the northern shore of Crete. But the idea that it put an end to Minoan civilization is not a sensible proposition; little better, in truth, than the associated chatter about the lost world of Atlantis. What does give the Thera eruption more than local significance is its ashfall, which offers archaeologists the chance of establishing synchronies as far afield as Egypt. Moreover dendrochronologists have recently come up with an exact date of 1628 BC for it. This has surprised the Egyptologists, who had been working with a date at least a century later. At the moment they are in denial.

1. The Hyksos era, the Second Intermediate Period of Egyptian historiography, is a lot more obscure than this précis implies: the existence of the fourteenth dynasty has never been verified, and the king list for the Hyksos has many uncertainties. At this time Nubia (between cataracts 1 and 2) combined with Kush (from 2 to a point above 3) to form a principality whose ruling house is shown as Egyptian, but could equally well have been Nilo-Saharan.

2. About 1700 BC northern China passed straight from the neolithic into a full Bronze Age. The absence of an evolutionary chalcolithic phase confirms the obvious assumption that the Chinese derived their bronze-working techniques from the Near East.

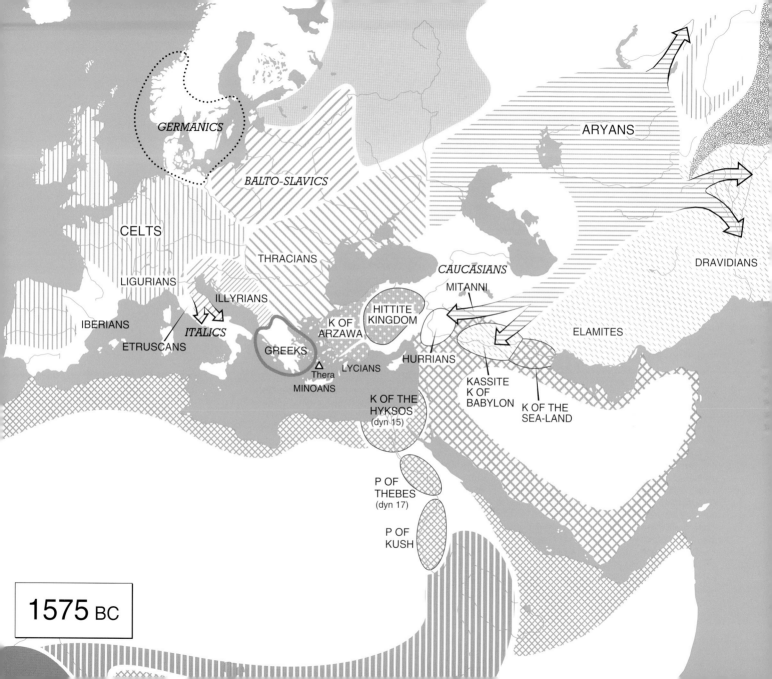

GERMANICS

BALTO-SLAVICS

CELTS

THRACIANS

LIGURIANS

ILLYRIANS

IBERIANS

*ITALICS*

ETRUSCANS

GREEKS

K OF
ARZAWA

HITTITE
KINGDOM

LYCIANS

△ Thera

MINOANS

CAUCASIANS

MITANNI

HURRIANS

ARYANS

DRAVIDIANS

ELAMITES

KASSITE
K OF
BABYLON

K OF THE
SEA-LAND

K OF THE
HYKSOS
(dyn 15)

P OF
THEBES
(dyn 17)

P OF
KUSH

1575 BC

The expulsion of the Hyksos from Egypt by Ahmose, Prince of Thebes, transformed the vassal seventeenth dynasty into the imperial eighteenth. Ahmose (ruling *c.* 1545 BC) pursued the Hyksos into Palestine, which became the first province of the fledgling Egyptian Empire; succeeding pharaohs went further, Tuthmosis I (*c.* 1485 BC) raiding among the Hurrians of Syria, Tuthmosis III (*c.* 1450 BC) making the Euphrates his frontier and, on occasion, crossing it.[1] However, a counter-offensive by the Hurrians under the leadership of the Mitanni succeeded in driving the Egyptians from Syria, and thereafter the eighteenth dynasty Empire never extended much beyond Byblos on the coast, and Palestine as regards the interior. A subsequent truce between the Egyptians and the Mitanni, at first sullen, became cordial as the power of the Hittites revived. The Hittite kings brought the states of western Anatolia (Lycia and Arzawa) to heel in the second quarter of the fourteenth century; towards its end Hittite armies appeared south of the Taurus once more. The invaders quickly broke the power of the Mitanni and took their place as masters of northern Syria.

Egypt, preoccupied with Akhenaten's religious revolution (*see* p. 44, n1), made no attempt to prevent or exploit the collapse of the Mitanni, and it was only with the accession of the next dynasty that Egypt intervened in Syria again. By then it was too late: the Hittites had consolidated their position and the nineteenth dynasty's most militant pharaohs, Seti I and Ramesses II, were both beaten off, the latter in a decisive battle at Kadesh (1275 BC). The Egyptians retained Palestine, though on a loose rein, with the Pharaoh's representatives adjudicating between the local rulers, rather than issuing orders. This was different from the situation in Kush, which had been a directly administered province since its conquest by Tuthmosis I.

Jewish history begins to come into focus during this period. Abraham was presumably an Amorite chieftain whose lineage moved to Egypt with, or in the wake of, the Hyksos. Conditions for the Semitic minority will have deteriorated after the Hyksos were expelled: the first historically identifiable bit of the Bible has the Israelites working as slave labourers on Pi-Ramesses, the new town Ramesses II built alongside Avaris in the eastern delta. From there they exited Egypt; then, after a sojourn in Sinai that only a people of strong nomad traditions could have survived, moved across the Negeb into Transjordan. Ascending Mount Nebo, their leader Moses was able to look across the river, into the promised land.

In Mesopotamia Assyria, which had been a vassal of the Mitanni in their heyday (1400 BC), regained its independence when the Mitanni were defeated by the Hittites (1325 BC). Fifty years later the Assyrians completed their recovery by annexing the remnants of the Mitannian state. In the south the Kassites of Babylon conquered the Kingdom of the Sea-Land (1450 BC). In the Aegean the Greeks extended their sway over the islands, including Crete. Both archaeology and legend suggest that the important Greek kingdoms at this time were Mycenae, overlord of the Peloponnese, Thebes, the most powerful state in central Greece, and Knossos, seat of King Minos of Crete. Archaeologists refer to the Greeks of the period as Mycenaeans, regardless of the fact that the Mycenaean kingdom was far from being all-embracing: Homeric scholars call them Achaeans, which is one of the terms that Homer uses, the other being Danaoi.

Further differentiation of the East Indo-European stock is now in order. The Aryan stem can be divided into Iranian, Indic and Scytho-Cimmerian branches, each with the separate geographical compartments needed to keep them moving apart linguistically. In darker Europe the notable event is the appearance of the *Lausitz* culture in Poland, conventionally taken as marking the emergence of the Slavs. The *Lausitz* people were the first to adopt a funeral rite soon to become widespread, cremation with burial of the ashes in an urn. The cemetery that results from this is called an urnfield, and the community concerned an *Urnfield* culture.

Minor points to note are the appearance of the Cypriote Kingdom of Alašiya – at this period a Hittite vassal – and the Italics' completion of their drive down the Italian peninsula.

---

[1] Tuthmosis I also conquered Kush and extended Egyptian control of the upper Nile to a point midway between cataracts 4 and 5.

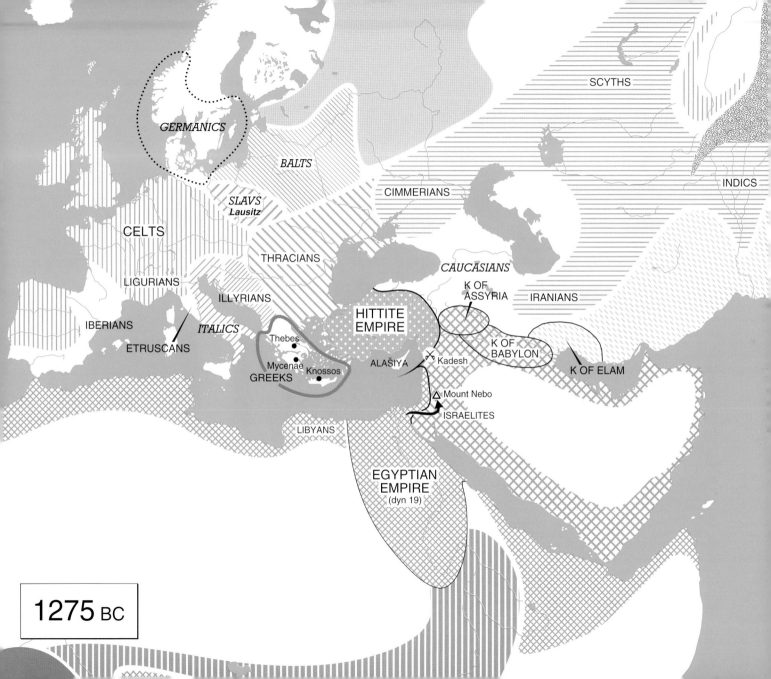

SCYTHS

INDICS

*GERMANICS*

*BALTS*

CIMMERIANS

*SLAVS*
*Lausitz*

*CAUCASIANS*

CELTS

K OF
ASSYRIA

IRANIANS

THRACIANS

LIGURIANS

ILLYRIANS

HITTITE
EMPIRE

IBERIANS

*ITALICS*

K OF
BABYLON

Thebes

ETRUSCANS

ALAŠIYA

Kadesh

K OF ELAM

Mycenae
Knossos

GREEKS

△ Mount Nebo

ISRAELITES

LIBYANS

EGYPTIAN
EMPIRE
(dyn 19)

1275 BC

The progress of literacy during the second millennium was far from smooth. In the east, important ground was lost when the unlettered Aryans overran eastern Iran and the Indus valley: Elamite cuneiform was subsequently restricted to the area of the Elamite Kingdom, while the Indus Valley script disappeared altogether. However, more than adequate compensation for this setback is to be found in the west where the Aegean communities became literate and, what is more, did so with a new and better form of writing, the open syllabary. The old logosyllabaries contained signs for all types of monosyllable and even some signs for disyllables: in contrast the new scripts restricted themselves to a single class, the open syllable, consisting of simple consonant-vowel combinations such as ma, me, mi, mo or mu. This reduces the number of signs needed from many hundreds to a mere eighty or so.

The evolutionary history of the open syllabary is unknown: some have seen its beginnings in the 'pseudo-hieroglyphic' of Byblos, but the dating of this is uncertain, and its decipherment even more so. A safer starting point is probably to be found in the symbols that occur on Cretan seals of the early second millennium. This 'Cretan hieroglyphic' subsequently developed into the as yet undeciphered Linear A script used by the Minoans in the sixteenth century BC. This is certainly an open syllabary, the oldest known for sure. By the date of this map what is essentially the same script was being used to write Greek, in which (fully deciphered) form it is known as Linear B. Another relative of Linear A, Cypro-Minoan, was in use on Cyprus for the (pre-Greek) language of the island: alas, it too falls in the undeciphered category. Luvian hieroglyphic, on the other hand, is well understood. Despite its name and peculiar appearance it is an open syllabary of the Aegean type: it probably came into use not much later than Linear A.[1]

The open syllabary was in its turn outmoded by the consonantal alphabet, a Syro-Palestinian invention that followed naturally from the use of an open syllabary for writing languages like Semitic – in which consonants dominate and vowels are relatively unimportant. When this is the case, only one sign is required for each class in the syllabary – one for m (any vowel), for example – and the total number of signs needed falls to about twenty. This is such a huge advance that it seems petty to point out that a set of signs for consonants (vowels understood) is not the same as a set consisting of separate signs for consonants and vowels and that a consonantal alphabet is not a true alphabet.[2]

There are consonantal alphabets in both cuneiform (Ugaritic) and a cursive based on Egyptian hieroglyphs (proto-Canaanite and proto-Sinaitic). The surprising thing about them is their date, some examples of proto-Canaanite being put as far back as the eighteenth century BC. This makes it entirely possible that the evolutionary sequence from open syllabary to consonantal alphabet given here is false, and that the open syllabary was in fact an expanded version of the consonantal alphabet for languages in which vowels needed specifying.

Though these developments are the most exciting aspect of second millennium literacy it should not be forgotten that, on a contemporary view, this was the golden age of cuneiform. It was used for a surprising variety of different languages: Indo-European (Hittite and the Aryan horse-training manuals of the Mitanni), Caucasian (Hurrian), and Elamo-Dravidian (Elamite) as well as Semitic and Sumerian (this last now a dead language though still taught in the scribal schools). It was the recognized mode for diplomatic communications: even the pharaohs of the proud eighteenth dynasty conducted their foreign correspondence in Akkadian cuneiform. And it was on the verge of its greatest success ever. Towards the end of the thirteenth century BC the Shang princes of North China began to use a script that is as clearly dependent on a near eastern prototype for its structure – it uses the same system of logosyllabic signs and determinatives – as it is distinct – and quintessentially Chinese – in its individual characters. In this encrypted form Sumer's greatest invention is still with us today.

1. It is usual to bring in the Phaistos disc at this point because it was found (on Crete) in a sixteenth-century BC context, and its forty-five different signs suggest that it is an open syllabary. However these are just about the only ways in which it fits in with what we know of second millennium writing systems. The signs have been impressed using punches, a technique otherwise unknown in the ancient world. The spiral layout is also unique. The clay it is made of has been handled in a peculiar, amateurish-looking way. Most important of all – it's a one-off: nothing like it has turned up in the ninety years since it was discovered. It has to be a hoax.

2. Grammatologists call consonantal alphabets abjads. This seems too ugly a word ever to catch on.

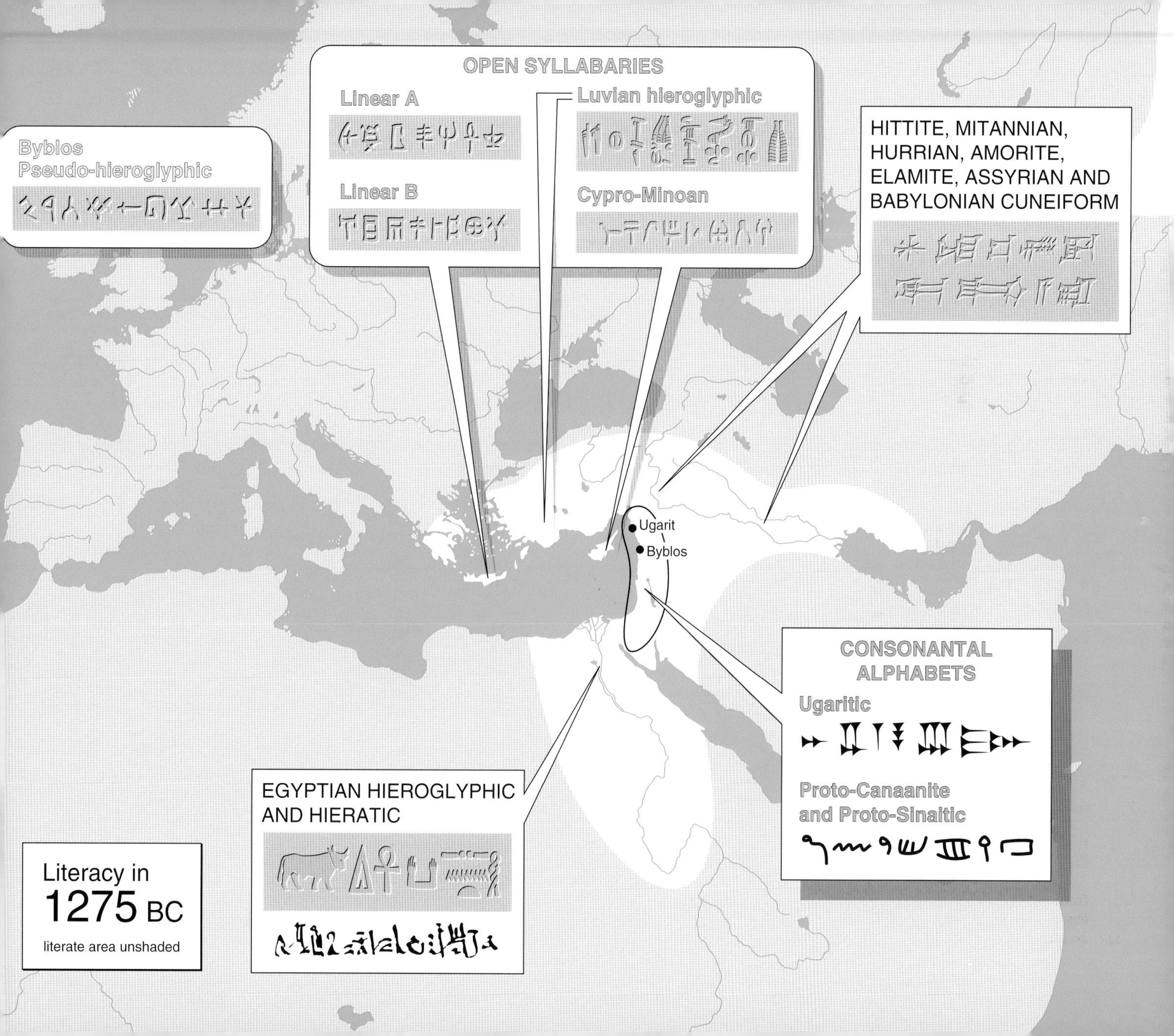

Byblos
Pseudo-hieroglyphic

**OPEN SYLLABARIES**

Linear A

Luvian hieroglyphic

Linear B

Cypro-Minoan

HITTITE, MITANNIAN,
HURRIAN, AMORITE,
ELAMITE, ASSYRIAN AND
BABYLONIAN CUNEIFORM

Ugarit

Byblos

**CONSONANTAL
ALPHABETS**

Ugaritic

Proto-Canaanite
and Proto-Sinaitic

EGYPTIAN HIEROGLYPHIC
AND HIERATIC

Literacy in
**1275** BC

literate area unshaded

The Late Bronze Age was a prosperous period. The population model used in this book suggests a figure of 25 million for the area of the map (out of a world total of 45 million) with several geographical regions – Spain, France and Italy in the west, Anatolia, Egypt, the Fertile Crescent and Iran in the east – having populations around the 2 million mark. In most areas, though, densities were still not high enough for town formation and the majority of Bronze Age people lived in small isolated communities, homesteads more often than hamlets, and hamlets more often than villages. The Near East was better focused, with true villages (having hundreds of inhabitants) scattered along the Nile valley and through the Fertile Crescent. The Fertile Crescent could also boast a dozen towns, a category for which we can now raise the qualifying threshold to 7,500. Egypt, despite its high population density, still had no centres of this size. Thebes and Memphis, the capitals of Upper and Lower Egypt, were loose associations of palace, necropolis and temple without anything much in the way of suburbs, and though Akhenaten did build an integrated administrative centre at Akhetaten, this was abandoned by his successor Tutankhamun.[1] The nature of Hattusas, the Hittite capital (perhaps more familiar under its modern name of Bogazkoy) is difficult to assess: its walls certainly enclose a large area but whether it had a population to match is questionable; this part of the world did not produce anything in the way of major towns in the remainder of antiquity and the site has a hollow, bombastic feel to it which puts one in mind of Charles Foster Kane. On the whole it seems safer to classify it as a royal residence rather than a town. As to the Mycenaeans' 'cities', they come in two varieties: castles like Mycenae and unfortified palaces like Knossos. Neither sort covered much more than a hectare, which means that, on the standard set in the Near East, they can't really be rated as royal residences, let alone towns.

What of trade? Here we get some helpful insights from the Amarna correspondence, the diplomatic archive left behind when Akhetaten (modern el-Amarna) was abandoned. There are letters to and from all the potentates of the Near East, and nearly every one of these diplomatic exchanges was accompanied by the dispatch of presents and a demand for presents in return. As regards Egypt it is clear that what Pharaoh's fellow monarchs wanted from him was gold. 'Gold is as dust in the land of Egypt' wrote the Mitannian king and it does seem that, thanks to mines in the Eastern Desert, the Egyptians had more than anyone else. The Pharaoh's ambassadors also took with them linen, and furniture inlaid with ivory and ebony. In return the rulers of the Near East sent horses and chariots, lapis, and the occasional iron weapon or ornament. Iron was a new, exciting, and very expensive technology at this time and only kings could afford it. The Egyptians were also interested in acquiring copper from Cyprus (a major producer from this time on), and glass from Tyre and Ascalon (the Levantine towns made a speciality of glass manufacture).

Two shipwrecks of the late Bronze Age have confirmed the picture gleaned from these documents. Both were found off the south Turkish coast: the first, tree-ring dated to 1316 BC, off Ulu Burun; the second, dated to around 1200 BC, off Cape Gelidonya. The Ulu Burun wreck was carrying 6 tons of Cypriot copper (almost exactly the 200 talents of copper requested by Pharaoh in one of the Armana letters), a ton of tin, some raw glass, 145 Palestinian amphorae containing incense, some cedar logs, tortoise-shells and hippo teeth, together with small articles made of ivory, ebony, and amber. The Cape Gelidonya ship, which was smaller, also carried both copper (1 ton) and tin (a little, in the form of foil). The suggestion is that both ships were travelling a route that ran anti-clockwise round the eastern Mediterranean, taking on raw glass and incense in Palestine, Anatolian copper and Iranian tin in Syria, and more copper in Cyprus. This merchandise would have been traded for Mycenaean pottery (well attested in the Levant) and gold, ivory and ebony in Egypt.

This trade route brought other, less welcome commodities to Egypt. In 1280 BC the normally inert Libyans of the Western Desert launched an assault on Egypt, which Ramesses II only beat back with considerable difficulty. Accompanying the Libyans, and doubtless responsible for stirring them up in the first place, were some bands of Sherdan 'from the midst of the Sea', formidable fighters whom Ramesses was subsequently pleased to hire as mercenaries. These Sherdan, with their characteristic horned helmets, appear among his forces at the Battle of Kadesh. A vase from Mycenae shows a line of warriors with similar horned helmets, so there is little doubt who the Sherdan were: the Mycenaean Greeks were testing the boundaries of the Aegean world.[2]

1. Akhenaten's move to Akhetaten was part of his attempt to make the Sun Disc, Aten, the supreme god in the Egyptian pantheon, at the expense of Amun of Thebes. Hence his personal change of name from Amenophis IV ('Amen is content') to Akhenaten ('Benefactor of Aten').

2. The old identification of the Sherdan as Sardinians, long discounted but recently revived, is not really a runner. Sardinia has always been one of history's dead ends, and pretending that it can have intervened in the distant and populous lands of the Levant is to put onomastics above common sense.

AMBER

TIN

LAPIS

TIN

Hattusas

COPPER

Cape Gelidonya
and Ulu Burun
shipwrecks

Carchemish

Assur

Dur-Kurigalzu

Nippur

Susa

Aleppo

Lagash

Babylon

Ur

Tyre

Damascus

COPPER

Hazor

Etesian winds April—Oct

Avaris

Memphis

Akhetaten

Thebes

GOLD

Towns and trade routes in
1275 BC

◆   town
☐   royal residence
◇   abandoned residence

IVORY
EBONY

Hittite annals make it clear that, by the beginning of the twelfth century BC, their western border was under threat. The records are not very specific as to who was causing the trouble but we know that three different peoples were involved: the Phrygians (a group of Thracian tribes who had crossed over from Europe), the Luvian peoples of western Anatolia (specifically the Carians and Lycians) and the Greeks of the Aegean islands. Under the weight of their attacks the Hittite defences collapsed, and in 1180 BC the Empire itself was swept away. The hegemony of central Anatolia passed to the Phrygians, while the Luvians overran the southern provinces where, in the areas either side of the Taurus, they set up a number of principalities that historians refer to as neo-Hittite. The Greeks took Cyprus.

This was far from being the end of the upheaval. The Phrygians became embroiled with the Assyrians, who rather confusingly refer to them as the Mushki. Other elements moved south through Syria (where they sacked Ugarit) and Palestine (where they destroyed Hazor, something the Israelites later took credit for). The Egyptians, who call these invaders the Sea Peoples, realized that they were next on the list. Ramesses III, the current Pharaoh, mobilized every available man, and the two sides clashed somewhere in the borderlands. Luckily for him, the land and sea battles that followed went Egypt's way. But the Sea Peoples, though rebuffed, were far from being a spent force. They settled in the coastal plain of Palestine (which actually gets its name from one of their component tribes, the Peleset, better known as the biblical Philistines), and soon established their rule over the quarelling Canaanites and Israelites of the interior.[1]

One might expect to get some useful information on this period from the many Greek legends that refer back to the Late Bronze Age. Unfortunately these rarely look outside the Aegean, completely ignoring the conquest of Cyprus, for example. Their usual focus is the war with Troy (in the 1180s?), an event which must have been of genuine importance because it caused King Agammemnon of Mycenae to mobilize all the forces at his command, but which is difficult to understand in terms of aims and results. A possible explanation has been seen in another legend of the period, the voyage of the Argo.

A generation before the Trojan war the Argo had sailed to Colchis, at the far end of the Black Sea, in search of the Golden Fleece (read precious metals generally?): maybe the Trojans subsequently decided to choke off Greek enterprise in this direction, and, in doing so, provoked Agammemnon's offensive. But if so, why did the Argo's voyage go unrepeated in the years after Troy's destruction? Maybe it was all about the peerless Helen after all.[2]

Less than a hundred years after the Trojan war, the Greek world was convulsed by an internal migration, the Dorian movement. The Dorians were illiterate northern Greeks who overthrew the Kingdom of Mycenae and occupied all the Peloponnese (bar its central core), plus Crete and the south Aegean islands as far east as Rhodes. The order that had characterized the Mycenaean world – its political structure, its aristocratic style, its literacy – was lost: Greece moved into a Dark Age of which we know exceedingly little.

Egypt also went into a decline. The successful defence of the country by Ramesses III gave his dynasty, the twentieth, the prestige needed to maintain itself in power for the next hundred years, but his successors were a lacklustre lot and, in the reign of Ramesses XI (1103–1070 BC), the Empire began to come unstitched. The first sign was the loss of Kush, which broke away sometime around 1080. An event of the same period, the expedition of Wenamun to Byblos in Phoenicia, demonstrated all too plainly the little account in which Egypt was now held abroad. Wenamun was a priest of Amun at Thebes: his mission was to obtain the cedarwood needed for a new ceremonial boat for the god's annual progress round his many temples. Before he even got to Byblos Wenamun was robbed by the Tjekker, originally one of the Sea Peoples, now settled at Dor on the Palestinian coast, and though he eventually made it to Byblos and, via Cyprus, back to Egypt, the off-hand treatment he received at his various ports of call stands in striking contrast to the way Pharaoh's representatives had been received in the Amarna period.

Assyria, on the other hand, was doing exceptionally well. During his long reign King Tiglath-Pilesar I (1115–1077 BC) fought vigorously on all fronts, rebuffing the Mushki in the north-west, and the

Aramaean nomads within the arc of the Fertile Crescent. Westward he reached the Mediterranean and extracted tribute – or, at least, handsome presents – from the princes of Phoenicia. But his most impressive achievement was the conquest of Babylon. The Assyrian briefly lorded it over all the lands between the Upper and Lower Seas.[3]

1. Though the Egyptians give names to several of the Sea Peoples we still don't know whether they were predominantly Greek or predominantly neo-Hittite. The identification of the Danunians with the town of Adana in Cilicia doesn't really help: the location is certainly neo-Hittite but the ruling house appears to have had Greek origins. In favour of a Greek identity is the statement in the Bible that the Philistines came from Caphtor (meaning Crete), and the archaeologists' classification of their pottery as Mycenaean.

2. Thebes and Knossos had both lost their exceptional status by the time of the Trojan war. The troubles that brought Thebes low, starting with the war of the Seven, were remembered in detail by later Greeks, but the downfall of Knossos is only vaguely indicated in the various legends featuring Minos and his progeny.

3. The Kassite dynasty of Babylon had been extinguished by the Elamites in 1157 BC: subsequent rulers constitute the fourth dynasty, alternatively known as the second dynasty of Isin.

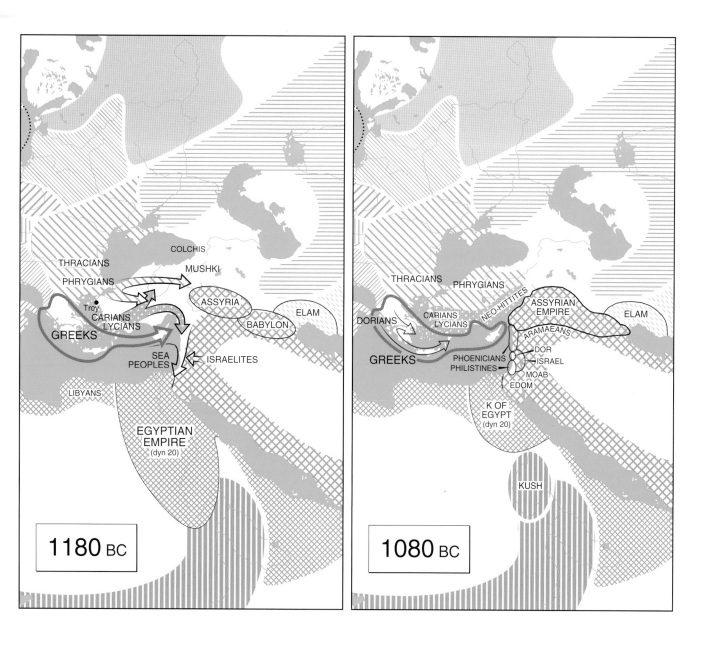

**1180 BC**

THRACIANS
PHRYGIANS
COLCHIS
MUSHKI
Troy
CARIANS
LYCIANS
ASSYRIA
ELAM
GREEKS
BABYLON
SEA
PEOPLES
ISRAELITES
LIBYANS
EGYPTIAN
EMPIRE
(dyn 20)

**1080 BC**

THRACIANS
PHRYGIANS
DORIANS
CARIANS
LYCIANS
NEO-HITTITES
ASSYRIAN
EMPIRE
ELAM
ARAMAEANS
GREEKS
PHOENICIANS
PHILISTINES
DOR
ISRAEL
MOAB
EDOM
K OF
EGYPT
(dyn 20)
KUSH

Aftershocks from the Dorian upheaval continued to trouble the Greek world for several generations after the Dorians themselves had settled down. Settlers from the west side of the Aegean began to colonize the east side, first the offshore islands (Lesbos, Chios, Samos), then the coast: gradually they created an 'Ionic sphere' to balance the 'Doric sphere' to the south. The creation of these two different traditions was important: by the classical period they were distinguishable at the dialect level. On the other hand, the differences between them should not be exaggerated: they were as one in looking down on the North Greeks whom they regarded as little better than barbarians (non-Greeks). A fourth group, consisting of the old Mycenaean stocks, was effectively sidelined by this time, being confined to Arcadia (the central Peloponnese), Pamphylia (the central section of the south Anatolian coast) and Cyprus.[1]

No documents survive from the Greek world of this date, which is hardly surprising as only the Cypriots were still literate. More unexpected is the lack of documentation in the Fertile Crescent, which remained fully literate, but was undergoing something of a Dark Age too. This was largely down to the Aramaeans, nomads from the Syrian desert first mentioned in the records of the Assyrian king Tiglath-Pilesar I. He had kept them in their place by vigorous campaigning but they got the upper hand over his successors, and the late eleventh century saw them spilling out over Syria and all but the heartland of Assyria itself. Assyria survived but only as an island in an Aramaean sea. Babylon was in little better case with its kingship passing through four different dynasties in less than a hundred years. Of Elam we know nothing at all.

Palestine, on the other hand, now enters recorded history, as represented by the Old Testament account of Israel's beginnings. Since arriving in the promised land in the late thirteenth century, the twelve Hebrew tribes had gradually elbowed aside the native Canaanites, becoming the dominant, though not the sole, element in the population. The invasion of the Sea Peoples in 1190 BC probably aided the process – as already noted it scuppered Hazor, the most powerful of the Canaanite principalities – but it had its downside too, because it established the Philistines on the coast, and the Philistines made themselves overlords of the interior as far as the Jordan. Try as they might, the Israelite judges (tribal leaders) found the task of breaking the Philistine grip beyond them: what was needed was not a local hero, like Samson, but a king of all Israel. A first attempt at this under Saul ended in disaster at the Battle of Gilboa where the Philistines slaughtered Saul and three of his sons. Subsequently David (990–970 BC) succeeded where Saul had failed, creating a kingdom that not only stood independently of the Philistines but was able to extract homage from the peoples of the interior – the Aramaeans of southern Syria, the Ammonites and Moabites of Transjordan, and the Edomites of the southern desert. David also eliminated the last strongholds of the Canaanites: one of them, Jerusalem, became the capital of his new state.

The year 1000 BC is conventionally taken as the starting point of the Near Eastern Iron Age. This is not unreasonable: iron weaponry rises from a mere 3 per cent of the whole (the rest being bronze) in the twelfth century, to 20 per cent in the eleventh and more than 50 per cent in the tenth. From being many times more expensive than bronze, iron had become cheaper. Left unanswered are questions as to where the new technology developed and how it spread. The traditional view is that both are associated with the Dorian movement. If so, the use of iron will then have spread from west to east via the east Mediterranean trade route. Compatible with this is the Bible's story of the Philistines' attempt to keep the Israelites in a position of military inferiority by forbidding them to manufacture any sort of iron tools.

In Egypt the Ramessid line had come to an end with the death of Ramesses XI in 1070 BC. The new sovereigns of the country, constituting the twenty-first dynasty, established their capital at Tanis, not far from Avaris/Pi-Ramesses in the eastern delta; they were content with a nominal role in Upper Egypt, which became, for all practical purposes, an independent vice-royalty. Control of this region was in the hands of the high priests of Amun at Thebes, who, as the office was hereditary during this period, can be counted as a separate, though unnumbered, dynasty.

The simple distribution of the Italics – all Italy west of the line drawn from the central Alps to the Tiber – was modified by the arrival of the Messapians, an Illyrian people, on the Adriatic coast, and the departure of the Sicels from the toe. The nature of Sicily's original inhabitants, whom the Greeks called Sicans, is unknown: classical authors had it that one group was Iberian. In the rest of Europe there is nothing to note except the expansion of the urnfield habit across central Europe and into the Italian and Iberian peninsulas. Despite many attempts to make its contour match the ethnolinguistic map, it doesn't.

1. These various dialects – Ionic, Doric, North-West Greek and Arcado-Cypriote – were to disappear in the freer intercourse of Hellenistic times when a development of Ionic became universal.

GERMANICS

CELTS

ILLYRIANS THRACIANS PHRYGIANS

ASSYRIA

SICELS

IONIANS NEO-HITTITES ARAMAEANS BABYLON ELAM

SICANS

DORIANS PHOENICIANS

ISRAEL

PHILISTINES

EDOM

K OF MIDIAN
EGYPT
(dyn 21)

limit of
iron
working

KUSH

980 BC

The Kingdom of Israel's prestige reached a peak under David's son and successor Solomon (965–931 BC), who enhanced Jerusalem's standing, and his own reputation, by building a Temple for the previously peripatetic Jehovah. He did not, however, maintain David's frontiers, ceding a border province to Tyre, and allowing the Aramaean principality of Damascus to recover its independence. After Solomon's death it was downhill all the way: the remaining tributaries rebelled and the Kingdom itself split into two unequal halves. The first, Judah, consisted of little more than Jerusalem and its environs; the second, Israel, inherited the bulk of the Hebrew territory, but lacked a proper capital prior to the building of Samaria (880 BC). Divided they were doomed. The first pharaoh of the twenty-second dynasty, an ex-soldier of Libyan stock, celebrated his accession with a razzia through Palestine which included a sack of Jerusalem (928 BC), but there was no lasting revival on the part of Egypt and it was the Damascenes who made the kings of Judah and Israel their vassals. Damascus, indeed, proved strong enough to stave off the otherwise irresistible Assyrians, who had re-established their control over northern Mesopotamia and reduced Babylon to dependence in the early ninth century and were now steadily advancing their frontier westward. Northern Syria and Cilicia fell to King Shalmaneser III (859–824 BC) and his successors kept up the pressure. The rhythm of their campaigns indicates the Assyrians' main problem; the area they sought to control – the northern half of the fertile crescent – lacked natural defences. Punitive expeditions were mounted yearly – eastward against the Zagros tribes (and beyond them the Iranian Medes, first identified at this time), southward against the ever contentious Babylonians, northward against the recently established Caucasian kingdom of Urartu, westward against the Aramaeans, neo-Hittites and Phrygians. Victories were constantly celebrated; constant victory was the condition on which the Assyrian Empire existed.

Paying tribute to Assyria as necessary but still, at this stage, effectively independent, were the Phoenician seaports, of which Tyre was now the most prominent. This position it owed to its merchant venturers, who not only established a near-monopoly of the old Bronze Age route to the Aegean, but pioneered an extension of this that eventually spanned the length of the Mediterranean. The achievement is almost undocumented. The basis for it appears to have been the development of latitude sailing, which gave Tyrian seamen the confidence to probe open waters. Checking their position against the noonday sun or, at night, the Little Bear and Pole Star, the ships first cut across the Ionian Sea to Sicily. After coasting round Sicily, they set sail for the southern coast of Sardinia and from there to Ibiza in the Balaearics. The final leg took them to the southern coast of Spain. There they hit the jackpot: cheap silver produced from the mines of the Rio Tinto region. The date at which this was first done is disputable. Ancient historians placed the discovery of Spain in the twelfth century, with Cadiz and a halfway post at Utica being founded about 1100 BC. No one believes this nowadays and some would regard a date of *c.* 820 BC, as suggested here, as still on the early side. Allowing for the fact that, in Sicily, the Phoenicians preceded the Greeks by at least one, more probably two generations, the latest possible date would be around 775 BC. This is also the latest feasible date for the founding of Carthage (traditionally given as 814 BC).

These and other uncertainties in the chronology mean that the 'limit of iron working' line on this map has to be taken with a particularly large grain of salt. Overland spread via Iran is thought to have taken knowledge of the technique to the borders of India by this time: on the other hand it seems clear that there was very little advance in the Balkan region, which remained the only part of Europe to have entered the Iron Age. Some compensation for this sluggishness is to be found in the maritime sphere, for the Phoenicians carried their Iron Age know-how with them as they sailed through the west Mediterranean: in a generation or two the natives they traded with will surely have acquired not just the tools and weapons that the Tyrian merchants wanted to sell them, but some knowledge of how to make such items for themselves. How far this process will have got by the late ninth century is debatable, but Sicily and Southern Italy are reasonable starting points.

GERMANICS

SCYTHS

CELTS

CIMMERIANS

←Tyrian route to Spain

THRACIANS

PHRYGIANS

URARTU

MEDES

ASSYRIAN
EMPIRE

ELAM

GREEKS

BABYLON

DAMASCUS

Tyre

ISRAEL

PHILISTINES

JUDAH

MOAB

EDOM

limit of
iron
working

K OF
EGYPT
(dyn 22)

KUSH

820 BC

Until the eighth century BC the chariot remained the only way of exploiting the speed and power of the horse on the battlefield. By the century's end this was no longer the case: the nomads of the Eurasian steppe, the Cimmerians and the Scyths, had become sufficiently adept at horse riding to create a modern-style cavalry force. They hadn't got saddles or stirrups so their seats weren't too stable, but they were able to use bow and arrow effectively, and the tactics they adopted – provoking attack, quickly retreating, then circling round to fire again – proved astonishingly effective, enabling relatively small bands of nomads to destroy much larger infantry armies. The first to feel the pain of this new style of warfare was the Urartuan monarchy. A force of Cimmerians appeared south of the Caucasus and, in 714 BC, overthrew the Urartuan king, Rusa I. From there the Cimmerians moved west, into Anatolia, where they won an even more astonishing victory, defeating and killing the Assyrian king, Sargon II (705 BC). Anatolia offered the Cimmerians the pasture they needed to support their lifestyle, so they decided to settle there: in 696 BC they put the Phrygian capital, Gordium, to the sack and replaced the Phrygian hegemony over the plateau with their own.[1]

The Assyrian defeat at the hands of the Cimmerians was highly unusual: this was an era when Assyria, even judged by its own aggressive standards, was exercising more military muscle, to better effect, than ever before. The run of success began in the reign of Tiglath-Pilesar III (745–727 BC) who destroyed the anti-Assyrian coalition built up by the Urartuans in Syria and Cilicia and then went on to annex two of Assyria's most dogged opponents, Damascus (732 BC) and Babylon (729 BC). By the end of his reign he had reduced the entire Fertile Crescent to obedience. Much of it consisted of Assyrian provinces ruled by governors-general: the rest was composed of vassal states paying heavy tribute. The ultimate fate of these vassals varied. For example, when Israel refused tribute its history was brought to an abrupt end by Sargon II, who sacked Samaria in 722 BC and deported the ten tribes that made up the northern Hebrew state. Judah, on the other hand, survived, though more by good luck than good management. Initially, its policy had been pro-Assyrian (simply because Israel was anti): subsequently Egyptian promises of support encouraged a bid for independence. Isaiah, not unreasonably, prophesied disaster, but as it turned out Assyria's King Sennacherib (705–681 BC) was forced from the field when the Angel of the Lord – without a word to Isaiah – struck down his army (701 BC). This event, which a passage in Herodotus suggests may have been an outbreak of bubonic plague, saved Jerusalem, but did not prevent Sennacherib from subsequently imposing a hefty increase in tribute. Egypt's come-uppance was delivered by the next Assyrian ruler, Esarhaddon (681–669 BC), who invaded the country, annexed the delta and restricted the kings of the twenty-fifth dynasty to the upper Nile (670 BC).[2]

During this period the Greeks took to their boats and, as in earlier days, began to push the envelope of the Greek world. Eastward the pioneers were Ionians from Miletus, who followed the route taken by the Argo all those centuries before and re-established contact with the Transcaucasians at the far end of the Black Sea. Colonies were subsequently established at two points on the route: Sinope, at the centre point of Turkey's northern coast, and Trapezus, at its eastern end. Westward the first explorers were also Ionian, this time from Euboea: they used the Phoenician route to get to the straits of Messina, then coasted north up the shin of Italy to Etruria. Colonies to support the trade that then developed with the Etruscans were set up at the straits and at Cumae, just north of the Bay of Naples. In both cases there is no doubt that what these Ionian explorers were after were sources of precious or useful metals, but the underpopulated coasts discovered during the pioneering voyages were soon helping to meet a different need. Greece had too many people and establishing overseas colonies was a good way of managing this problem. The result was that the stretches of coast nearest the homeland – the shores of the Sea of Marmara in the east and the sole of Italy, and the east coast of Sicily in the west – were soon dotted with purely agricultural Greek communities.[3]

Within Greece itself the main event was the emergence of Sparta as the leading power. The Spartans, the Dorian conquerors of the south-east quarter of the Peloponnese, were unusual in two ways: they kept themselves totally separate from the people they had subordinated and they made soldiering their sole occupation. A long war in the second half of the eighth century won them control of Messene (the south-west quarter of the Peloponnese) where they immediately introduced the same social regime: the inhabitants became helots (near enough slaves) owned by and working for the Spartan elite. This confirmed Sparta's place at the head of the list of Greek states. Not that the Spartan style of fighting was anything special: they used armoured spearmen (hoplites) drawn up in a close packed formation (the phalanx) in the same way as other Greeks. But they trained harder and did it better. From puberty the young men lived in barracks and when they went to war the Spartan mother had only one injunction for her son: 'Come back with your shield, or on it.'

---

**1.** The Cimmerian move south of the Caucasus was very likely precipitated by pressure from the Scyths who were advancing westward at this time. Subsequently the Scyths dispersed or absorbed those of the Cimmerians who elected to stay behind and the entire European steppe passed under their control. The Scyths did not occupy the Crimea, which remained in the possession of a Thracian people, the Tauri.

At this time Assyrian records give us a first mention of the Arabs of Saba, corresponding to modern-day Yemen. They also give us our first detailed picture of Cyprus whose twelve constituent communities began paying tribute in the reign of Tiglath-Pilesar III. Ten of the twelve were Greek, one a pre-Greek ('EteoCypriote') survival, and one a relatively recent Phoenician foundation. Other points to note on the map are the Iranian movement into the eastern half of Elam (which brings the Persians into their historical homeland) and the emergence of the Kingdom of Lydia in western Anatolia (presumably a result of the Phrygians' collapse).

**2.** The pharaohs of the twenty-fifth dynasty were Kushites. The lineage appears in Kush *c.* 785 BC and had conquered Egypt (and was resident there) by 715 BC. At the same time the southern frontier of this Kushitic-Egyptian Empire was advanced upriver to the confluence of the White and Blue Niles.

**3.** In Sicily the arrival of the Greeks forced the Tyrians to withdraw to the far end of the island. Elsewhere in the West Mediterranean the Phoenicians were prospering and their settlements multiplying.

All this maritime activity meant that the use of iron became general in the Mediterranean lands. Curiously it didn't manage the short hop from Palestine to Egypt: the Assyrian invasion found the country still in the Bronze Age.

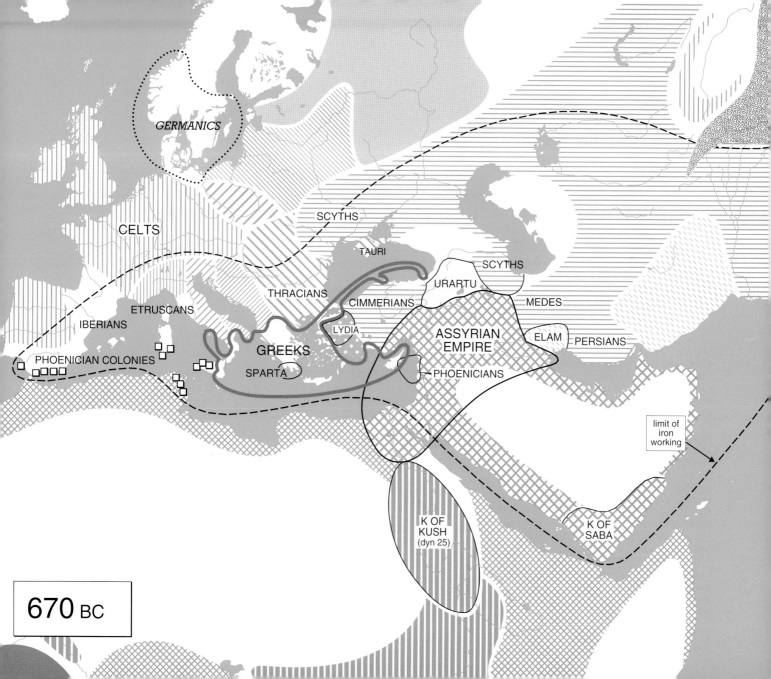

GERMANICS

CELTS

SCYTHS

TAURI

THRACIANS

SCYTHS

URARTU

CIMMERIANS

MEDES

ETRUSCANS

IBERIANS

LYDIA

GREEKS

ASSYRIAN
EMPIRE

ELAM

PERSIANS

PHOENICIAN COLONIES

SPARTA

PHOENICIANS

limit of
iron
working

K OF
KUSH
(dyn 25)

K OF
SABA

670 BC

The contraction of the literate world caused by the irruption of the Dorians into Greece, and the Phrygians into Anatolia, persisted for 400 years: then, in the eighth century BC, the lost ground was recovered by a new writing system, the true alphabet. This was invented by the Greeks, spread rapidly through their expanding sphere, and was taken up by many of their neighbours – on the east the Phrygians, Lydians, Carians and Lycians; in the west the Etruscans. Every bit as important as this geographical success was the qualitative leap forward that the true alphabet represented. Previously writing had been so complicated that only a few people – less than one in a hundred – ever learnt how to do it. These were the scribes who kept society's accounts and, in the more sophisticated states, some record of events. The true alphabet was simple enough for anyone interested to master quickly, and the possibility of male literacy rates of 10, 20, even 30 per cent became a genuine prospect.

The Greeks took their letter forms from the consonantal alphabets developed in the Levant in the second millennium BC. The early history of these has already been recounted: of the two forms in existence in 1275 BC, the date of the last map on this topic, one, the Ugaritic cuneiform alphabet, disappeared during the upheavals caused by the Sea Peoples. The other, the Proto-Canaanite/Proto-Sinaitic script, survived, evolved and was simplified and standardized until by the year 1000 it had emerged as the 22-letter consonantal alphabet of the Phoenicians. Tyrian traders brought this to the Aegean area and sometime around 800 BC, somewhere in central Greece (later tradition said at Thebes) it was adapted for the writing of Greek. Half the letters corresponded to Greek consonants and were taken over as they stood: five which didn't – and this is the critical modification – were used to represent vowels. At last the world had a simple and unambiguous writing system that would do for all but tonal languages. It was the first flicker of the information age.

The breakthrough to the true alphabet impressed contemporaries less than it does us. The Near East stuck with the consonantal prototype, and so did the Phoenician colonies in the western Mediterranean. As a result the alphabet-using world split into two halves, one characterized by consonantal alphabets and the other by true alphabets. And the older form won just as many converts as the newer. The Assyrian bureaucracy used Aramaic, the 'inland' version of Phoenician, in its day-to-day correspondence: the royal scribes of Israel, Judah, Ammon and Moab wrote in variants of the same script. Aramaic was also the basis of the alphabet used by the desert peoples: this is termed South Arabian, because that is where most surviving inscriptions come from, but at this time the only certain examples are from the north of the peninsula.

Pre-alphabetic writing systems retained a place in the scheme of things, particularly when long-established societies felt the need to emphasize their authority in traditional ways. The neo-Hittites carved most of their formal inscriptions in Luvian hieroglyphic, though alphabetic examples, both Phoenician and Aramaic, are known. The Assyrian, Babylonian and Elamite monarchs always used cuneiform on their monuments, as also in their archives. The Urartuans used both cuneiform and an as yet undeciphered hieroglyphic script of their own invention. The Egyptians, of course, remained wedded to their ancient script in its hieroglyphic and hieratic variants. A curious survival is the Cypriote syllabary, descended from the Linear B of the Bronze Age, and used for both Greek and EteoCypriote.

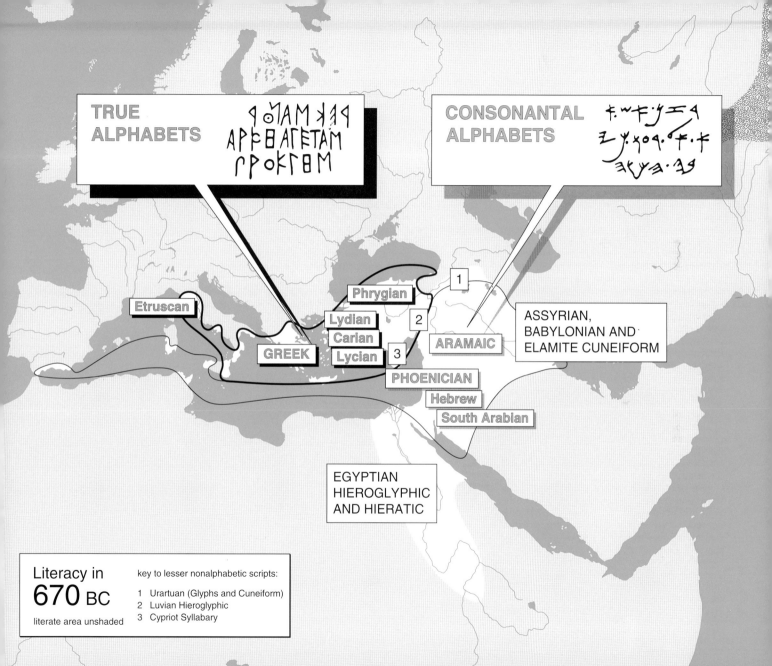

TRUE ALPHABETS

CONSONANTAL ALPHABETS

Etruscan

Phrygian

Lydian
Carian
Lycian

GREEK

1

2

3

ARAMAIC

ASSYRIAN, BABYLONIAN AND ELAMITE CUNEIFORM

PHOENICIAN

Hebrew

South Arabian

EGYPTIAN HIEROGLYPHIC AND HIERATIC

Literacy in
**670** BC

literate area unshaded

key to lesser nonalphabetic scripts:

1 Urartuan (Glyphs and Cuneiform)
2 Luvian Hieroglyphic
3 Cypriot Syllabary

The striking difference between this map and its predecessor in the towns and trade routes series is the way seafarers are now exploiting the whole of the Mediterranean. In the far west the locally based Phoenicians are collecting the output of the silver mines of the Rio Tinto and putting it into general circulation. In the north west Phoenicians and Greeks are purchasing low-cost iron (from Elba) and copper (from mainland Etruria) from the Etruscans. In the Black Sea it's still more a matter of reconnaissance than useful returns but there is increasing Greek activity on all its shores. And in the Levant the old seasonal wheel is still turning, sucking in the new resources and circulating the traditional goods and manufactures of the region: Egyptian papyrus, linen and faience, African ivory and ebony, Levantine glassware and textiles, Arabian resins.

Resins were a relatively recent addition to this list. The demand for them was stronger than you might think: in the form of balsam, myrrh and frankincense, they were applied as unguents, used as perfumes and burnt as incense. The difficulty was marketing the stuff: the long journey from the source of supply in Saba (modern day Yemen) to the consumers in the towns of the Fertile Crescent had some formidably harsh stages; watering points were often too far apart and too unreliable for the Near East's usual beast of burden, the donkey. Domestication of the one animal that could cope with these conditions, the camel, seems to have occurred around 1200 BC, well in time for the Queen of Sheba (read Saba) to visit Solomon in the mid-tenth century. By the date of this map camel caravans were certainly moving through the Hejaz ('the corridor') on a regular basis and Arabian resins had become a common article of commerce.[1]

More trade means more prosperous trading towns, and there is little doubt that by this time the most important nodes in the near eastern trading network had achieved urban status. Tyre and Sidon, the leading seaports of Phoenicia, are the most convincing candidates. But this ranking – implying a population of around 7,500 – is no longer that impressive: there are now places with two or even four times that number. The beginnings of the increase in scale can be put back to the ninth century when the Assyrian king Ashurnasirpal II built himself a new capital at Calah. The inscriptions celebrating its completion (in 879 BC) include one which numbers its inhabitants at 16,000. This is a figure to treasure as it's almost the only direct statement of a city's population to survive from antiquity. It also provides a basis for estimating the population of Nineveh, Assyria's capital in its seventh-century heyday. By then the Assyrian Empire was twice the size it had been in Ashurnasirpal's time and, as measured on the ground, its capital was twice as big (Nineveh 720 ha. as against Calah 358): it seems reasonable to translate this into a population figure of 30,000.

These unprecedented statistics – compare the 50 ha. of Assyria's traditional capital Assur – reflect the special nature of the later Assyrian Empire. Previously empires had been about prestige rather than transfers of wealth. Presents passed back and forth between the suzerain and his vassal kings: the name of the game was honour and acclaim. The Assyrian empire was a much grimmer creation. To sustain the army that upheld the Empire, huge amounts of material were needed: flocks to feed it, textiles to clothe it, weapons to arm it. Assyrian clerks became used to dealing in thousands and tens of thousands: subject peoples were treated as commodities and marched to wherever their labour was needed. The same inscription that numbers Calah's inhabitants numbers the labourers used to build the new city at 47,074. This focussing of resources explains why the Assyrian capitals were the first towns of compelling magnitude. And why the Assyrians were so widely hated.[2]

1. The camel concerned is the Arabian one-humped camel or dromedary. It is to be distinguished from the Bactrian two-humped camel of central Asia, which had been domesticated much earlier, in the third millennium BC.

2. On the map Calah is shown with a population at the 7,500 level rather than the 16,000 of its metropolitan heyday. The assumption is that Nineveh's rise will have been at least partly at Calah's expense.

TIN

AMBER

LAPIS

TIN

SILVER

IRON

COPPER

Greek routes

COPPER

**NINEVEH**
Calah
◆Assur
◆Susa
**Babylon**
◆

West
Phoenician
routes

East
Phoenician
routes

Tyre
Sidon ◆Damascus

Memphis ◆

Arab routes

GOLD

RESINS

Towns and trade routes in
**670** BC

towns, estimated populations
●     30,000
●     15,000
◆     7,500

IVORY
EBONY

The Assyrians' constant campaigning continued under Esarhaddon's son Ashurbanipal (669–627 BC). New lands were conquered (Upper Egypt in 663 BC, western Elam in 647 BC) and old foes beaten yet again (the Medes in 653 BC, the Babylonians in 648 BC). But, unlike his predecessors, Ashurbanipal seems to have realized that this couldn't go on forever, that instead of feverishly hacking away at its enemies Assyria needed to get some friends. Early on in his reign he decided to entrust Egypt to a local princeling, Psammetichus of Sais, and withdraw from the country altogether, a move that effectively shut down one battlefront. Then, in the 650s, he made an alliance with the Scyths and persuaded them to attack the Medes, which they did to such good effect that the Medes were out of the frame for a generation (652–625 BC). This removed a threat that had been uncomfortably close to home. When Ashurbanipal died, the Empire had never looked stronger.

In fact its time was fast running out. In 627 BC the Chaldean prince, Nabopolasar,[1] raised the standard of revolt in southern Mesopotamia; fortune favoured his cause and by 616 BC he had freed all Babylonia. This was the signal for the Medes to resume hostilities: with the Assyrians facing south they were able to swoop down on Assur and put it to the sack (614 BC). The blow to the Empire's prestige – the Empire that for two centuries had not seen its cities under even passing threat – proved mortal: it tipped the Scyths into changing sides, producing an anti-Assyrian coalition too strong to be successfully resisted. In 612 BC, after breaking what was left of the Assyrian defences, the armies of the Medes, Scyths and Babylonians converged on Nineveh, took the hated city and gutted it, along with every other place of any importance in the country around. Assyria became an empty land.

The war wasn't quite over. Remnants of the Assyrian army were collecting at Harran, and Pharaoh Necho II, Psammetichus' son, seeing a splendid opportunity to regain Egypt's ancient empire in Syria and Palestine and a perfect buffer for these provinces in a dependent Assyria, was offering to march to their support. But by the time Necho got there the town had fallen to the Medes and with it went any possibility of an Assyrian revival (609 BC).

For a few years Necho made the Euphrates his frontier, then his complete defeat at the hands of Nebuchadnezzar, Nabopolasar's son and heir, at the battle of Carchemish, put an end to this Egyptian fantasy (605 BC).[2]

The Scyths now decided to return to the Russian steppe, leaving the two remaining members of the alliance, the Babylonians and Medes, free to carve up the entire Near East. Nebuchadnezzar got the Fertile Crescent bar Assyria, plus Cilicia, western Elam and the northern half of Arabia. The Medes got Assyria plus Urartu and a free hand in Anatolia. The Caucasian Urartuans had disappeared by this time: the country was in the hands of a Phrygian people, the Armenians, who had presumably moved in in the chaos following the Cimmerian invasion. The Armenians submitted to the Medes, who went on to annihilate the Cimmerians. This liberated the Lydians of western Anatolia, who subsequently proved strong enough to stop the Medes from advancing further. Nebuchadnezzar's vassal, the king of Cilicia, brokered a peace between the two, which put the frontier on the Halys (585 BC).

The Greeks continued their overseas expansion during this period, consolidating their hold on Sicily and southern Italy, and planting a whole raft of new colonies on the northern shores of the Aegean and Sea of Marmara. They also colonized the western and northern coasts of the Black Sea, focussing particularly on the Cimmerian Bosporus, the modern-day Strait of Kerch. Another venture was to Libya, where the colony of Cyrene began the process of transforming this sector of the coast (still known as Cyrenaica) into a Greek enclave. These were all agricultural communities of the traditional Greek sort, though some of those in the Sea of Marmara and Black Sea were soon to start developing commercial fisheries. One enterprise, however, had a clearly mercantile aim: the move past Etruria to the south of France and the north-east corner of Spain where the colonies of Massilia (Marseilles) and Emporion were founded in 600 BC and 575 BC respectively. The idea was to find a way to the Spanish silver mines that circumvented the Phoenician grip on the direct route from Sicily. It was a challenge that demanded a Phoenician response.[3]

In Italy, note the Etruscans' expansion at the

expense of the Italics – north across the Apennines and into the Po valley, and south along the Mediterranean coast. One of the local communities that passed under Etruscan control as a result of the southward move was Rome, where an Etruscan dynasty was installed in the closing years of the seventh century.

**1.** The Chaldeans were Babylonia's equivalent of the Aramaeans, nomads who had infiltrated the area some time before the mid ninth century when their presence is first recorded. By the eighth century they had become the dominant political force in the region.

**2.** Judah got it both coming and going; its army was annihilated by Necho on his way north and Jerusalem taken by Nebuchadnezzar on his way south (597 BC). Ten years later an Egyptian-inspired revolt led to Nebuchadnezzar's return, a second capture of the city and the deportation to Babylon of the two tribes of Judah (586 BC).

Necho's hopes of an Egyptian revival were not entirely frustrated. About the date of this map, Cyprus and Cyrene became tributaries, and, as the Kushites had been chased back to the second cataract in 593 BC, the outline of the Egyptian state ruled by this (26th) dynasty compares favourably with its immediate predecessors'.

**3.** The Greeks believed that the silver mines lay in a 'Kingdom of Tartessus' but this seems mythical. The peoples of Spain were, and long remained, fragmented: it's most unlikely that the mines were under unified political control.

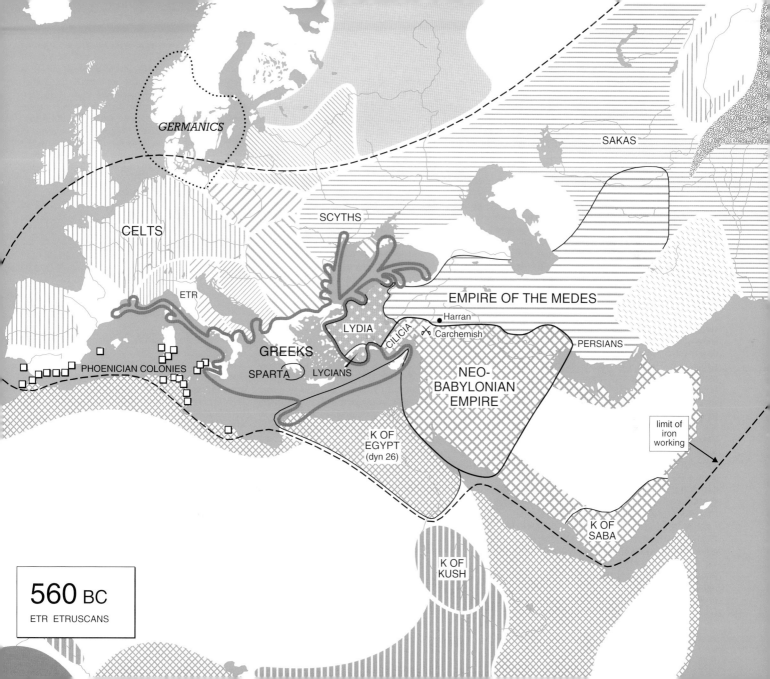

GERMANICS

SAKAS

CELTS

SCYTHS

EMPIRE OF THE MEDES

ETR

Harran

Carchemish

LYDIA

PERSIANS

CILICIA

GREEKS

NEO-
BABYLONIAN
EMPIRE

SPARTA

LYCIANS

PHOENICIAN COLONIES

limit of
iron
working

K OF
EGYPT
(dyn 26)

K OF
SABA

K OF
KUSH

560 BC

ETR ETRUSCANS

In 550 BC there was a falling-out between Astyages, King of the Medes, and his subordinate, the Persian king, Cyrus I. Against expectation, Astyages lost the subsequent battle: Cyrus emerged as the new ruler of the Iranian peoples, and the Medes had to share the rewards of Empire with Cyrus' countrymen, the Persians. History was to simplify this accommodation. Cyrus became Cyrus the Great, creator of the mighty Persian Empire and founder of its ruling Achaemenid dynasty. The achievements of the Medes were largely forgotten.

Cyrus certainly expanded the frontier of the Iranian world. First came a war with Lydia, where King Croesus had been showing signs of dissatisfaction with the Halys frontier. In 547 BC the Lydian and Persian armies fought a drawn battle somewhere near the river, after which Croesus sent his men home for the winter. Cyrus, far from doing the same, followed Croesus back to Sardis and put the city under siege. In the spring Sardis fell, and Lydia with it. Meanwhile, King Nabonidus of Babylon was busy alienating his subjects by trying to promote the Moon God, Sin, over Bel Marduk, the capital's traditional deity. For ten years the rituals uniting god and ruler went unperformed as Nabonidus sulked in his desert retreat of Tema: by the time he returned to Babylon and took over the reins of government from his son Balshazzar, the situation was beyond repair – the adherents of Marduk had called on Cyrus to intervene, and Persian troops were closing in on the city (539 BC). The new year saw Cyrus' son Cambyses installed as king and ceremonially 'taking the hands of Bel'. In between the Lydian and Babylonian campaigns, or after the latter, or both, Cyrus extended the Empire eastward: we have no details but he certainly got as far as the Transoxian garrison town later sources call Cyropolis. It was somewhere in this region, fighting a Saka tribe, that he met his death (530 BC).

Cyrus was, by the standards of his time, a benign ruler. He not only refrained from the fearsome revenges, exactions and deportations practised by the Assyrians and Babylonians, he freed many of the people they had dispossessed. The two tribes of Judah, discovered languishing in exile by the waters of Babylon, were encouraged to return home and rebuild Jerusalem, and even given public funds to help them do so. The result was a Jewish commitment to Achaemenid rule that lasted as long as the dynasty. On the other hand, however benign his policies, Cyrus was still an autocrat and everyone had to toe the line he drew. Where Croesus, for example, had tolerated the independence of the Lycians and Ionian Greeks, Cyrus was having none of it: both peoples were ordered to bend the knee, or else. The Ionians appealed to their brethren across the sea and somewhat surprisingly the Spartans sent an embassy that told the Persians to leave Ionia alone. 'Who are the Spartans?' asked a puzzled Cyrus, but whatever reply he got hardly mattered: the Ionians decided to submit, the Spartan delegates went off home, and the Empire's western boundary found what appeared to be a natural resting place on the shoreline of Asia.

Cyrus' son and successor Cambyses added Egypt to the Achaemenid realm. A hard-fought battle at the Egyptian frontier post of Pelusium decided the fate of the country (525 BC); Cambyses deposed the last Pharaoh of the twenty-sixth (Saite) dynasty and took his place as first Pharaoh of the twenty-seventh. The Egyptian dependencies of Cyrene and Cyprus quickly adjusted to the new order. At this point, according to Herodotus, Cambyses went mad, killing the sacred Apis bull just for laughs and mocking hard-core Egyptian superstitions. There is no evidence to support this story – the Apis bull that died during his visit was buried with full honours and a representation of a mourning Cambyses – so it is more likely that all he did was deprive the priesthood of some of its excessive revenues and get libelled in consequence. However, the end of Cambyses' reign was certainly less glorious than the beginning: the eastern provinces rose in revolt and Cambyses himself died unexpectedly, possibly in a riding accident, probably in some more sinister way. As his only brother, who had been acting as Viceroy of the East, disappeared about the same time, the Persian throne, the most powerful position in the world, was up for grabs.

The man who grabbed it was Darius I (522–486 BC), an Achaemenid noble who soon disposed of the various satraps (provincial governors) inclined to dispute his authority. He then set the wheels of empire in motion again, probing the frontier regions in search of places worth conquering. One expedition reached Peshawar, on the far side of Afghanistan; from there, Scylax, a Carian officer in Darius' service, sailed the length of the Indus, returning home via the Arabian Sea and Persian Gulf. Subsequently an Indian satrapy was organized: estimates of its extent vary from a minimum covering just the Kabul valley to a maximum embracing all the lands as far as the Indus. In the west Darius' achievements are better documented. First he edged forward in the Aegean, occupying the offshore islands of Lesbos, Chios and Samos. Then he built a bridge of boats across the Hellespont (it took 200 of them to do it) and personally led an army into Europe. His aim was to subdue the Scyths of South Russia, so he struck north, crossed the Danube (another bridge), and advanced across the steppe. But the Scyths retreated before him, and Darius could find no way to catch them. Baffled, he retreated to Asia, leaving subordinates to organize the area south of the Danube into the Satrapy of Thrace (c. 515 BC).

The Ionians made no difficulties about supporting Darius' expeditions, even those aimed at fellow Greeks. Indeed it was the Milesians who proposed the next such move, against Naxos in 499 BC. But Naxos didn't fall and the Milesians, fearing that they would be blamed for the failure of the operation, decided on rebellion. Fanned by nascent pan-Hellenic sentiment, the revolt spread rapidly through Ionia and from there to Caria and Cyprus. Messengers were dispatched to seek support from mainland Greece and though this time the Spartans refused to get involved, Athens and Eretria sent

**Between 550 and 525 BC Carthage turned what had always been a leading position among the Phoenician settlements in the west into outright control of all of them. The result was a maritime empire that could deploy armies as well as fleets to defend its interests, and the result of that was the defeat of the Greek attempt to settle Corsica (c. 535 BC) and the end of the Greek dream of tapping into the Spanish silver trade. The Ebro became the effective dividing line between Carthaginian and Greek (i.e. Massiliote) spheres.**

**Also visible on this map are the first indications of expansion by the Germanics, a westward movement along the North Sea coast.**

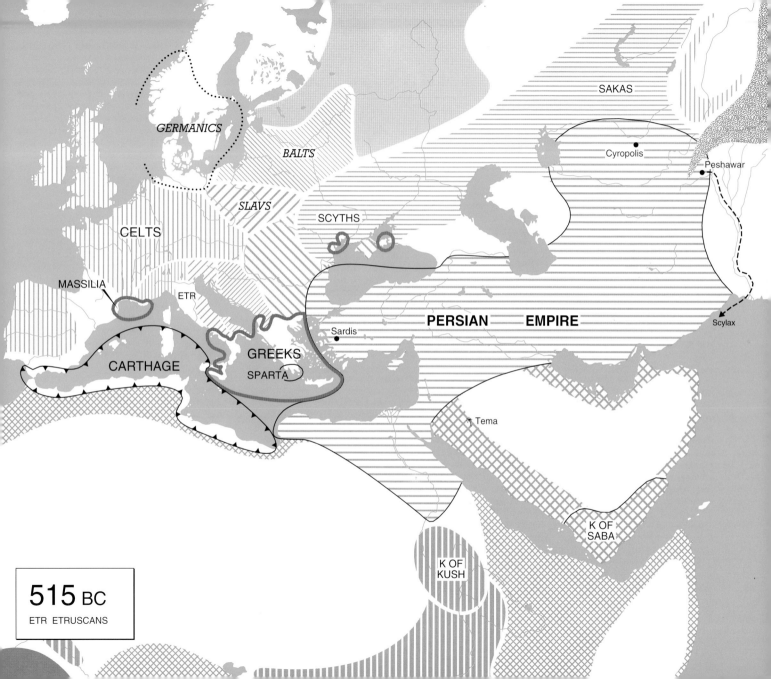

GERMANICS

BALTS

SLAVS

SAKAS

CELTS

Cyropolis

Peshawar

SCYTHS

MASSILIA

ETR

PERSIAN    EMPIRE

Sardis

Scylax

CARTHAGE

GREEKS

SPARTA

Tema

K OF
SABA

K OF
KUSH

515 BC
ETR ETRUSCANS

troops. Their contingents joined a rebel army that marched on Sardis, the seat of the Persian satrap, and succeeded in taking the lower town. That proved to be the high point of the revolt. The citadel held out, and Persian reinforcements badly cut up the Greek force as it made its way back to the coast. One by one the rebel communities were reduced and, after five years, the revolt was extinguished. All that remained to be done was punish Athens and Eretria for their intervention.

If Darius had Eretria and Athens as his immediate targets his longer-range plans encompassed all Greece: in 491 BC he sent envoys to the peninsula demanding 'earth and water', the traditional tokens of surrender, from everyone including the Spartans. But Greek opinion was hardening too. The Spartans offered the Athenians an alliance and both of them executed Darius' envoys. There was no going back now. All eyes turned to the north, where the Persians had the army that had subjugated Thrace, plus a considerable fleet. When news came that the fleet had been wrecked off Mount Athos in a winter storm, Greece breathed easier – an invasion without naval support seemed unlikely – but Darius insisted that operations begin in 490 BC, albeit on a reduced scale. A new fleet was assembled in Phoenicia: it was given the task of taking out Eretria and Athens, and by doing so showing the Greeks what their fate would be if they continued to defy the Great King. Darius had none of Cyrus' disdain for terror.

The Persian fleet moved against Eretria first, stopping only to subdue Naxos and Carystos en route. A six-day assault and some undercover negotiations induced Eretria to surrender: it was razed to the ground and its citizens sold into slavery. Then the Persians sailed down to the eastern side of Attica (the Athenian peninsula) and disembarked on the plain of Marathon. This, they reckoned, was the place where their cavalry could be used to best advantage. The Athenians, who had no cavalry at all, recognized the tactical problem. They marched their army – at around 9,000 strong probably the numerical equal of the Persians' – across the peninsula to the edge of the plain, but took care to make camp in the foothills, where the Persian horse couldn't operate effectively. For a week the two sides watched each other, the Athenians edging their camp forward when they felt it was safe to do so, the Persians becoming a bit sloppy about getting their cavalry into line in the mornings. By dawn on the ninth day the Athenian general, Miltiades, had the opportunity he needed: the gap between the two armies was down to a mile and the Persian cavalry was nowhere to be seen. The order to attack was speedily executed. The line of hoplites swept onto the plain and over the open ground, both flanks wheeling in to crowd the Persians together. The battle that followed was sternly contested, but everywhere the armoured Greeks fared better than their lightly armed foes. The Persians broke, and ran for their ships. By midday it was all over: Athens had won a famous victory.

Marathon, understandably enough, immediately assumed mythic importance for the Athenians but, in truth, it was no more than a minor check for the Persians. Their resources, immensely greater than those of any Greek state, remained unimpaired, and Darius now began planning the overland campaign which would allow these resources to be brought to bear. He died before the preparations were complete and it was his son Xerxes (486–465 BC) who eventually assembled the famous host which, if not to be numbered in the millions of later oratory, was certainly far larger than any previously seen in Europe. At a minimum some 150,000 men crossed the bridge of boats that had been constructed at the Hellespont: from there Xerxes, his army and his fleet set off along the north coast of the Aegean. A canal had been dug across the base of the Athos peninsula to enable the fleet to avoid the treacherous waters off its tip – and also, no doubt, to demonstrate that not even the forces of nature could thwart the advance of the Great King.

The most northerly Greek state, the Kingdom of Macedon, had already submitted to Xerxes' envoys: Thessaly did not resist either. However, the Spartan-led Greek league had sent an army to hold the pass of Thermopylae, and a fleet to guard its flank, and it was here that the battle for the peninsula began. The army was pretty much a scratch force. The Spartans had provided its general, Leonidas, and he had with him his personal guard of 300 hoplites, but total strength was no more than 5,000, and if it was to do its job – which was to hang on till the main Greek force came up – then it needed every advantage of position. The narrow pass was, on the face of it, ideal, but could be outflanked by a path through the hills overlooking it. On the third day of the fighting the Persians found the path and drove off the few troops watching it. When he heard the news Leonidas sent most of his army home but chose to stay himself along with his fellow Spartans and 1,000 Thebans, the Greeks most immediately threatened by the Persian advance. Attacked on both sides, the Thebans soon surrendered, but Leonidas and the 300 fought until the last of them was cut down. Such was the Spartan way.

The Persians resumed their march, entering Thebes (which changed sides) and Athens (which had been evacuated). Several years earlier the Athenians had decided that their hopes for a second Marathon lay not on land, where Sparta would inevitably play the main role, but at sea, and by building 200 ships – more than all the other Greek states put together – they had ensured that theirs would be the leading role in the naval war. Now Athens had to face the consequences of this decision: the fleet ferried the non-combatants from Attica to the Peloponnese, then joined the other Greek ships guarding the new – and final – defence line across the Peloponnesian isthmus. A few days later, under the watchful eye of Xerxes himself, the Persian fleet made its move. Battle was joined in the channel between the island of Salamis and the coast of Attica: the Greek fleet made better use of the confined space and its cohesion and tactics proved equally superior. By the end of the day the Persian navy had been crushed and the threat of further Persian advance dispelled. A disgusted Xerxes returned to Asia, leaving his general Mardonius to consolidate Persian rule in the area already won.

The next year the Spartans took the offensive, leading the forces of the League out of the Peloponnese and into the foothills overlooking the Boeotian plain. Mardonius sent his cavalry against the Greeks' supply lines and they did their work so well that the Greek army began to pull back in some disorder. Mardonius, keen to exploit his advantage, followed up with the main force only to find himself at grips with a hoplite army on ground that favoured it and not him. It was Marathon all over

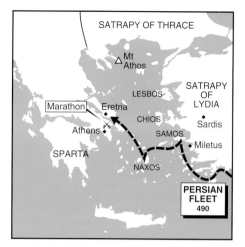

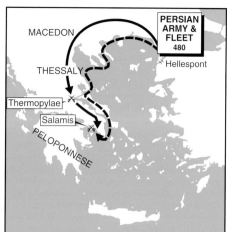

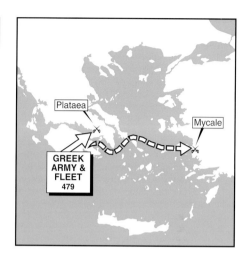

again, but on a far bigger scale. The battle, named for the nearby town of Plataea, destroyed the bulk of the forces Xerxes had left behind; the remainder perished in the months that followed when the north of the peninsula was liberated. The Persian navy was finished off in the same campaign. The Greek fleet chased it from Samos, the haven to which it had fled after Salamis, to Mycale, where the sailors abandoned their ships and retreated to a stockade. With the Athenians in the lead, the Greeks landed, burnt the ships and stormed the stockade. Then they sailed north and seized the Hellespont.

The Athenians certainly had a lot to be proud about. They had made all the right decisions and, as a result, won a series of fine victories: Marathon, Salamis and now Mycale. By their own estimate they had 'saved all Greece from slavery', and they were not chary of saying so on their many war memorials. The Spartans, famously a people of few words, took a more restrained line. The inscription on the trophy they erected (on behalf of the League) at Delphi simply said 'These fought in the war', followed by the names of the thirty states that did. But even the Spartans felt that something more was needed in the case of Leonidas and the 300. So they

asked Simonides, the most admired poet of the day, for some lines for the memorial under construction at Thermopylae. Taking a leaf from the Spartan book, he came up with the shortest, and best remembered, of all his epitaphs:

> STRANGER
> GO TELL THE SPARTANS
> THAT WE KEEP THE GROUND
> THEY BID US HOLD

Once the Persian invasion had been defeated, Sparta's horizon contracted to the coastline of the Peloponnese and it was left to Athens to exploit the Greek military superiority that the war had revealed. At first progress was rapid: within a few years the Athenian fleet had liberated all the Greek communities on the shores of the Aegean and Sea of Marmara, and was looking to do the same in Cyprus. But Cyprus proved an island too far: by 470 BC the Persians had won this particular battle and it was apparent that a balance had been struck between the Aegean power of Athens and the Levantine resources of the Persian Empire. It was not, however, in the Athenian nature to accept this, nor, in truth, was it in their interest. Liberated Greek communities had all been enrolled in an anti-Persian League in which Athens, needless to say, had the decisive voice. And all of them paid dues to the League treasury (on the island of Delos) based on the taxes previously paid to Persia. If the war was over there was no need for the League, and Athens would lose the revenues that had raised her into a different class from any other Greek state. So the war went on.

It was, nonetheless, difficult to find a profitable way of expressing this continuing belligerence. Another expedition was made to Cyprus, followed by a massive effort to sustain an anti-Persian rebellion in Egypt (459–454 BC). Neither succeeded, and troubles blew up within the League as a result. Athens reacted with vigour: the League treasury was transferred from Delos to Athens and it was made clear to all member states that there was no question of anyone leaving. The metamorphosis of the supposedly voluntary Delian League into an Athenian empire was now complete (454 BC). Athens also tidied up its strategy by formally abandoning any idea of enlarging its home base. Squabbles with Corinth had led to Athens placing garrisons in areas adjacent to Attica, notably Megara and Boeotia: these were ejected by the locals in 446 BC and Athens made no attempt to reinstate them. Instead the Athenians declared their commitment to a purely maritime empire by building walls linking the city of Athens to Piraeus, its port. If war threatened, the Athenians would simply man walls and fleet, and the rest of the peninsula – including the rest of Attica – would have to look after itself.

There remained the problem of finding a justification for the Empire. If it wasn't possible to make further advances in the east, then Athens would have to look west, along the sea routes to southern Italy and Sicily. This meant facing down Corinth, which had traditionally dominated trade in this direction. In itself this wasn't difficult, but Corinth was allied with Sparta, and though the Spartans were reluctant to move, their relationship with Athens was not what it had been. Theirs was a traditional society, proud of its ways and conscious of its prestige: the Athenians – innovative, cocksure and greedy – represented everything they distrusted. But when the Spartans finally did declare war they found themselves unable to get to grips with their opponents. The population of Attica took refuge within the 'Long Walls' and whatever damage the Spartans did to the Attic harvest was equalled by the damage done to Sparta's coastal lands by the Athenian fleet. The ten year war (431–421 BC) ended in a draw, which was, in a way, a victory for Athens. The Athenians celebrated by preparing a major expedition to bring Sicily into their empire. The armada – 100 warships carrying 5,000 hoplites – set sail in 415 BC.

Meanwhile, the western Greeks had been fighting the Etruscans and Carthaginians, and making a fairly good job of it. In particular the Greeks of Cumae defeated Lars Porsenna of Clusium, one of the most important Etruscan kings, at Aricia in Latium in 504 BC. Subsequently the Romans, in a coup that was presumably related to this defeat, expelled the Etruscan king, Tarquin the Proud, and adopted a republican constitution (traditionally in 509 BC, but surely after, rather than before, Aricia). But if the Etruscans were fading by the end of the sixth century BC, the Carthaginians were not, and early on in the fifth they landed an army in Sicily that was so formidable that contemporaries compared it with the host of Xerxes, then being marshalled in the east. It was to suffer a similar fate. Advancing against Himera, the nearest Greek settlement, it was attacked by a Syracusan-led Greek army and effectively annihilated. This in the same year as Salamis (480 BC) – later historians improved the coincidence to the same day.

While Himera freed the Sicilian Greeks from external threat their brethren in south-western Italy were less fortunate. The problem was not the Etruscans – thanks to Syracusan aid Cumae was able to see off a final Etruscan offensive in 474 BC – but the hill tribes of the Apennines, who were now spilling out of the valleys and on to the plains. This made life difficult for the plains dwellers both in Latium, where the Romans had a hard time coping with the local mountain men, the Volsci and Aequi, and in Campania, where both Etruscan Capua and Greek Cumae fell to the Samnites, the people of the south-central Apennines, in the 420s. By the end of the century, Naples and Velia were the only survivors in what had once been a continuous chain of Greek settlements along the shin of the Italian foot.[1]

At the southern end of the Red Sea note the colonization of the west coast – modern Eritrea – by settlers from the opposite, Arabian side. This Semitic intrusion separated the northernmost Cushitic tribe, the Beja, from their relatives in southern Eritrea, the Danakil. In due course – sooner rather than later, apparently – the newcomers moved into the mountainous interior, which was to get its medieval name, Abyssinia, from one of their tribes, the Habesh (and the name of its language, Geez, from another, the Ag'azi).

Iron-working is now general throughout our area. In Europe only the Lapps remain ignorant of the technology: in Asia it has spread to the borders of China. Knowledge of iron-working has also travelled up the Nile as far as the sixth cataract: from there it will spread through the Sahel, reaching the Niger by the end of the third century BC.[2]

---

1. Campania is the area round Capua, for which Cumae and Naples acted as seaports. Latium is the area between Rome and Campania, Etruria the area between Rome and the Arno.

2. New entries on this map include: the Sarmatians, a Scythian people occupying the steppe to the east of the Don, Khwarizm (the land around the lower Oxus) and Hyrcania (the southern shore of the Caspian), ex-Persian provinces that have slipped out of Persian control; and a new culture, named after the (later) Swiss site of *La Téne*, which has developed in the Celtic heartland, the mid-Rhine/upper Danube region. *La Téne* craftsmen were the first to show the fascination with spiral design that became the hallmark of late-Celtic art.

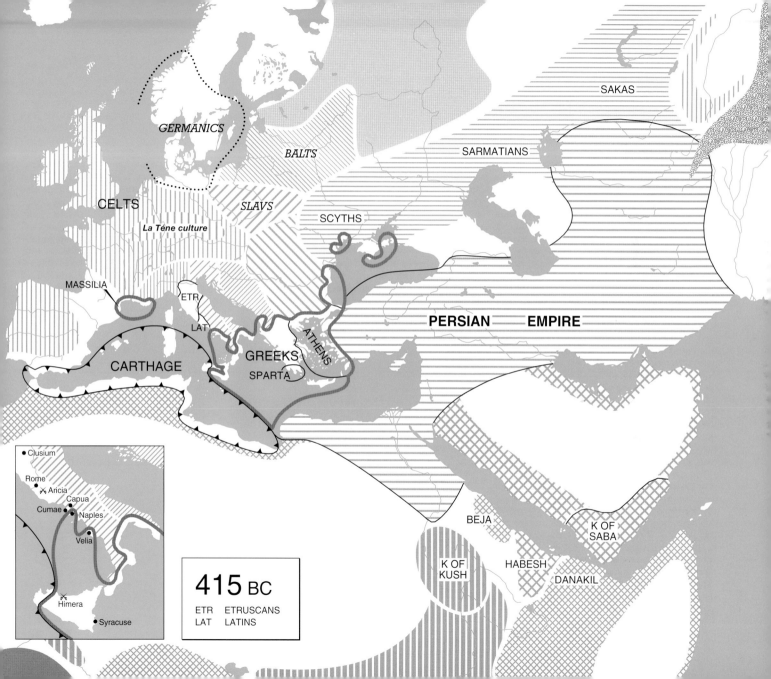

GERMANICS

BALTS

SAKAS

SARMATIANS

CELTS

SLAVS

*La Tène culture*

SCYTHS

MASSILIA

ETR

LAT

PERSIAN    EMPIRE

CARTHAGE

GREEKS

ATHENS

SPARTA

BEJA

K OF
SABA

K OF
KUSH

HABESH

DANAKIL

● Clusium

Rome ●
✕ Aricia
Capua ●
Cumae ● ● Naples

Velia ●

✕ Himera

● Syracuse

## 415 BC

ETR    ETRUSCANS
LAT    LATINS

According to the database used to construct this map, some 40 million people lived in our area in the late fifth century BC out of a global total of 110 million. The Persian Empire, the region's biggest political unit, contained some 16 million people. By comparison, peninsular Greece and the Aegean islands had a population of only 2.5 million, of whom perhaps half lived in states that contested the Persian advance.

Given this enormous disparity in numbers, how did the Persians manage to do so badly? Logistics provide part of the answer, drastically reducing the force that the Persians could bring to bear. A seaborne army had to be small and, as was shown at Marathon, could easily be matched by the Greeks. Even with a land-based advance there was a limit to the number of troops that could be supported, and an even lower limit to the force that could be sustained in the longer term. There is no reason to doubt that, when he first entered the peninsula, Xerxes' army outnumbered any force the Greeks could raise. But he took many of the best troops home with him, and the army of occupation he left behind is unlikely to have been larger than the force mustered by the Spartan League in 479 BC. Another part of the answer is provided by the local geography. Almost everywhere in Greece, the terrain favoured foot above horse, which meant that the odds were on the side with the most effective infantry. First Marathon, then Plataea, proved that heavy infantry on the Greek model was superior to the lightly armed style preferred by the Persians. In the final analysis, on the killing ground of the battlefield, it was the hoplite, the Greek armoured spearman, who won the war.

The hoplite panoply – helmet, breastplate and greaves – had a long history in the Aegean. It existed in Homer's day and, before that, in the time of the Sea Peoples. But if the warrior was essentially the same from the Late Bronze Age through the Early Iron Age, the nature of warfare changed entirely. Homeric battles were fought by hero-kings and their war bands, as witness Achilles and his Myrmidons. The Iron Age state, on the other hand, deployed its entire citizen body in a mass formation, the phalanx. This was a highly effective way of expressing military power – Athens, for example, with a mere 30,000 citizens, was able to send 9,000 hoplites to Marathon – but the social revolution underlying the change is equally important. The new citizen armies not only defended the state, they had a say in its running. Where Homeric states had been ruled by king and council, the society that emerged in the Early Iron Age used a king, council and assembly system, with all citizens attending the assembly. Moreover there was a strong tendency to drop the king. There was a shift in power within the social pyramid, from an aristocratic state to a more egalitarian one. This is the basis for saying that the Greeks were free, in a way that the subjects of the Persian king were not.

Greek states varied a great deal in the extent to which they institutionalized this change. The backwoods state of Macedon not only kept its king, it allowed him a near monopoly of executive power: once crowned he could do pretty much as he pleased. The Spartans, ever conservative, also retained their kings, but only as figureheads: power was vested in a council of elders. The Athenians, famously, went the whole hog, and made the assembly sovereign. All Athenian citizens (meaning free-born native males of military age) had the right, and indeed obligation, to attend the assembly and vote on its proposals, just as they had the right and obligation to bear arms. The conflict between Sparta and Athens consequently took on an ideological dimension. Sparta imposed oligarchic constitutions where it could, and Athens democracies. The difference is important, but it's worth remembering that the idea that the assembly had to register its consent in some manner was general, and that the assembly existed, in the form of the army, in all states. Even Macedon.

Another interesting point is that democracy depended on demography: an assembly could only function with the necessary regularity if the majority of its citizens lived within walking distance of the meeting place. So the possibility of democracy arose from the fact that, after Egypt, Greece had the highest population density of any country in our area. In fact Early Iron Age Greece was conspicuously overpopulated. Whereas Egypt could feed its people and usually have surplus grain for export, the Greeks could only just get by in good years: in bad years some of them had to up stakes and emigrate. This happened so often that by the eighth century there was an established procedure for collecting and dispatching colonists (who weren't allowed to return) and this continued in use throughout the classical period. It didn't solve the problem – Greece was still living at the Malthusian limit in the late fifth century – but it eased it. So of course did the constant wars.

The ability to sustain high rates of loss can be taken as a measure of the degree of overpopulation. Here Athens is the paradigm. Casualty lists that would have broken a state in better demographic balance – even the devastating plague of 431 BC – failed to stop the dispatch of armadas overseas, and the planting of colonies within and without the empire. The Athenian achievement seems to have had its roots in a population dynamic that, for more than a century, proved unstoppable. The Spartan situation was the exact opposite: the effective roll call was always low because citizenship was restricted to the ruling caste. According to Aristotle, if Sparta had had a normal social structure it could have fielded 30,000 hoplites: as it was it managed only about 5,000 at Plataea (presumably an all-out effort), and thereafter the number steadily fell. Such decline is almost inevitable for groups that refuse to recruit new members: in the case of Sparta it meant that hoplite turnout was down to 3,500 by the date of this map.

Population in
**415 BC**

⅄ 250,000

⅄ 125,000

areas averaging 10 or
more persons per km²
left unshaded

The various versions of the alphabet continued their advance during the fifth and fourth centuries. Westward the most important gains were in Italy, where all the native peoples acquired at least the rudiments of literacy. The scripts they adopted were variations of the Etruscan: the Lepontic and Venetic alphabets were used to write the Celto-Ligurian and Venetic languages, the Oscan alphabet the various dialects of Italic spoken in the central and southern Apennines. The one with the future, of course, was the Latin alphabet, at this stage restricted to Rome and its environs. In the heel of the peninsula the Messapians found an unmodified Greek alphabet sufficed for their Illyrian tongue.

The east remained wedded to the consonantal alphabet. Persian bureaucrats, like their Assyrian predecessors, used Aramaic in their correspondence, and it was in the form of Aramaic that the peoples of the more easterly provinces made their first acquaintance with literacy. Aramaic was also gaining the upper hand over its Phoenician relative, Aramaic-derived square Hebrew letters displacing the original Phoenician-derived linear script (though the changeover was not completed until the days of the Maccabees) while the Nabataeans of the Syrian and Jordanian borderlands opted for an Aramaic-based alphabet to replace the South Arabian one that had been used by their forebears. The only success notched up by the Phoenician alphabet – an important one, for sure – was its dissemination through the western Mediterranean area now dominated by the Carthaginians.

Pre-alphabetic scripts were still much in evidence. All Egyptian inscriptions continued to be written in hieroglyphs: there was, however, a change in the cursive form from hieratic to a shorthand style known as demotic. This enabled the Egyptian scribes to match one of the advantages conferred by the alphabet, speed of writing, but, because demotic was only the same old logosyllabary in a repackaged form, it did nothing for ease of understanding; it was as complex and ambiguous as its predecessor.

Further east, cuneiform was also keeping its end up. Lower Mesopotamia continued to use the Babylonian form, and the Persian chancellery the Elamite version. And, as with Egyptian hieroglyphs, cuneiform remained the preferred mode for official inscriptions. A good example is Darius' account of his rise to power carved on a cliff face at Behistun, overlooking the road from Ecbatana to Babylon. The inscription is trilingual, with parallel versions in Persian, Babylonian and Elamite. All three are written in cuneiform, which, as far as Persian is concerned, meant inventing an entirely new variant of the script. This Persian cuneiform is an open syllabary, so it is not as archaic as it looks, but the archaic look was what mattered to Darius. Dignity demanded it.[1]

Other pre-alphabetic scripts, lacking this sort of patronage, were long gone by the date of this map. Assyrian and Urartuan cuneiform (and the Urartuan glyphs) vanished when the Assyrian and Urartuan empires fell. Luvian hieroglyphic had disappeared even earlier, during the Assyrians' piecemeal destruction of the neo-Hittite principalities.

Two undeciphered scripts are interesting. One is an alphabet used at Side, on the south coast of Anatolia, for the unknown local language – presumably a variety of Luvian. The other is Iberian, which existed in three variants: south-western, south-eastern ('Baetican') and north-eastern ('Levantine'). The general assumption is that the language belongs to the largely extinct group of which Basque is the only survivor today. The script is an odd combination of alphabet (true alphabet, with vowels) and syllabary (open syllables only), which makes it difficult to classify. As with Sidetic, it is the obscurities of the language, not the script, which is holding up the decipherment.

---

1. Between 1835 and 1847, Henry Rawlinson, an English officer serving with the Persian army, managed to make a complete copy of this immense and almost inaccessible inscription. This gave him the material he needed to decipher the Persian text, the first cuneiform script to be read in modern times. Babylonian cuneiform took longer to comprehend, but by the 1850s Rawlinson, along with other scholars, had got the hang of it, and the work of recovering Mesopotamia's ancient past could begin.

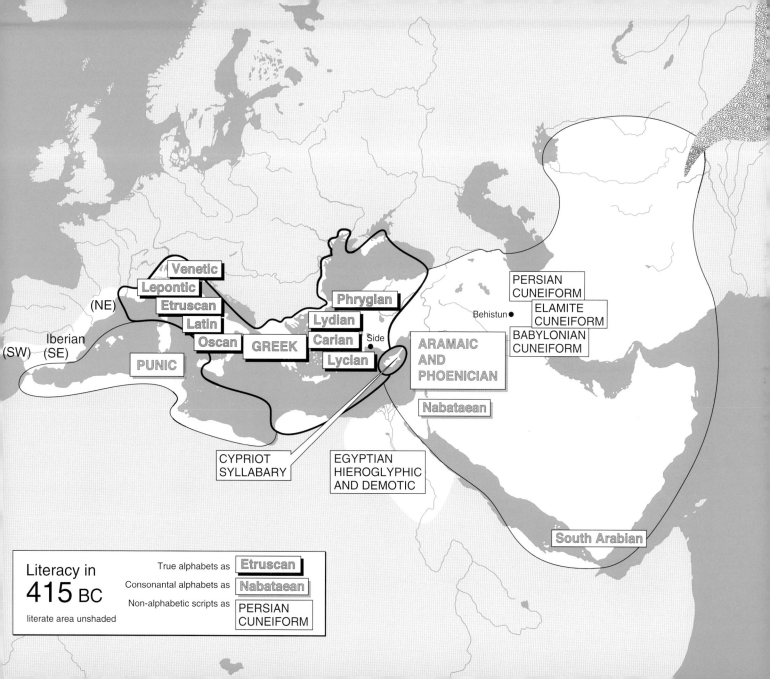

Venetic

Lepontic

Etruscan

(NE)

Latin

Oscan

GREEK

PUNIC

Iberian
(SE)

(SW)

Phrygian

Lydian

Carian

Side

Lycian

ARAMAIC
AND
PHOENICIAN

Nabataean

PERSIAN
CUNEIFORM

Behistun

ELAMITE
CUNEIFORM

BABYLONIAN
CUNEIFORM

CYPRIOT
SYLLABARY

EGYPTIAN
HIEROGLYPHIC
AND DEMOTIC

South Arabian

Literacy in
415 BC

literate area unshaded

True alphabets as    Etruscan

Consonantal alphabets as    Nabataean

Non-alphabetic scripts as    PERSIAN
CUNEIFORM

In the fifth century the city of Athens was the showplace of Greece. Supporting its glories, and adding to them in the brief interludes of peace, was a state revenue on a scale hitherto unknown in the peninsula. All the sources of wealth known to the ancient world contributed to this income: the Athenians had industries (potteries and metal-working shops whose products were in demand throughout the Mediterranean), significant mineral deposits (silver mines at Laurion on the southern tip of Attica), a cash-oriented agriculture (the oil, wine and honey of the Attic hills), and a commercial network centered on Piraeus that must have yielded significant dues. But, more important than any of these, they had the tribute paid by their Aegean 'allies': 600 talents a year out of a total revenue of 1,000. This was the input that enabled so many Athenians to live in the city instead of the country and make the running of the state, rather than the running of their farms, their main business. By contrast, it has been calculated that the fine pottery industry, for all its Mediterranean-wide success, never employed more than a handful of workers, and consequently can hardly have made more than a marginal contribution to the Athenian economy.

The most direct expression of Athens' wealth was its size. What data we have suggest that at its peak in the late fifth century the city's population was about 35,000, a figure way above the norm for Greek urban centres. In fact the only place in peninsular Greece that could hold a candle to it was Piraeus, the city's port, with perhaps 7,500 year-round inhabitants (double that when the fleet was fitting out, but that doesn't count). Elsewhere in the Greek world Syracuse will have been a match for Piraeus, but there was no other town that could match Syracuse, let alone Athens. The city was in a class of its own. No wonder it dominated Aegean trade. It also influenced places much further away. The development of wheat farming and anchovy fishing by the Greek communities on the Black Sea littoral owed a great deal to the needs of Athens.

Given its exceptional population and resources it is not surprising to find that Athens became the cultural capital of the Greek world. It was an exciting time to hold this position. Thanks to their pioneering of the alphabet the Greeks had achieved an unprecedented level of literacy. Horizons had also been widened by the colonization programme, while the growth of commerce, and more particularly the increasing use of money, challenged the traditional forms of society.[1] These factors combined to produce the 'Ionian awakening' of the sixth century, in which, for the first time, the spirit of enquiry was allowed free play. Athens' unique contribution was the size of its audience. It was in the Theatre of Dionysos, at the foot of the Athenian acropolis, that Aeschylus, Sophocles and Euripides presented the tragedies that mark the starting point of western drama. It was in Plato's Academy and Aristotle's Lyceum that the new philosophies were expounded and the first codifications of knowledge attempted. Here Herodotus read his *History*, the first work to deserve that title, and Thucydides found the objectivity that has been the historians' grail ever since. Through the fifth and fourth centuries Athens was the place to be, not just because it was the most magnificent city in the Greek world – though with its all-marble acropolis it was certainly that – but because it had the buzz that goes with a mixture of money and talent, and a consciousness of superiority. The city was, in its own estimation, 'an education to Greece'.

Others differed. To her enemies, Greek as well as foreign, Athens was simply a predatory imperial power. Even her so-called allies – the 190 Aegean communities that constituted the Athenian Empire – saw little profit in the association. They had no vote in the Athenian assembly, no say in how high the empire's taxes would be nor how they would be spent. What they had paid to the Great King, they now paid to the Athenian state; the rest was horse feathers.[2]

1. Coinage has its beginnings in the hallmarked electrum slugs produced by the Lydians in the later seventh century. Electrum, a naturally occurring gold-silver alloy, was initially regarded as a metal in its own right: only when its true nature became apparent in the mid sixth century did the Lydians begin striking gold and silver separately. The Greeks – first the Ionians, then the maritime communities of the peninsula such as Aegina, Corinth and Athens – started their silver coinage shortly after. The most widely used Greek currency, the owl-stamped coinage of Athens (the owl was the sacred bird of the goddess Athena) dates from 520 BC: the Persian equivalent is the coinage issued by Darius in both gold (with an image of the king drawing his bow) and silver.

2. The Persian Empire, with twenty times the revenue of Athens, might be expected to have produced an equivalent crop of cities, but the Persians were not an urban people, and under their rule the Near East gained few new towns. The more centralized administration imposed on Egypt may have pushed Memphis up to the 7,500 mark, but that's about it. In fact, the whole empire, enormous though it was, contained only one large city, Babylon, and that had been inherited from the previous regime. Babylon benefited from the fact that the Great King spent the winter months there, but each spring the court moved to Persepolis, Darius' palace complex in Fars, and Susa and Ecbatana were also visited on a regular basis. This peripatetic habit meant that no single centre attained metropolitan status: the 'capital' was wherever the court happened to be.

Worth a brief mention is the Nile–Red Sea canal begun by Necho II and finished by Darius. It was not a success: the northerly winds that prevail in the upper part of the Red Sea made access difficult and shippers preferred to continue as before, transferring their goods to and from the upper Nile via the Wadi Hammamat.

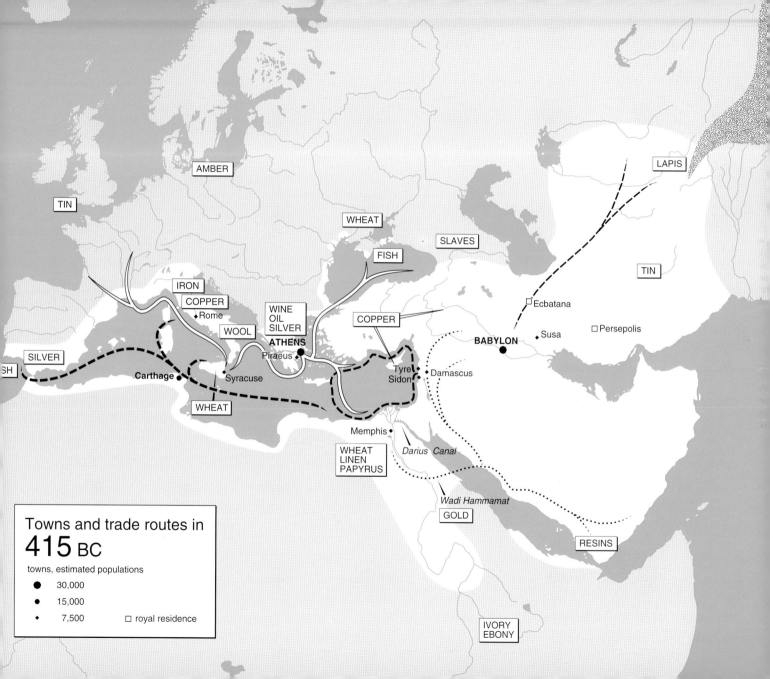

AMBER

TIN

LAPIS

WHEAT

SLAVES

TIN

FISH

IRON

COPPER

□ Ecbatana

◆ Rome

WOOL

WINE
OIL
SILVER

COPPER

BABYLON ●

□ Persepolis

◆ Susa

ATHENS

Piraeus ◆

SILVER

SH

Carthage ●

Syracuse ◆

Tyre
Sidon

◆ Damascus

WHEAT

Memphis ◆

WHEAT
LINEN
PAPYRUS

Darius Canal

Wadi Hammamat

GOLD

RESINS

IVORY
EBONY

## Towns and trade routes in
# 415 BC

towns, estimated populations

●     30,000

●     15,000

◆     7,500     □ royal residence

If the Athenians were to establish themselves in Sicily they had to capture Syracuse, and quickly too. This proved to be more than they could manage: all their assaults failed and, as the weeks passed, the besiegers gradually became the besieged. A second fleet, almost as large as the original armada, failed to restore the situation and, in 413 BC, the entire expedition had to surrender. It was a staggering blow to Athenian pretensions. Ten thousand hoplites, half of them native Athenians, had been lost, along with 200 warships. The empire's enemies immediately closed in for the kill. Sparta sent an army to occupy Attica, many of Athens' 'allies' changed sides and, most important of all, the Persians promised the subsidies needed to create a Spartan-officered fleet. The Athenians fought back as best they could, and for a few years managed to hold on to the Hellespont, the vital link with the wheatfields of south Russia. Then, in 405, the Spartan admiral, Lysander, caught the Athenian fleet napping at Aegospotami, on the European side of the straits, and all but annihilated it. A starving Athens surrendered the next year: its walls were razed and its empire dismantled.

For the next few years Sparta assumed the mantle of Athens, and acted as arbiter of the Aegean. This led to a break with Persia which consequently switched its subsidies to Athens, enabling the city to rebuild both its walls and its fleet. The only way Sparta could get back into the Persians' good books was to recognize their claim to the east coast of the Aegean, and this, despite a chorus of disapproval from the rest of the Greek world, they proceeded to do (386 BC). Without risking battle himself, simply by paying Greek to fight Greek, the Great King had won back a useful strip of territory. The Aegean islanders were so alarmed that they agreed to the reconstitution of the Athenian Empire (378 BC), though at much lower rates of tax than Athens had levied in the old days.[1]

Athens was not the only power to challenge Syracuse for the hegemony of Sicily during this period; in 409 BC the Carthaginians began a series of punitive campaigns against the western Greek settlements, which went so well that they decided to go for the whole island. By 396 BC they were under the walls of Syracuse, but once again the city held

out and, as their losses mounted, the Carthaginians began to have second thoughts. The peace treaty of 392 BC restored the pre-war frontiers, and Syracuse returned to her old position as protector and master of the Greek (and Sicel) communities on the island. The settlements in the toe of Italy also sought her protection at this time, but this Syracusan empire was a restless, unstable affair. In ruthlessness the Athens of the west was the equal of Athens itself, but it shared few of its other features and certainly wasn't an education to anyone.

The transition from fifth to fourth centuries marks an important development in the story of the Celts. From the archaeologist's point of view this is the period when the *La Téne* culture triumphs, becoming the defining style of all the peoples living between the Loire and the Danube. And the historian is able to recognize this as the distribution of the Gauls, the core element of the Celtic world. This world was now in a state of flux. The northernmost tribes, the group later known as the Belgae, were in the process of shifting from Germany across the Rhine into Belgium: in doing so they displaced the existing tenants, the Parisi, most of whom moved south-west, to the Paris basin, though a minority chose a more adventurous option, crossing the Channel and coasting north to Yorkshire. Other Gallic tribes moved east down the Danube, west into Atlantic and Mediterranean France, and south into Italy. It was the invasion of Italy that attracted the most attention at the time. The Etruscan element in the Po Valley had been weakened as a result of the northward advance of the Umbrians, the Italic people of the north-central Apennines. Now both Etruscans and Umbrians were swept aside by an inrush of Gallic tribes that settled much of the north Italian plain and raided deep into the rest of the peninsula. Rome, which had just consolidated its position as the leading city of Latium by eliminating Veii (396 BC), the nearest of the Etruscan communities, was put to the sack by one Gallic band (386 BC); another reached down the Adriatic coast almost to the heel. The Gallic invasions set the seal on the Etruscans' decline: the last time they are known to have taken any offensive action is in 415 BC, when they contributed to the Athenian expedition against Syracuse.

Featured for the first time on this map is the north Greek kingdom of Macedon. For some time past the Macedonians had been edging eastwards at the expense of the Thracians and their kings now reigned over what was, by Greek standards, an unusually large territory. But though they reigned, they did not rule: the clans of the interior paid no more than lip service to the monarchy, while the people of the coastal communities were colonists from further south, with their own laws and purely local allegiances.

Note the creation of the Bosporan principality from the various Greek settlements to either side of the Cimmerian Bosporus (c. 400 BC). The ruling house was Thracian, but the area was considered part of the Greek world, and is shown as such on the map. In the Yemen the south Arabian kingdom of Saba split four ways (c. 410 BC).

1. 'My best soldiers seem to be my archers' was the Great King's comment, 'archers' being the colloquial term for the Persian gold coin, officially a 'daric', which bore an image of him drawing his bow.

Persia's success in recovering its Aegean seaboard was offset by the loss of Egypt, which recovered its independence under a sequence of native dynasties (28th, 29th and 30th, starting c. 405 BC). Even more worrying for the empire's leadership was the failure to find a counter to the hoplite. This was tellingly illustrated by the 'march of the ten thousand', an army of Greek mercenaries hired by a brother of the Persian king for an attempt on the throne. In 401 BC this Greek force marched from Sardis to Cunaxa, just short of Babylon, where they beat the best army the Great King could raise. Unfortunately for the ten thousand the would-be usurper was killed in the battle so the only course open to them was to fight their way out again. This leg of their march was an even more remarkable achievement, for they were deep in enemy territory, every man's hand was against them, and they had no cavalry to protect their flanks. But they did it.

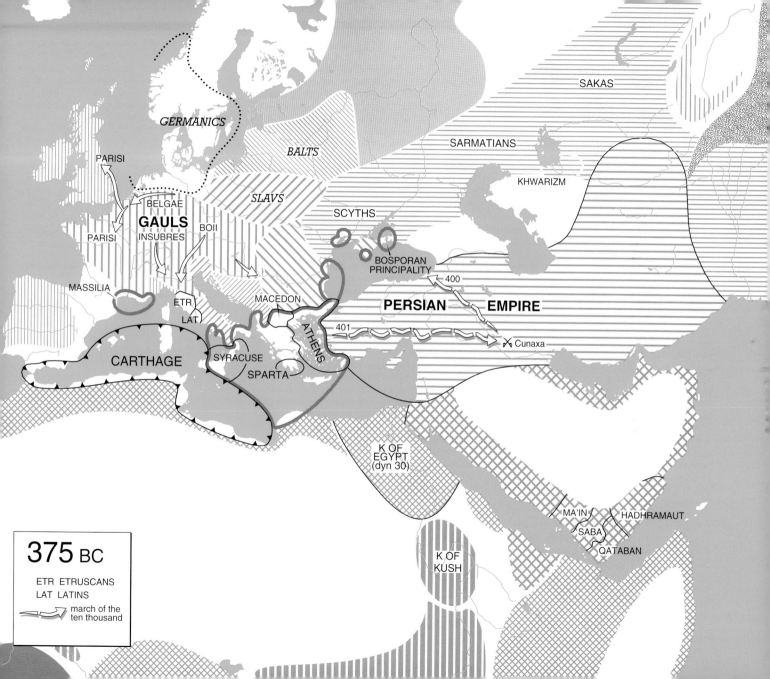

PARISI

GERMANICS

BALTS

SAKAS

SARMATIANS

KHWARIZM

BELGAE

SLAVS

**GAULS**

BOII

SCYTHS

INSUBRES

BOSPORAN
PRINCIPALITY

PARISI

MASSILIA

ETR

MACEDON

LAT

**PERSIAN    EMPIRE**

400

401

ATHENS

Cunaxa

CARTHAGE

SYRACUSE

SPARTA

K OF
EGYPT
(dyn 30)

MA'IN

HADHRAMAUT

SABA

QATABAN

K OF
KUSH

In the opening years of his reign, Philip II of Macedon (359–336 BC) transformed the levy of his backwoods state into the largest and most efficient force in Greece. First he established his authority over the kingdom and its borderlands, then he annexed the nearer parts of Illyria and Thrace. The silver mines these areas contained financed the increase in the size of the army: its effectiveness was established by constant campaigning. As early as 352 BC, when he gained control of Thessaly, the established powers of Greece had their warning; but, intent on a squabble over the sanctuary of Delphi – they called it the Sacred War – they put off forming an anti-Macedonian coalition until the last possible moment. By then Philip was unstoppable. At the Battle of Chaeronea he crushed the combined forces of Thebes and Athens (338 BC): subsequently they and all the other states of Greece were forcibly enrolled in a pan-Hellenic League that took its orders from Philip.[1]

Master of Greece, Philip now looked east. The purpose of the League, he announced, was to support a Macedonian-led invasion of Persia. His enemies scoffed that this was merely an excuse for the tyranny of Greek over Greek, but Philip was entirely sincere, and this became apparent as his recruiting agents went to work. He had sound reasons for confidence. The Persians might have recovered Egypt (343 BC) but as they were now relying on Greek mercenaries to do their fighting for them, Philip, at the head of the best army ever raised in Greece, looked a certain winner. It was not to be. On the eve of his departure for Asia he was assassinated by a member of his bodyguard. Rumour fingered Philip's colourful Epirote wife Olympias (Philip had just acquired an additional bride) but, as is usual in such cases, it was more probably the work of a lone malcontent. The Macedonian crown passed to Olympias' son, the 20-year-old Alexander.[2]

Young he might be, but lacking in confidence Alexander was not. He marched into Greece with such speed that the Hellenic League had no chance to do anything but congratulate him on his accession: then he headed north for the Danube and the few Thracian tribes that had managed to fend off his father's attentions. After making a show of force in this area (and receiving an embassy from the Gauls,

now infiltrating the middle Danube), he moved westward to impress the Illyrians, then, on the news that Thebes had rebelled, back into Greece again. The city was stormed, its walls razed and its history ended. There was to be no slackening of Macedon's grip on Greece.

The next spring Alexander crossed the Hellespont, seeking immediate battle. The local satraps obliged (overruling the commander of their Greek mercenaries who favoured a scorched earth policy) and the two sides met at the River Granicus. Alexander's furious attack gained him a complete victory, put Anatolia at his mercy and relieved him of his most pressing money worries. The rest of the year was spent tidying up: then, in 333 BC, he crossed the Taurus and took the coast road into Syria. The Persian king, Darius III, was close by with the main force of the Empire: he waited till Alexander had passed by, then moved in behind him. Alexander faced about, and the armies met at Issus. This was a harder fought battle than Granicus, but Alexander's cavalry charge won the field, and the day ended with the Persians fleeing eastwards. Alexander resumed his southward march, reaching Egypt in 332 BC. There he made a couple of side trips, one to found the city of Alexandria, intended to replace Memphis as capital of Egypt, the other a personal pilgrimage to the Temple of Zeus-Ammon in the oasis of Siwa.[3]

Darius now sent a peace offer based on the status quo, which Philip would surely have accepted; Alexander, conscious of his destiny, marched on. In the battle of Gaugamela he destroyed the last Persian army and won the remaining provinces of the Empire; then he disappeared beyond the Greek horizon, spending the last years of his brief life in minor campaigns on, or, in the case of India, beyond the ancient Persian frontier. His army needed only competent leadership to win its set-piece battles, and it was in the conduct of these secondary operations that Alexander's genius was tested and triumphed. In inexorable succession citadels were scaled, hill tribes ambushed, and the horsemen of the steppe outrun. He loved every minute of it, only leaving India because his troops refused point-blank to march to the Ganges. When he died (of a fever, at Babylon, a year after his return from India) he was said to be planning campaigns against

Arabia and Carthage, but in seeking fresh worlds to conquer he was ignoring the needs of an already colossal achievement. Bithynia and Cappadocia were still defying his lieutenants: worse still the only heirs to his Empire were a mentally challenged half-brother and an infant son, born posthumously to his Persian wife, Roxanne.

Rome's humiliation by the Gauls did her no lasting damage. The city never lost its primacy among the Latin communities and, in 338 BC, after a brief struggle with the other members of the Latin League, Rome was able to turn this primacy into dominance. At the same time, Roman control was extended down the coast as far as Naples (327 BC). This brought Rome into conflict with the Samnites, the confederation of hill tribes that dominated Campania.

1. The Spartans refused to join, which mattered less than it would have in earlier days: the Thebans had knocked them off the top of the Greek military table in 371 BC, and ensured that they stayed down by freeing Messene. The Spartan king Agis III attempted a comeback while Alexander was in Asia but was easily defeated by his viceroy (331 BC).

2. Epirus was a satellite kingdom set up by Philip as part of his programme for stabilizing Macedonia's borders. Olympias came with the territory.

3. Philip's final recruiting drive had inflated his forces to a size that could only be sustained if there was a quick victory over Persia. Granicus and Issus were steps in the right direction, but still left Alexander with insufficient funds for a fleet. As a result, a Phoenician squadron operating in the Aegean was able to stir up a lot of trouble and Alexander only solved this particular problem when he took Tyre (in 332 BC, after a seven-month siege), completing his occupation of the Phoenician coastline.

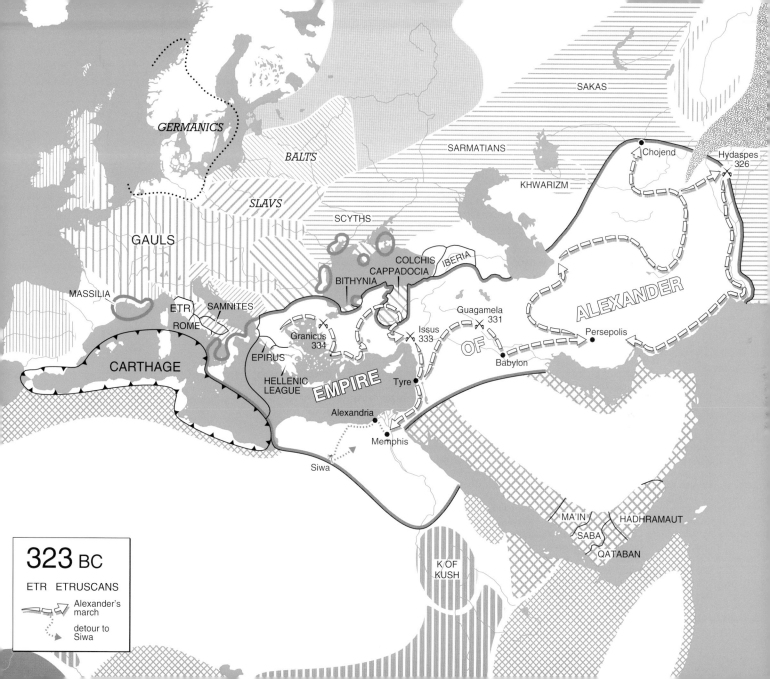

GERMANICS

SAKAS

BALTS

SLAVS

SARMATIANS

KHWARIZM

Chojend

Hydaspes
326

GAULS

SCYTHS

COLCHIS
CAPPADOCIA
BITHYNIA

IBERIA

ALEXANDER

MASSILIA

ETR
ROME

SAMNITES

Granicus
334

Guagamela
331

Issus
333

OF

Persepolis

CARTHAGE

EPIRUS

HELLENIC
LEAGUE

EMPIRE

Tyre

Babylon

Alexandria

Memphis

MA'IN

SABA

HADHRAMAUT

Siwa

QATABAN

K/OF
KUSH

## 323 BC

ETR ETRUSCANS

Alexander's
march

detour to
Siwa

Although for a few years after Alexander's death a central authority was maintained, lack of a capable royal successor made it inevitable that power would devolve on the generals in the provinces. In little more than a decade generals had become kings: Cassander in Macedon, Lysimachus in Thrace, Antigonus in Anatolia and Syria, Ptolemy in Egypt and Seleucus in the East. Of them all, only the 70-year-old Antigonus had the will to restore the unity of the Empire. He had the advantages of central position and command of the sea, and by clever propaganda was able to seduce the Hellenic League from its allegiance to Cassander, but his failure to disguise his ambition prompted his rivals to combine against him. As a result, at the critical battle of Ipsus, Antigonus had to face the united armies of Cassander, Lysimachus and Seleucus (301 BC). The old man went down fighting. Seleucus took Syria and Cilicia as his share of the spoils, and Lysimachus took Anatolia, while Ptolemy, who in his careful way had been too late for the battle, obtained Palestine and Cyprus. Antigonus' son, Demetrius, had escaped to his fleet and, although he was to be heard from again, he had only the resources – and mentality – of a freebooter. The imperial idea was dead.

Whatever their quarrels, the successor kingdoms generally maintained the perimeter of Alexander's empire. In some areas they even improved on it. Cappadocia was brought under control in the immediate post-Alexander period, while Lysander conquered the northern half of Thrace. On the other side of the ledger was the loss of the satrapies of Armenia and Atropatene, which drifted out of the Macedonian orbit during this period. The biggest subtraction, however, was at the eastern end of the Empire, where Seleucus ceded the Indian province on which Alexander had lavished so much of his attention to Chandragupta Maurya (c. 305 BC). Chandragupta, king of Magadha, doubtless inspired by Alexander's example, was busy extending the boundaries of his kingdom beyond the Ganges basin, its traditional area of concern: he paid Seleucus off with 500 war elephants which, so the story goes, helped tilt the battle of Ipsus Seleucus' way.

The traditional states of Greece don't figure much in the wars of the successors and the only one that does is a relative newcomer, Rhodes. Founded in 407 BC by the union of the three communities that had previously divided the island, Rhodes subsequently edged Athens out of its place as the leading commercial port of the Aegean. By the date of this map it was strong enough to withstand a famous siege by Demetrius (305–4 BC), a success that enabled it to remain outside the Island League set up in the Anti-gonid interest.

While Greek attention was concentrated on the exploitation of the East, the position of the western colonists was deteriorating. In Sicily, in 311 BC, the Carthaginians defeated the Syracusans and conquered all Sicily bar Syracuse itself. Thanks to a brilliantly conceived counter-blow at the city of Carthage, the Syracusans were able to obtain the restitution of Greek Sicily (306 BC), but the struggle was clearly becoming unequal. This was even more true in Italy where the Greeks had never been able to do much more than keep the local tribes at bay and where the accelerating advance of Roman power carried a challenge that they could not hope to meet. In some of the local wars Tarentum, the leading city of southern Italy, had employed Epirote and Spartan condottieri; the need now was for an Alexander.

Rome's main achievement during this period was bringing the Samnites to heel. Fighting in the hill country where the Samnites lived was difficult: on one occasion the entire Roman army, which at this time consisted of two legions of 4,000 men apiece, got itself trapped in a valley and had to be extricated under a humiliating truce.[1] But gradually, by forging alliances with the surrounding tribes and planting colonies of Roman citizens among them, the Romans encircled the Samnite heartland and were able to bring the necessary pressure to bear. In 304 BC they got the peace terms they wanted. Just as important, the undertakings the allied states had given during the war remained in force. Rome's handshake had turned into a permanent grip.

Note the appearance of the Nabataean Arabs at the northern end of the Hejaz trade route. Intrigued by reports of their wealth, Antigonus made an unsuccessful grab at Petra, their treasure house, in 312 BC.

1. Rome had replaced her kings with a pair of annually elected consuls. Normally they took a legion each but they sometimes campaigned together, exercising joint command. This was always tricky and, as in this case in the Second Samnite War and, more famously, at Cannae, the result could be a real cock-up.

The consuls were nominated by the Senate, Rome's equivalent of the Greek council of elders, which was also responsible for deciding on policy. Both nominations and policies had to be confirmed by the vote of the people, and decrees were issued in the name of both – *Senatus Populus Que Romanum*, hence SPQR. In practice the people always voted yes, and the only restraint on the oligarchy was the fear that they might not.

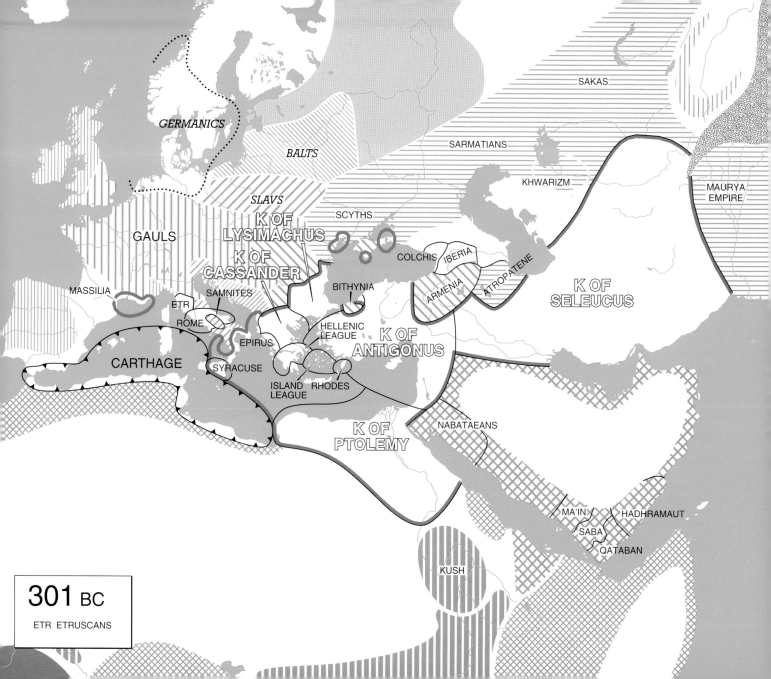

GERMANICS

BALTS

SAKAS

SARMATIANS

SLAVS

KHWARIZM

MAURYA
EMPIRE

GAULS

K OF
LYSIMACHUS

SCYTHS

K OF
CASSANDER

COLCHIS   IBERIA

ATROPATENE

K OF
SELEUCUS

MASSILIA

SAMNITES

BITHYNIA

ARMENIA

ETR

ROME

HELLENIC
LEAGUE

K OF
ANTIGONUS

EPIRUS

CARTHAGE

SYRACUSE

ISLAND   RHODES
LEAGUE

NABATAEANS

K OF
PTOLEMY

MA'IN   HADHRAMAUT

SABA

QATABAN

KUSH

301 BC

ETR ETRUSCANS

The battle of Ipsus did not put an end to the wars of Alexander's successors. By virtue of his fleet, Demetrius was able to control the Aegean and much of mainland Greece, and shortly after Cassander's death he was able to seize Macedon (298 BC). Lysimachus forced him out again, his fleet deserted to Ptolemy and, after a last wandering campaign in Anatolia, he ended up a prisoner of Seleucus. Lysimachus was the next to go, killed in battle by Seleucus at Corupedium in Ionia (280 BC). Macedon and the mantle of Alexander his for the taking, Seleucus crossed to Europe, only to be assassinated as he stepped out of the boat. And then from the north came the Gauls, pouring into Macedon, peninsular Greece and Thrace (279 BC). Demetrius' son, Antigonus II, cleaned them out of Macedon and seized the throne (which was to remain in his house thereafter), but the invaders retained control of Thrace, and three tribes which crossed the Hellespont were able to set up a robber state in north central Anatolia (Galatia, founded around the date of this map).[1] The political fragmentation of Asia Minor was carried a stage further when Ptolemy II used his sea power to relieve Antiochus, Seleucus' son and heir, of much of his western seaboard. Ptolemy's new-found fleet turned out to be an exceedingly useful asset. With it he was able to dominate the Aegean littoral and, in the event of trouble with either of his rivals, it was now an easy matter for him to raise Greece against Antigonus or Ionia against Antiochus. However, though trouble remained endemic, a balance had at last been struck and the successor states had assumed their definitive form.

To champion the cause of Hellenism against the Romans, the Tarentines picked Pyrrhus, King of Epirus, who was always game for a war. He arrived in Italy in 281 BC with a considerable army and even larger ambitions. Unfortunately for him, the opportune moment for intervention had passed, for in the opening decades of the century the Romans had finally mastered their native enemies – the Etruscans, Samnites and nearer Gauls – and though Pyrrhus won his battles, he failed to raise the country. When, in 278 BC, the Sicilian Greeks appealed to him for help against a new Carthaginian offensive, he preferred the chance of dramatic victories in a new theatre to the task of grinding away at the Romans. His success was indeed rapid and for a moment he was able to regard Sicily as his second kingdom. The Sicilian Greeks, however, were no keener to surrender their freedom to Pyrrhus than to Carthage; they revolted and he abandoned them, as next year he abandoned the Italian Greeks for a war with Antigonus II. He overran Macedon, lost it, and was attempting the conquest of the Peloponnese when he was killed in a skirmish (272 BC). Only then could the bewildered Romans be sure they had won.[2]

Both Macedonian control over the Hellenic League and the League itself disappeared during the wars of the successors. By garrisoning strategic points Antigonus II was able to keep a grip on the peninsula but he was never strong enough to marshal its member states into a subservient system. For a while the old pieces in the Greek war-game, Sparta and Athens, are on the board again, jostled by such newcomers as Epirus and Aetolia: where once Persia had paid, now it was Ptolemy.

Some time between this map and the preceding one the Kingdom of Kush shifted its capital from Napata (between the third and fourth cataracts) to Meroe (between the fifth and sixth). Subsequent to this move it is referred to as the Kingdom of Meroe.

1. More important than Galatia is another newcomer to the Anatolian scene, the Kingdom of Pontus. This was founded by a Persian noble who took advantage of the wars of the successors to gain control of the area bordering the Black Sea (the proper title of the Kingdom is Pontic [meaning Maritime] Cappadocia). Like Bithynia, Pontus benefited from the arrival of the Gauls who served as a useful screen against Seleucid intervention. The same is true of Paphlagonia, a minor principality that served as a buffer between Bithynia and Pontus.

The final element in the political fragmentation of this region is the reappearance of the Greek colonies founded in the seventh and sixth centuries and last seen on map 560 BC. The one on the Bithynia–Paphlagonia border is Heraclea: the next one along is Sinope, to which those further east looked for leadership.

2. Eventually the Epirotes lost patience with their over-ambitious kings, and in 232 BC the monarchy was abolished.

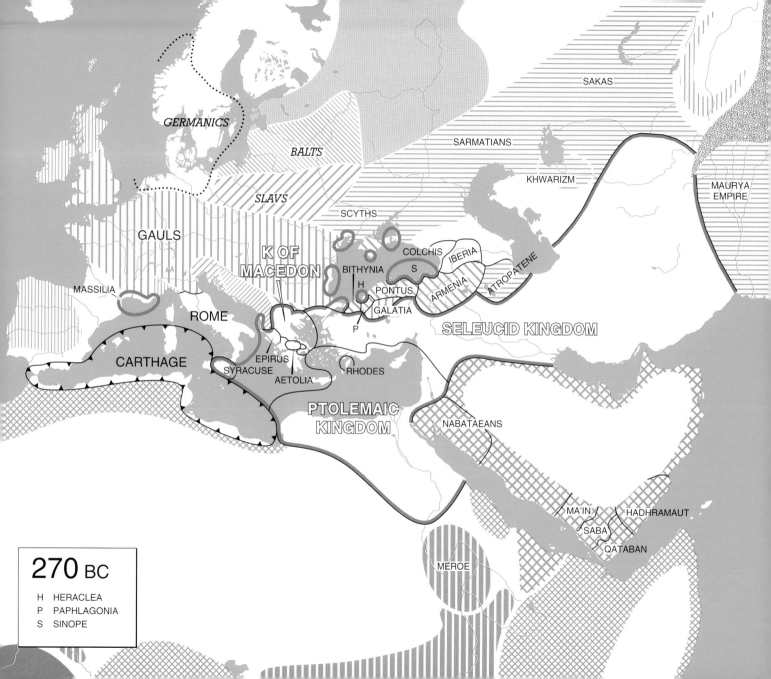

GERMANICS

BALTS

SAKAS

SARMATIANS

KHWARIZM

MAURYA
EMPIRE

SLAVS

SCYTHS

GAULS

K OF
MACEDON

COLCHIS
IBERIA
BITHYNIA
S
ATROPATENE
H
PONTUS
ARMENIA
MASSILIA
GALATIA
ROME
P

SELEUCID KINGDOM

CARTHAGE
EPIRUS
SYRACUSE
AETOLIA
RHODES

PTOLEMAIC
KINGDOM

NABATAEANS

MA'IN
SABA
HADHRAMAUT
QATABAN

MEROE

## 270 BC

H  HERACLEA
P  PAPHLAGONIA
S  SINOPE

Italy mastered, the Romans looked to Sicily. Initially the Syracusans and Carthaginians combined against them but the Syracusans quickly changed sides and what became known as the First Punic War (264–241 BC) focused on whether Rome or Carthage was going to gain possession of the island.[1] Eventually the Romans came out on top but this local success by the legions was less significant than the creation of a Roman navy and the disappearance, after repeated defeats, of the Carthaginian fleet. The imperial outlook fostered by the possession of this new weapon was soon apparent. Sardinia (along with Corsica) was lifted from Carthage in 237 BC when the Carthaginians were embroiled with the Berbers of the hinterland (now organizing into the kingdoms of Numidia and Mauretania); a campaign to eliminate piracy in the Adriatic led to Corfu and part of southern Illyria becoming Roman protectorates (229 BC).

Defeated she might be, but Carthage was not yet prepared to relinquish her role as a Mediterranean power. There was no attempt to rebuild the navy: instead the foothold in Spain, previously used purely for trade, was expanded into an imperial province covering the entire southern half of the Iberian peninsula. At the same time the Berber rulers of north Africa were drawn into alliances that committed them to the Carthaginian cause. Between them Africa and Spain provided the manpower needed for an army able to meet the Romans in the field. To the Romans these were alarming developments. They decided to challenge the Carthaginian position before it became even stronger, and in 220 BC offered the small but mettlesome Spanish town of Saguntum – well within the Carthaginian sphere, which extended as far north as the Ebro – a formal alliance. This proved a more than adequate provocation. Hannibal, the Carthaginian proconsul in Spain, took Saguntum by storm; the Roman delegation sent to demand his punishment returned from Carthage empty-handed.

Of the Macedonian successor states Ptolemaic Egypt was making the best showing at this time: its fleet dominated the Levant and the eastern shore of the Aegean where most of the Greek states acknowledged Ptolemaic suzerainty. The kingdom of Macedon was also scoring well. A challenge by

Sparta gave King Antigonus III the opportunity to intervene in the Peloponnese, crush Sparta and draft all the states of peninsular Greece (bar Athens and Aetolia) into a revived Hellenic League. By comparison the Seleucid Empire was struggling. It was too big to be easily held together and already bits were breaking off in the east – Bactria under a Greek dynasty and Parthia under native Iranian rulers (both c. 250 BC). Its western possessions also posed problems. To maintain access to Anatolia the Seleucids had to recognize the semi-independent status of Cappadocia (under a native dynast) while its efforts to impose its authority on the Aegean seaboard were constantly thwarted by the Ptolemies and by Pergamum – originally the stronghold of a minor Macedonian general but since 262 BC a player in its own right.[2]

Note that by the date of this map the Romans had defeated and were in the process of absorbing the Gauls of the Po valley – Cisalpine Gaul (Gaul this side of the Alps) to Latin geographers. The Italics of the north-east corner of Italy, the Veneti, no friends of the Gauls, came over to the Romans voluntarily. So did the last of the western Greek colonies, Massilia and Syracuse.

The Indian Empire of the Mauryas, which had reached a peak under the devout buddhist Asoka (268–231 BC), was now in precipitous decline: it is possible that the portion of the empire visible in this map had already become an independent kingdom under one of Asoka's sons.

---

1. Punic, a contracted form of Phoenician, is used as a synonym for Carthaginian.

2. The north-western borderlands of Armenia split off in the 230s, the northernmost part becoming the principality of Lesser Armenia, the southern part being absorbed by Cappadocia.

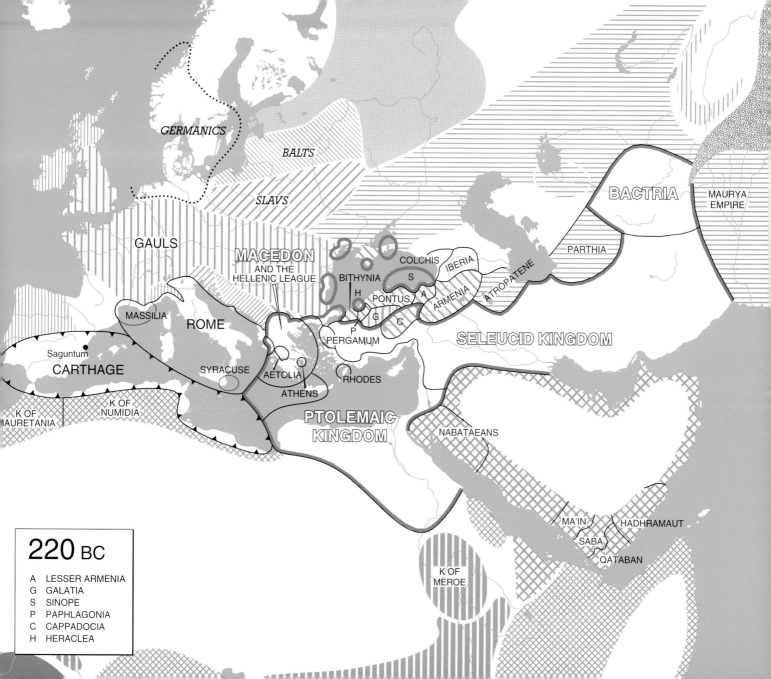

GERMANICS

BALTS

SLAVS

GAULS

MACEDON
AND THE
HELLENIC LEAGUE

COLCHIS

BITHYNIA
S
IBERIA

H
PONTUS
A
ARMENIA

BACTRIA

MAURYA
EMPIRE

PARTHIA

ATROPATENE

MASSILIA

ROME
G

P
C

PERGAMUM
SELEUCID KINGDOM

Saguntum

CARTHAGE

SYRACUSE

AETOLIA

ATHENS

RHODES

K OF
MAURETANIA

K OF
NUMIDIA

PTOLEMAIC
KINGDOM

NABATAEANS

MA'IN
HADHRAMAUT

SABA

QATABAN

K OF
MEROE

## 220 BC

A   LESSER ARMENIA
G   GALATIA
S   SINOPE
P   PAPHLAGONIA
C   CAPPADOCIA
H   HERACLEA

Confident in their command of the sea, the Romans envisaged their second conflict with Carthage in purely offensive terms. One consul would invade Spain, the other Africa: each would take with him the now standard consular army of two legions, plus contingents from the allied states of Italy. A further two legions would be stationed in Cisalpine Gaul which was only half conquered and needed a garrison, but that was a local matter. The war would be fought overseas.

Hannibal took a different view. It was clear to him that the resources of a united Italy far outweighed those at the disposal of Carthage, and that a defensive war, no matter how brilliantly conducted, would end up with Spain going the way of Sicily. There was no mileage at all in this sort of replay of the First Punic War. But there was a possible way of winning, or at least forcing a draw: attack Rome's Italian base and seduce her allies from their current allegiance. With that as his strategic aim, Hannibal assembled his army and, after making the appropriate arrangements for the defence of Spain, set out for Italy (spring 218 BC).

The first stage of Hannibal's march took him across the Ebro frontier and into southern Gaul. He crossed the Rhône (missing the Roman army travelling in the opposite direction), then the Alps (probably by the Col de la Traversette), appearing in the Po valley in time to fight and win a couple of battles before the end of the year – first at the Ticino, against the legions of Cisalpine Gaul, then at the Trebbia, over the consular army originally intended for Africa but now hastily recalled for the defence of the north. The next year he moved into Etruria. The Roman consul Flaminius caught up with him on the shores of Lake Trasimene where Hannibal had laid a trap that effectively destroyed the entire force. No one in Rome could remember such a defeat: two legions and a consul slaughtered. Obviously the Roman state would have to exert its full strength in the next campaign, and as Hannibal moved off south to make a demonstration raid through Campania, the senators made their preparations for a maximum effort. The consuls for 216 BC combined their armies: when Hannibal resumed his southward march they closed up behind him, confident that not even he could withstand a force of four

legions, plus auxiliaries. Hannibal turned and faced them on ground of his choosing near the hamlet of Cannae. The battle that followed provided a fitting climax to his long march. His cavalry swept the Roman horse from the field: his infantry line, carefully arranged so that it could yield ground without losing cohesion, managed to contain the Roman legions' steamroller advance long enough for the victorious cavalry to return and start cutting at the Romans' backs. The Romans were too crowded to redeploy successfully, and, their impetus lost, too off-balance to fight their way out of the encirclement. By the end of the day the largest army Rome had ever fielded had been all but annihilated.

Cannae produced the cracks in Rome's Italian dominion that Hannibal was looking for. Many of the Campanians and Samnites came over to the Carthaginian side in the aftermath of the battle, as did the Italic peoples of the south-west, the Lucanians and Brutii. Later the Greek towns along the sole of the Italian foot declared for Carthage too, as did Syracuse in Sicily. But the results were not quite what Hannibal had expected. Roman strength seemed little affected: the number of legions raised each year rose steadily, five years after Cannae reaching a peak of twenty-five. And the communities that defected proved more of a handicap than a help to Hannibal: he had to protect them from Roman attack, which meant that he lost the strategic initiative. The war became a matter of march and countermarch, siege and attempted relief, with the Romans, pushing forward at every point where Hannibal wasn't, gradually gaining the upper hand. They retook Capua in 212 BC, Syracuse in 211 BC, and Tarentum in 209 BC. Hannibal was still capable of dishing out sharp punishments – in 208 BC he defeated and killed both of the consuls in turn, and in 206 BC he saw off Metellus, the conqueror of Syracuse – but every year the area under his control got smaller. By 205 BC, he was cooped up in the toe of the peninsula, still too formidable to be attacked directly but no longer really able to influence events.

By this time the Romans had a hero of their own in Publius Scipio. He had made his name by taking New Carthage, the capital of Punic Spain, in 209 BC. After conquering the rest of the province, he

returned to Rome in 206 BC to celebrate a well-earned triumph, and push for an invasion of Africa. He got his way and in 204 BC he set sail from Sicily with two legions, landing within 30 miles (50 km) of Carthage itself. The next year he won a convincing victory over the Carthaginian home army at Great Plains. Facing disaster the Carthaginians negotiated a truce, the terms of which included the recall of Hannibal. He, as might be expected, insisted on one more trial of arms, but was defeated in his turn, at Zama, in 202 BC. Carthage was left with no option but surrender to Scipio – Scipio Africanus as he was now to be known – on terms that were formally ratified by the Roman Senate the next year.[1]

The long war had tested the limits of Rome's resources. In 209 BC the annual call-up had been rejected by twelve of the thirty Latin colonies on the grounds that they had no more men to send. But the Romans themselves, most of the Latins and most of the allied states continued to meet their commitments year after year until the war was won. The Romans may not have had a general of Hannibal's genius, but they had war-winning weapons in their steadfastness, and in the confidence of both Senate and people that in the end victory would be theirs.

1. Before he left, Hannibal put on record what he and his army had achieved in the thirteen years since setting out from New Carthage. The monument, in the form of an inscribed column, was set up on a promontory just south of Croton, his final headquarters. A generation later it was seen by the Greek historian Polybius, who took from it his figures for the strength of the Carthaginian army when it first arrived in Italy – 20,000 infantry (12,000 African, 8,000 Iberian) and 6,000 cavalry. There doesn't seem to have been any mention of elephants, the thing Hannibal's march is remembered for today, but elsewhere Polybius says that he set out with thirty-seven, and that a few survived the crossing of the Alps and saw action at the Trebbia.

The local North African breed, which provided the Carthaginians with their war elephants, was hunted out of existence during the Roman period. Unlike sub-Saharan African elephants, they seem to have been relatively easy to train, but whether they repaid the effort put into them is moot. The only time Hannibal ever had a significant number – at Zama, where he is said to have had eighty – they signally failed to win the day for him. Apparently they were a bit on the small side, for elephants, which can't have helped.

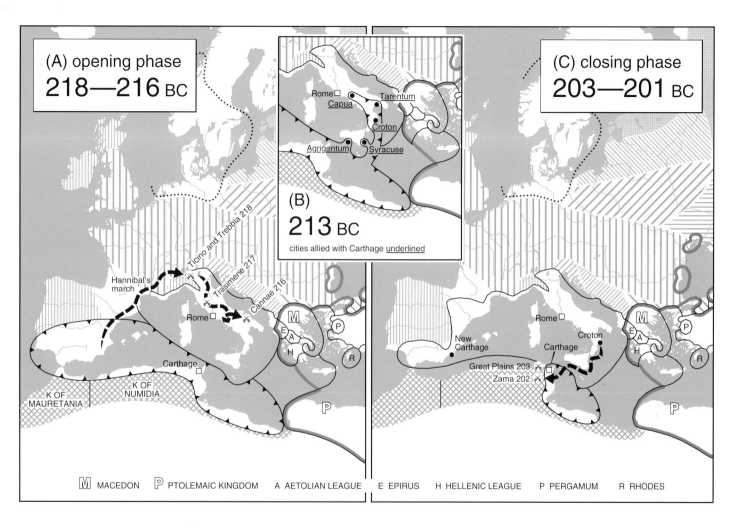

**(A) opening phase**
**218—216 BC**

**(B)**
**213 BC**
cities allied with Carthage underlined

Rome □
Capua
Tarentum
Croton
Agrigentum
Syracuse

**(C) closing phase**
**203—201 BC**

Ticino and Trebbia 218
Trasimene 217
Cannae 216
Hannibal's march
Rome □
Carthage □
M
E
A
H
P
R
P
K OF MAURETANIA
K OF NUMIDIA

New Carthage
Rome □
Great Plains 203
Zama 202
Carthage □
Croton
M
E
A
H
P
R
P

Ⓜ MACEDON   Ⓟ PTOLEMAIC KINGDOM   A AETOLIAN LEAGUE      E EPIRUS   H HELLENIC LEAGUE   P PERGAMUM   R RHODES

THE SECOND PUNIC WAR 218–201 BC

Rome's victory in the Second Punic War put the entire western half of the Mediterranean at her disposal. Two new provinces (Near Spain, centred on the Ebro valley, and Far Spain, centred on the Guadalquivir) were added to the two already existing (Sardinia and Sicily); the remaining stretches of coast were left to the locals – the south of France to the Greeks of Massilia, present day Algeria to the Numidians and present day Tunisia, plus Tripolitania, to the Carthaginians. But these governments, whether favoured like Massilia, or disdained like Carthage, were at the beck and call of Rome, the sole source of political authority in the region. The classical world was now divided between the dour might of this relative newcomer, and the splintered, squabbling arena of Hellenism.

Within the Hellenistic sphere the main event was a joint advance by Philip V of Macedon and the Seleucid monarch Antiochus III against the Egyptian Empire, in disarray since the death of Ptolemy IV in 203 BC. The idea was to lop off some of Egypt's outlying provinces and, after winning a battle at Panium in 200 BC, Antiochus duly got Palestine, the bit he particularly wanted. Philip did less well: his piecemeal acquisitions in the eastern Aegean were of little use in themselves, and they upset the mini-powers of the region, Pergamum and Rhodes. The two of them decided to call on Rome to intervene. Although the case their ambassadors had to make – that Macedonian gains in this area somehow posed a threat to the Roman state – was pretty far-fetched, the Senate was inclined to bend a friendly ear, for Philip had made an alliance with Hannibal during the recent war and there was a score to settle. At the time the dispatch of a fleet and a coalition with the Aetolians and Pergamenes had served to keep Philip in check: now the resources were available to teach him a sharper lesson. In 198 BC a consular army of two legions landed in Greece, charged with ending Macedon's hegemony in the peninsula.

Philip had only one card to play, the brute force of the Macedonian phalanx. An experienced Roman general was later to say that the onslaught of a phalanx was the most frightening thing he had ever seen in his life, but it was no longer the war-winning weapon it had been. A Roman legion was a more flexible formation, and once its swordsmen were in among them, the lines of Macedonian pikes quickly lost order and discipline. At the battle of Cynoscephalae, in Thessaly, Philip's army was completely defeated: he was forced to withdraw within the confines of Macedonia and renounce any wider ambitions. The Senate declared that the rest of Greece was now 'free', by which it meant free to do anything it had cleared with the Senate first.

The creation of a Roman protectorate over Greece shifted the boundary between Roman and Greek spheres to somewhere in the Aegean region. Quite where exactly was left unstated but the Senate was inclined to take a broad view, and include towns that the Seleucids had traditionally regarded as subordinate. King Antiochus III, who had spent twenty-five years painstakingly rebuilding the Seleucid position, was not prepared to accept this, and his many victories meant that he was not that impressed by Rome's defeat of Macedon either. In the east he had conquered Armenia (212 BC), checked the Parthians and Bactrians (209–206 BC), and even advanced into India to collect a tribute of elephants (205 BC). In the west he had gained Palestine, the object of many fruitless campaigns by his predecessors, and had made a good start towards reasserting the Seleucid position in the Aegean. He decided to continue with this task regardless of Rome. And at first events justified his policy. Though the Roman Senators accepted the pleas of two Asian Greek towns, Lampsacus and Smyrna, for protection, and ordered the king to pull back from the whole area, they did nothing when he did not do so. This made Antiochus over-bold: first he gave a place at his court to Rome's arch-enemy, Hannibal, then he moved over to the offensive. The Aetolians, discontent with the meagre rewards the Roman alliance had brought them, invited the king to deliver Greece from the Roman yoke. In 192 BC Antiochus took up the challenge, though no one apart from the Aetolians was very pleased to see him.

On the Russian steppe the Sarmatians disposed of the Scyths, driving the defeated remnants into the Danube delta and the Crimea (where the Tauri disappear). The Thracians dispersed the Gauls who had been lording it over them since the 270s. Pontus won control of the stretch of Black Sea littoral east of Sinope.

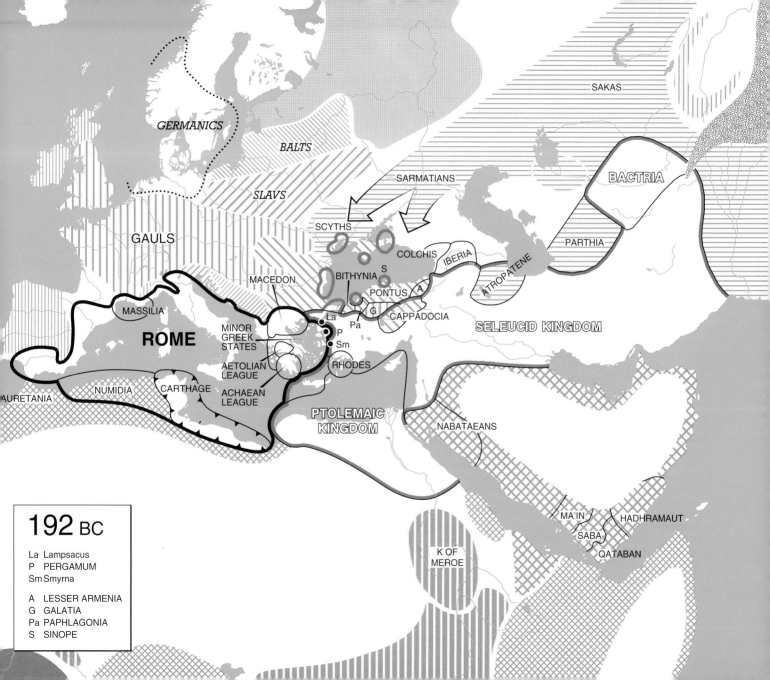

GERMANICS

BALTS

SLAVS

GAULS

SARMATIANS

SAKAS

BACTRIA

SCYTHS

COLCHIS

IBERIA

PARTHIA

ATROPATENE

MASSILIA

MACEDON

BITHYNIA

S

PONTUS

A

SELEUCID KINGDOM

ROME

MINOR
GREEK
STATES

La

P

Sm

G

Pa

CAPPADOCIA

AETOLIAN
LEAGUE

RHODES

ACHAEAN
LEAGUE

MAURETANIA

NUMIDIA

CARTHAGE

PTOLEMAIC
KINGDOM

NABATAEANS

K OF
MEROE

MA'IN

HADHRAMAUT

SABA

QATABAN

## 192 BC

La Lampsacus
P  PERGAMUM
Sm Smyrna

A  LESSER ARMENIA
G  GALATIA
Pa PAPHLAGONIA
S  SINOPE

At first glance the inheritors of Alexander's empire appear to have spun a sorry tale of division and dissension: the unity of purpose Macedon had brought to the Greek world was lost, the energies of its all-conquering army wasted in pointless feuding. But appearances are misleading. The hundred years after Alexander's death witnessed the triumph of Hellenism – the Greek lifestyle – throughout the Near East. Greek became the language not just of the elite, but also of the bureaucracy and the marketplace. New towns were built for Greek settlers: old towns were reconstituted on Greek lines. And it is arguable that far from being slowed down by the breakup of the empire, this process – easily the most important consequence of Alexander's expedition – was speeded up by it, for it put the successor kings into competition with each other as regards Greek immigrants. The 150,000 Greeks who moved to Egypt would hardly have done so if the Ptolemies hadn't been offering attractive terms.

The Hellenistic world was in every sense bigger than its Classical predecessor. Athens in its heyday had had an income of 1,000 talents a year: the sum the Ptolemys extracted from Egypt was twelve to fifteen times greater than this. In addition, Egypt produced a wheat surplus that could be sold on the Aegean market, or used to subsidize allied states. It was these relatively enormous resources that powered the Hellenization of Egypt and underpinned the most visible expression of this process, the rapid growth of Alexandria. From the start the city had been planned as a rival to Athens: it soon left the Attic capital far behind and by the date of this map was an easy number one in the Greek world – indeed in the world at large. And it was entirely Greek. Only Greeks were allowed to become citizens and they lived there in the same way they had at home. A direct connection with Rhodes ensured the availability of everything necessary to this lifestyle: royal patronage attracted the academics needed to make the city the intellectual, as well as the commercial, capital of the Mediterranean.

The Seleucids had no city to match Alexandria, indeed for a long time they were unsure exactly where their capital was going to be – anyway their needs were quite different. Where the Ptolemies could run the Nile valley from a single city at its mouth, the Seleucids needed garrisons at strategic points throughout their empire. As against the two Greek cities that the Ptolemies founded (Alexandria, plus the relatively minor Ptolemais in upper Egypt), the Seleucids set up more than thirty. Of them all only two find a place on the map: Seleucia-on-the-Tigris, in the process of replacing Babylon as the capital of Mesopotamia, and Antioch, metropolis of Syria and increasingly viewed as the capital of the empire as a whole. But compared to Alexandria, Antioch was only a city of the second rank, along with Athens (in gentle decline), Carthage (static) and Rome (rising).

These ranks, it should be noted, are each a notch higher than they were in the previous towns and trade routes map, with 15,000 now needed to get on to the bottom rung, as against 7,500 previously. On this basis the urban population in 415 BC would have been no more than 75,000, as against the 345,000 of this map. The more than four-fold increase is another measure of the economic progress made in the Hellenistic age. The progress was, however, quantitative rather than qualitative: there was no significant change in the commodities moving through the Mediterranean network. Wheat and wine remained the only items traded in bulk, wheat flowing from Egypt to the Aegean, and wine from the Aegean to Egypt and from Italy to Gaul. The low cost of Egyptian wheat put the Black Sea producers out of business: exports from this area had ceased by the third century.

Note that the literate area has now been enlarged by the addition of India, where two scripts derived from the Aramaic consonantal alphabet have come into use, Brahmi (used by Asoka in his inscriptions) and Kharoshthi. In the part of north Africa under Carthaginian influence the Berbers were beginning to use a consonantal alphabet of Phoenician type.

AMBER

TIN

FISH

TIN

IRON
COPPER

COPPER

● ROME

Salonika

● Pergamum

COPPER

WINE

● Ephesus

● ANTIOCH

Seleucia

ATHENS

● Babylon

WHEAT

Rhodes

COPPER
SILVER

Tyre

WINE
OIL

● CARTHAGE

Syracuse

ALEXANDRIA

Memphis ●

WHEAT
LINEN
PAPYRUS

GOLD

RESINS

IVORY
EBONY

Towns and trade routes in
**192** BC

towns, estimated populations

◉   90,000

●   30,000

•   15,000

The Romans quickly pushed Antiochus out of Greece and, crossing to Asia, routed his forces in a battle near Magnesia (190 BC). The peace they then imposed on the Seleucid monarch was not unduly harsh – all Antiochus had to give up was Anatolia – but the fact of his defeat immediately undid his life-work. Armenia, Atropatene and Parthia repudiated his suzerainty and new kingdoms rose up in Elymais (Elam) and Persia. Parthia subsequently underwent a rapid expansion. King Mithradates I (170–138 BC) defeated the Bactrians, conquered Media, and imposed his overlordship on Elymais and Persia: by the end of his reign the Parthian realm was at least the equal of the Seleucid, now reduced to Cilicia, Syria, Palestine and Mesopotamia.[1]

Not wishing to bring Anatolia under direct rule, the Roman Senate contented itself with aggrandizing its allies Pergamum and Rhodes, the parts that were left over being declared 'free', meaning, as ever, locally self-governing but in every other way subordinate.[2] Nearer home this policy was becoming inappropriate. After two more flare-ups with Macedon (in 171–168 BC and 148 BC) the Senators moved to annex it. Shortly afterwards a squabble in Greece proper ended the Romans' patience with Greek factionalism and the peninsula was placed under the authority of the governor of Macedonia (146 BC). The same year wrote the final chapter of a more bitter story. Confident in Roman support the Numidians had been nibbling at the Carthaginian remnant; in 151 BC there was open warfare along the frontier between the two. Rome seized a legalistic pretext (Carthage was not allowed to go to war without Rome's permission) to destroy the hated city, whose territory became another Roman province. There were now six of these: Sicily, Sardinia (including Corsica), Near and Far Spain, Macedon and Africa (meaning the bit we refer to as Tunisia; Tripolitania was given to Numidia). During these years the Roman frontier was also edged forward in northern Italy (notably in Istria) and Spain.

In 170 BC the Yuezhi – Indo-European nomads living on the borders of China – were crushingly defeated by the Xiongnu – an equally pastoral, but Altaic, people living further north, in Outer Mongolia. The Yuezhi fled westward in a two-pronged migration that brings them onto the east-ern corner of the map: the smaller group occupied the Tarim basin, the larger the steppe south of Lake Balkash. At this stage, we have only the Chinese name for them, and we do not know whether to class them as Aryans (as the shading used here suggests) or Tocharians (a more attractive if less likely hypothesis). At the western end of the steppe we can now recognize three separate elements within the Sarmatian nation, the Jazyges between the Danube and the Dnieper, the Roxolani between the Dnieper and the Don, and the Alans east of the Don.

In India, feeble inheritors of Maurya provinces lost first the Kabul valley and then the upper reaches of the Indus to the Bactrian Greeks; the new conquests became a separate kingdom under Menander, long remembered for protecting the local Buddhists from the tide of Hindu reaction, now running strongly elsewhere in the subcontinent. Menander's kingdom soon outshone its Bactrian parent, stripped of its western borderlands by the Parthians, and of Transoxiana by the Sakas (around the date of this map).

[1]. Armenia came in three parts at this time, Commagene, Sophene, and Armenia proper. Lesser Armenia, on the Black Sea coast, had been annexed by Pontus (as had Sinope, in 183 BC).

[2]. The Roman Senate could be irritable as well as generous; twenty years later, following a tactless display of independence by a Rhodian embassy, the senators revoked their grant to Rhodes (of southern Caria and Lycia) and, not content with this, declared Delos, in the central Aegean, a tax-free port, purely to undermine Rhodes' trading position.

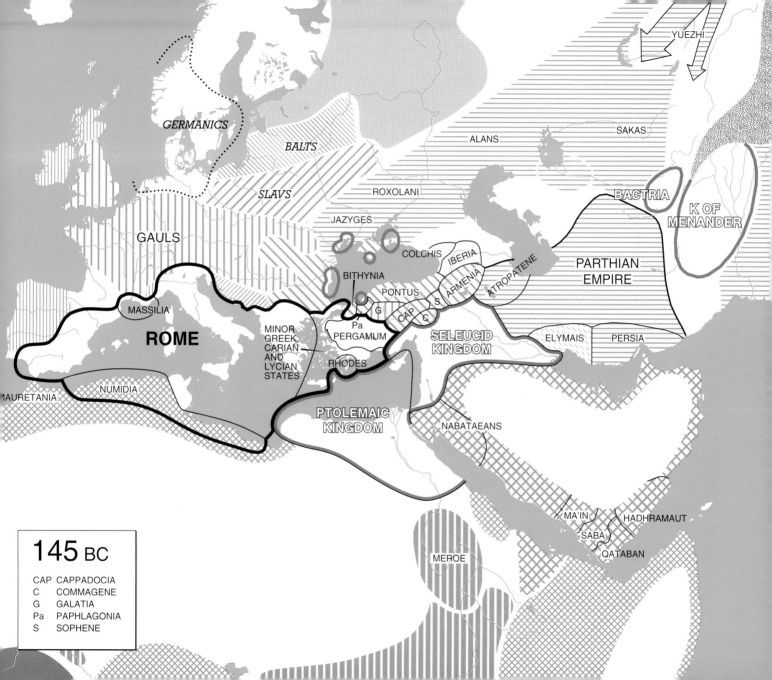

GERMANICS

BALTS

SLAVS

GAULS

YUEZHI

ALANS

SAKAS

ROXOLANI

BACTRIA

K OF MENANDER

JAZYGES

COLCHIS

IBERIA

PARTHIAN EMPIRE

BITHYNIA

ARMENIA

ATROPATENE

MASSILIA

PONTUS

G

S

CAP

C

**ROME**

Pa
PERGAMUM

MINOR
GREEK,
CARIAN
AND
LYCIAN
STATES

SELEUCID
KINGDOM

ELYMAIS

PERSIA

RHODES

MAURETANIA

NUMIDIA

NABATAEANS

PTOLEMAIC
KINGDOM

MA'IN

HADHRAMAUT

SABA

MEROE

QATABAN

## 145 BC

CAP CAPPADOCIA
C   COMMAGENE
G   GALATIA
Pa  PAPHLAGONIA
S   SOPHENE

Around 130 BC the Yuezhi completed their westward migration by occupying Transoxiana. This displaced a slew of Saka tribes that wreaked havoc in Bactria and the eastern provinces of the Parthian Empire. The Greek Kingdom of Bactria was swept away in their first rush, and a Parthian king who tried to stem the tide lost his life as well as his army. It wasn't till the 90s that his successors succeeded in re-establishing their eastern frontier. Some Sakas chose to remain as Parthian subjects, particularly in the province subsequently known as Seistan (i.e. Sakastan), but King Maues led his part of the horde across the Sulaiman range into India. There he wrested the Indus lands from the feeble descendants of Menander. The surviving Indo-Greeks retreated into the Kabul valley where the last of their rulers, Hermaeus, was to hold court for a few years more. Meanwhile Seistan had become the fief of the Surens, a Parthian lineage that had played a prominent part in the reconquest.

Much earlier, in 141 BC, the Parthians had taken Mesopotamia from the Seleucids. This suggested that it was only a matter of time before they scooped up the remaining bits of the Seleucid Empire – Syria, Cilicia and Palestine – but this never happened. First the Saka invasion forced the Parthians to turn east, then they fell to squabbling among themselves. The easy pickings went instead to the Armenian king, Tigranes, who, after repudiating the Parthian overlordship imposed on him at his accession, relieved his late masters of Atropatene and northern Mesopotamia and then moved on to seize Cilicia and most of Syria (83 BC). The broom was wielded too rapidly to sweep clean: in 74 BC the cities of Seleucia-in-Syria and Acre still harboured Seleucid princes, several inland towns were in the hands of the Ituraean and Nabataean Arabs, and most of Palestine in the possession of a resurgent Jewish state.[1]

The obvious supremacy of Rome in the Mediterranean world and the apparent inevitability of her further advance led the last king of Pergamum to will his state to Rome (133 BC). Cyrene was another bequest (96 BC: it had been a Ptolemaic sub-kingdom since 144 BC), as was, somewhat later, Bithynia (75 BC). During the same period Egypt and the states of central Anatolia became officially Roman-protected. But if all was going smoothly enough at the periphery of the Empire there were increasing problems at the centre, where the famous partnership between Senate and People was coming unstuck. The People had acquired an agenda of their own, with land for veterans and bread for the urban poor as the lead items: the Senate had doubts about the necessity for either and was grudging in its response. Just as important, the People tended to idolize successful generals and vote to continue their commands, something that struck at the root of the Senators' collegiate principle. Taken together these developments suggested a nightmare scenario in which a military hero pandered to the demands of an organized Popular party. This would put the institutions of the republic in the gravest danger: Rome could even – heaven forbid – find itself being ruled by a Dictator, a king in all but name.[2]

The nightmare came a step nearer reality in the person of Marius, a general who made his reputation in a war with King Jugurtha of Numidia (112–105 BC). This was a minor affair that the Senate had allowed to drag on for far too long: Marius brought it to a speedy conclusion (after which Numidia was markedly reduced in size): popular demand then insisted that he be put in charge of the defence of Italy, which was under threat from the Cimbri and Teutones. These two Celtic tribes had been on the move since about 115 BC, when they had abandoned their lands on the middle Danube and set off downstream in search of fairer fields. Subsequently, they had reversed course and headed for Gaul. On the way they defeated a Roman army sent to intercept them: once there they won further victories over both Romans and natives. Now, emboldened by their many successes, they planned a two-pronged invasion of north Italy (102 BC). Marius annihilated the horde that attempted the coastal route, and, though in doing so he had to allow the other an unopposed entry to the Po valley via the Alps, he caught and destroyed this group the following year.[3]

Marius had now served an unprecedented six terms as consul, and the Senate determined to make the least possible use of his services in future. They refused him command of the eastern provinces where punishment was overdue for Mithradates VI of Pontus (during the decade 110–100 BC, Mithradates had annexed the Bosporan kingdom, the Crimea, and the Roman-protected states of Galatia and Cappadocia) and he was allowed only a minor part in the Social War of 91–88 BC in which the Italian provincials, provoked by the Romans' refusal to allow them full citizenship, rose in rebellion. The repression of the Italians proved not too difficult once the extension of the franchise had been promised: success in achieving this bolstered the reputation of Sulla, Marius' only serious rival. To nobody's surprise it was Sulla who was then given the coveted command in the East.

Before he left, Sulla used his legions to consolidate the Senate's position. Marius, fearing for his life, fled to Africa. Meanwhile Mithradates had used the opportunity presented by the Social War to overrun all Anatolia and even invade Greece (89–88 BC). Sulla drove him back into his own territory and forced him to sue for peace, but the terms imposed – Mithradates kept his kingdom – were conspicuously lenient, for while Sulla had been engaged in the campaign, Marius had returned to Rome, overthrown the Senate and instituted the sort of Popular government that the Senators had been dreading. Sulla hurried home to find Marius dead of a stroke; his veterans made short work of the Popular levies. The restoration of Senatorial rule that followed was even bloodier than its previous overthrow.

**1.** The Jews had edged out of the Seleucid Empire in the middle years of the second century. A rebellion led by Judas Maccabeus (167–161 BC) failed in a military sense but opened the way for a compromise in which his brother Jonathan acquired the title of High Priest along with considerable local autonomy (152 BC). When Seleucid authority collapsed (in 129 BC, after a disastrous attempt to recover Mesopotamia), this Jewish principality found itself free.

**2.** The constitution allowed for a short-term dictatorship if the state was in extreme danger. The last time this had been done was after Trasimene, when it was thought that Hannibal was going to march on Rome.

**3.** Though their name was once used as a synonym for Germanic, the Teutones were Celts, not German speakers. Classical historians often used the term German geographically and when they said that the Belgae or Bastarnae were Germans they meant only that these Celtic peoples had originally lived in Germany (that is, east of the Rhine and north of the upper Danube). The same

(continued on page 92)

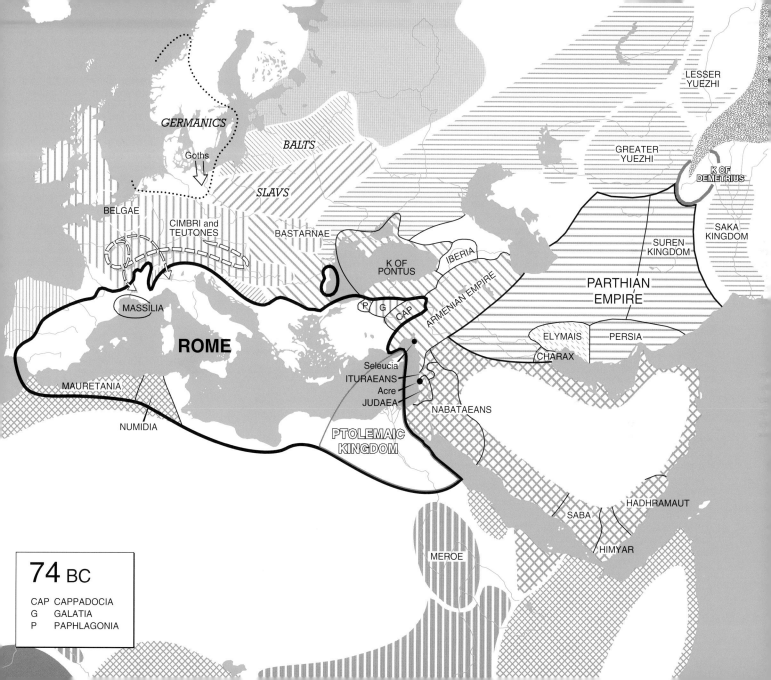

GERMANICS

Goths

BALTS

SLAVS

BELGAE

CIMBRI and
TEUTONES

BASTARNAE

MASSILIA

**ROME**

K OF
PONTUS

IBERIA

ARMENIAN EMPIRE

GREATER
YUEZHI

LESSER
YUEZHI

K OF
DEMETRIUS

SAKA
KINGDOM

SUREN
KINGDOM

PARTHIAN
EMPIRE

PERSIA

ELYMAIS

CHARAX

R  G

CAP

MAURETANIA

NUMIDIA

Seleucia
ITURAEANS

Acre

JUDAEA

NABATAEANS

*PTOLEMAIC
KINGDOM*

MEROE

SABA

HIMYAR

HADHRAMAUT

**74** BC

CAP CAPPADOCIA
G   GALATIA
P   PAPHLAGONIA

The Senatorial government that Sulla had reinstated made a reasonable go of things after his death in 78 BC. Not that there weren't problems: there was a rebellion to be suppressed in Spain, and a bad attack of piracy in the Mediterranean, something that had to be attended to with dispatch because it threatened the food supply of the capital. And then there was Mithradates (again). In each case the Senate turned to Pompey, the ablest of Sulla's lieutenants. He did not disappoint. He put down the Spanish revolt (76–71 BC), swept the pirates from the seas (67 BC), and then moved against Mithradates. This time Mithradates had as his ally Tigranes of Armenia; but Tigranes' jerry-built empire did not survive its first major test. Pompey's victories were quick and conclusive: he followed them up by making the direct settlement of eastern affairs that the Senate had been avoiding for the last century (64 BC). The whole coastline from Pontus to the borders of Egypt was incorporated in the Empire, and the kingdoms of the interior given definitive status as Roman vassals. In the north the Bosporan Kingdom, Colchis, Iberia and Armenia were added to the area under Roman suzerainty, which extended, in theory at least, as far as the Albani of the eastern Caucasus. In Syria there was a new Roman province, plus a list of dependent minor principalities that included Emesa, Ituraea, Judaea and the extensive, if sparsely populated, Nabataean Kingdom.

The Senate had every reason to be grateful to Pompey, who had eliminated the Empire's enemies, significantly extended its boundaries and nearly tripled its revenues (from 8,350 to 22,500 talents). But that was the problem: he had done so much that the political reflex was to cut him down to size. Waiting until he had disbanded his army before showing their hand, the Senators rebuffed the very reasonable demands he made on his soldiers' behalf. Furious, Pompey turned to the enemies of the Senatorial oligarchy; Julius Caesar, who controlled the remnant of Marius' old Popular party, and Marcus Crassus, the archetypal plutocrat, all too eager to buy himself into history. The Senate found itself pushed to one side by this triumvirate (three-man junta) and thereafter Pompey ruled in Rome while Caesar and Crassus took up the military commands they coveted. Both hoped to gain victories to rival Pompey's and both indulged in gratuitous aggression to satisfy this ambition. Caesar, in a remorseless series of campaigns between 58 and 51 BC, conquered Gaul, put the Roman frontier on the Rhine, and invested his whole enterprise with romance by reconnoitring the hitherto fabulous island of Britain. These successes won him the devotion of an army that by the end of the decade had become the most formidable in the Roman world. Crassus also made his mark. Leading the legions of the East against Parthia, he was barely across the frontier when his force was cut off and shot to pieces by the Saka bowmen of the Parthians' Suren general. Crassus perished in the debacle (at Carrhae, 53 BC). It seemed as if Pompey's eastern settlement would be overthrown by the victors; but as Parthian quarrelled with Suren and Caesar with Pompey, the war petered out. Only Armenia and Iberia passed out of Roman control.

Caesar's mounting reputation cast a shadow over Pompey's, and the Senate moved quickly to exploit the resulting coolness between the two. Reminding the conservative-minded Pompey that it was his duty to protect the constitution, the Senators persuaded him to break with Caesar: they had no doubt that he could handle the upstart, and that they could handle him. But Caesar moved too fast for the new allies, seizing Italy in a lightning campaign, and, before the year was out, Spain as well (49 BC). In 48 BC, at Pharsalus, he won a complete victory over the army Pompey had gathered in Greece, and from there he went on to make a clean sweep of the East (47 BC), Africa (46 BC) and Spain, which had revolted again (45 BC). The man who had gone into politics to pay his debts returned to Rome with the Empire in his pocket – he now became Dictator for life – and Cleopatra, the last of the Ptolemies, on his arm. Caesar's political administration was like his generalship, active and efficient, but behind the urgency of the reformer lay the restlessness of an opportunist. In the midst of preparations for invasions of Parthia and Dacia – both unnecessary as Parthia was quiet and the Dacian kingdom collapsed of its own accord within a few years – he was assassinated by a clique of Senatorial diehards (44 BC).

In darker Europe the Germanic peoples were now pressing southwards, into previously Celtic central Germany, while the Slavs of south Russia were beginning to push north at the expense of the Balts. In the Far East the Chinese, who had been pursuing a forward policy against the nomads living beyond the Great Wall ever since the reign of the Emperor Wu Di (141–87 BC), brought the Tarim basin under their control in 49 BC. The protectorate they set up there remained in force till AD 23, so on this map and the next China, in the shape of this western outlier of the mighty Han Empire, makes its first and last appearances in the atlas. In India, the power of the Saka Kingdom of the Indus valley was broken by the Suren.

---

*(footnotes continued from 74 BC text)*

applies to the Cimbri and Teutones though in the case of the Cimbri the Romans did come to believe (incorrectly) that they had been dealing with people from the Germanic area (specifically Jutland). In their defence it can be said that there is nothing unacceptable in the idea that the original impetus for these various displacements lay in the Germanic north. There was steady southward pressure from this area from now on, probably stoked up by migration from Scandinavia. The Goths, for example, held that they had migrated from an original homeland in southern Sweden about this time, and they were far from being the only Germanic tribe to claim a Scandinavian origin.

Some changes in Arabia require a mention. The Arab trading post of Charax, just inside Parthian territory, had a spell as an independent state in the 120s but soon reverted to vassal status. The Kingdom of Qataban in the Yemen passed into the hands of the Himyarite Arabs; Ma'in was conquered by Saba.

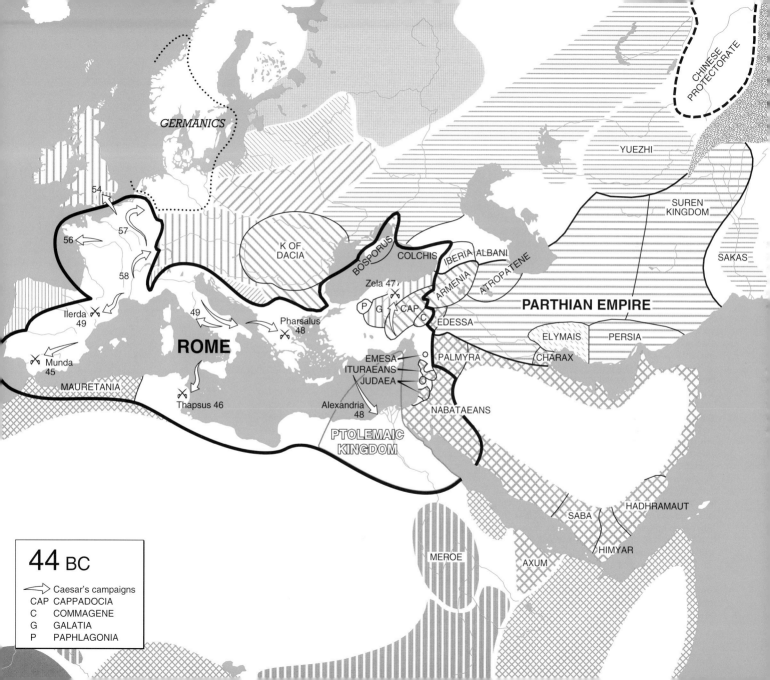

GERMANICS

54
57
56
58

Ilerda
49

Munda
45

MAURETANIA

ROME

49

Thapsus 46

Pharsalus
48

Alexandria
48

PTOLEMAIC
KINGDOM

MEROE

AXUM

K OF
DACIA

BOSPORUS

COLCHIS

IBERIA ALBANI

ARMENIA ATROPATENE

Zela 47

P   G   CAP
C

EDESSA

EMESA
ITURAEANS
JUDAEA

PALMYRA

NABATAEANS

PARTHIAN EMPIRE

ELYMAIS   PERSIA

CHARAX

YUEZHI

CHINESE
PROTECTORATE

SUREN
KINGDOM

SAKAS

SABA   HADHRAMAUT

HIMYAR

44 BC

➤ Caesar's campaigns
CAP  CAPPADOCIA
C    COMMAGENE
G    GALATIA
P    PAPHLAGONIA

Though Caesar's assassination was the signal for political reaction, the old order had clearly had its day: once Caesar's heir, Octavius, and Caesar's lieutenant, Antony, had come to terms with one another, it took only the single battle of Philippi (42 BC) to make an end of the Senatorial party. The Empire was then divided between the victors, Antony, the most experienced general, taking the East and the Parthian problem, and Octavius the West, while Africa was temporarily given to Lepidus, a myopic grandee whom Anthony and Octavius had been carrying around to reassure the conservatives.

Antony found war with Parthia brought few rewards. He managed to reimpose Roman suzerainty on Iberia and Armenia, but casualties were heavy and the replacements Octavius kept promising never seemed to arrive. Cleopatra was his dangerous consolation, Antony failing to see that in re-creating the Empire of the Ptolemies for her he was alienating his depleted legions. When the inevitable break with Octavius came they followed him to the battlefield of Actium, in western Greece, but once there promptly deserted him (31 BC). Chased back to Alexandria, Antony committed suicide, as did Cleopatra after her capture; her son by Caesar was tidied away into a small box.

Octavius celebrated the fact that his sway was now unchallenged by taking the new name of Augustus (27 BC). He then proceeded to give the Empire the first spell of coherent government it had had since the beginning of the century. One of his first moves was to defuse the Parthian situation. He saw that the Parthians lacked the power to sustain an offensive: once he had restored Rome's moral and strategic position by obtaining the return of the standards lost at Carrhae, and reasserting, yet again, Rome's suzerainty over Armenia and Iberia (20 BC), he felt able to declare the matter closed and turn his attention elsewhere. There was a lot to do. First came tidying up operations in the Alps and Spain (conquest completed in 19 BC), then a major push that took the line of the Roman frontier in Europe up to the Danube (14–8 BC). The success of these operations suggested another, an advance from the Rhine to the Elbe, which, if followed by the occupation of Bohemia, would result in a substantial shortening of the Roman line. Phase 1, which saw the legions move into the north-western quarter of Germany, was completed by 9 BC. But then the newly acquired Danubian provinces rose in a rebellion that took three years to suppress (AD 6–9). And no sooner was that job done than a revolt in Germany opened with a catastrophic Roman defeat: all three of the legions that formed the garrison of the province were surprised and destroyed as they marched through the Teutoburger Wald (AD 9). Augustus, recognizing that he was asking more of his army than it could manage, gave up on his master plan and the Roman frontier was re-established on the Rhine.[1]

As well as being enlarged the empire was also simplified. Five of Rome's vassal states were annexed: Egypt and Cyprus in 30 BC, after Actium; Galatia in 25 BC, Paphlagonia in 6 BC, and Judaea in AD 6. Judaea had been part of a kingdom created for Rome's tried and true ally Herod the Great in 37 BC. At his death in 4 BC this kingdom was divided between his three surviving sons, Archelaus getting Judaea proper, Herod Antipas Galilee and a bit of Transjordan, and Philip the Golan and other lands to the north-east. Archelaus proved incompetent and was soon deposed: the other two principalities survived into Tiberius' reign.[2]

Before Augustus the Romans had raised armies for specific tasks, disbanding them when these were accomplished. Augustus created a standing army of twenty-five legions whose positions in the year of his death are marked on the map. The equivalent of a twenty-sixth legion, the Praetorian Guard, garrisoned Italy and protected the Emperor's person. Each legion consisted of about 5,000 men (ten cohorts of 480 men each). In addition to the 130,000 legionaries and guards (recruited from Roman citizens) there was an approximately equal number of auxiliary troops (provincials or even barbarians). The distribution of the cohort-sized auxiliary units roughly follows that of the legions.

These legions were the source of Augustus' power. However, throughout his reign he worked to conciliate the Senatorial class and encourage its participation (in roles chosen by him) in the new hierarchy. He restored a pretence of constitutionalism by accumulating traditional offices until these were sufficient to explain and legitimize his pre-eminent position; he returned the government of the paci-fied provinces to the Senate while retaining under his personal control the more 'difficult' ones (which contained the legions) and Egypt (whose wheat provided the citizens of Rome with much of their bread). Caesar's dazzling talents had kept the Mediterranean world in turmoil: the grey genius of Augustus created peace and prosperity, and the machinery for its continuance. He used men well, shunned the spectacular, and died in bed.

**1.** Meanwhile the Germans (i.e. the continental as opposed to Scandinavian Germanics) had made important advances southward at the expense of the Celts, occupying Bohemia (where the Marcomanni displaced the Celtic Boii), Moravia (occupied by the Quadi), and, in the east, Pomerania and Brandenburg (we think: there's no hard information on this area).

**2.** Two new client states were acquired, Thrace and Palmyra, and a new one set up, Pontus, which included Caucasian Colchis.

In the 20s BC Augustus had a look at his southern border to see if there was anything worth conquering in this direction. Expeditions to the Fezzan oases, up the Nile as far as Napata, and to Marib in Saba showed that there wasn't. There is one development to note in this area, however, the appearance of the kingdom of Axum on the Red Sea coast. This is the first political expression of the long-standing Semitic colonization of Eritrea and Tigre.

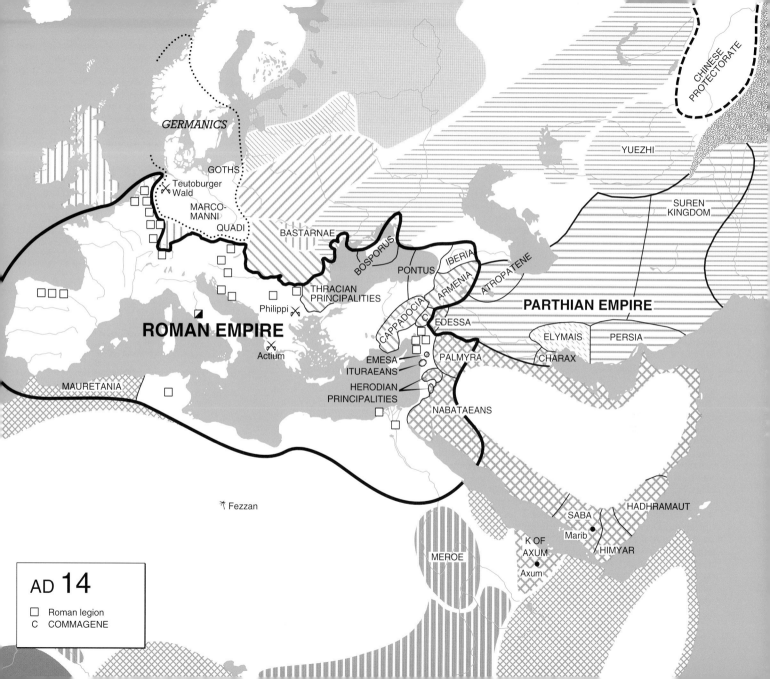

GERMANICS

GOTHS

Teutoburger
Wald

MARCO-
MANNI

QUADI

BASTARNAE

BOSPORUS

PONTUS

IBERIA

ATROPATENE

ARMENIA

THRACIAN
PRINCIPALITIES

Philippi

CAPPADOCIA

C

EDESSA

**PARTHIAN EMPIRE**

YUEZHI

SUREN
KINGDOM

CHINESE
PROTECTORATE

**ROMAN EMPIRE**

Actium

EMESA

ITURAEANS

HERODIAN
PRINCIPALITIES

PALMYRA

NABATAEANS

ELYMAIS

PERSIA

CHARAX

MAURETANIA

Fezzan

MEROE

K OF
AXUM

Axum

SABA

Marib

HADHRAMAUT

HIMYAR

AD **14**

□ Roman legion
C COMMAGENE

The most important economic consequence of the growth of Roman power was the growth of Rome itself. We know from the records of the wheat dole that in Augustus' day the city's population was around 250,000, making it more than twice the size of Alexandria, the previous world record holder. Feeding and watering this unprecedented number of people was a correspondingly mammoth task, at the very limit of the technology of the time. Alexandria had been able to grow to the size it did because it was sitting on the perfect agricultural base: a country that generated a reliable surplus of cereals, with a central conduit, the Nile, that led straight to the greedy metropolis. Rome had no such advantages and supplying it was always a problem. The authorities were able to meet the need for water by building the great series of aqueducts whose arcades still march across the campagna. But from an early stage, wheat had to be brought in from overseas. The first provinces – Sicily, Sardinia and Africa – paid much of their taxes in cereals. In the last days of the republic these traditional sources of supply were no longer sufficient. The answer was found in Egypt, which was forced to take on a double burden, Rome as well as Alexandria. The inevitable result was a steady impoverishment of the country, for Rome, unlike Alexandria, gave nothing in return. This decline, which in time began to drag Alexandria down too, worried the Romans not at all.

Shipping wheat on the scale Rome required meant building ships to match, monsters of 1,000 tons or more. With the simple sails of the time, they had difficulty making the trip to Rome against the north-westerly winds that prevail in the summer months (no one went to sea in the winter). A captain who could get to the Anatolian coast by passing to the left of Cyprus was doing well: all too often the winds forced the ships to take the long way round the Levant. Once at Rhodes it was relatively simple to get to Crete, the jumping-off point for the crucial leg, the long haul across the open sea to Malta. The final stage was just a matter of coasting north via Syracuse and Pozzuoli. The whole trip could easily take seventy days, as against the twenty required for the return journey, with the same winds now helping instead of hindering, and allowing the captains

to set a direct course from the Straits of Messina to Alexandria.[1]

Apart from the rearrangement of the Mediterranean trading network for the benefit of Rome, the last century BC saw the first direct contacts established between the Mediterranean world on the one hand and China and India on the other. The opening of the route from China, the famous 'silk road', obviously relates to Chinese military activity in the Tarim basin. This brought a measure of security to 2,000 of the 4,400 miles (3,200 out of 7,000 km) that separate Changan, China's western capital, from Antioch, the Mediterranean's nearest entrepôt. Much of the remainder was covered by the existing Iranian network, which stretched from the frontier of the Roman Empire to the banks of the Jaxartes. All that was needed was to connect the two systems. This meant finding a caravan-friendly pass over the Pamirs, something that seems to have been done in the latter part of the first century BC. The silk road was now complete. It ran from Changan via Yunmen (the last gate in the Great Wall) and Lop Nor to the Tarim. The caravans then skirted the Tarim's central desert, the Takla Makan, using routes to the north or south of it: either way, they ended up at Kashgar, the last place under Chinese protection. On the other side of the Pamirs the road ran from Samarkand via Marv (the terminal oasis of the Murghab river) and Hamadan to Seleucia-on-the-Tigris. The final stage from Seleucia to Antioch (or Tyre) was handled by Palmyra, whose prosperity dates from this period. The Palmyrenes' desert routes enabled them to bypass the militarized sector of the Romano–Parthian frontier, where trade must often have been frustrated.

The route to India was a lot simpler. In theory it had been open since the Bronze Age but, in practice, there seems to have been very little traffic along the coast of the Arabian Sea during the last millennium BC. All this changed in the days of the last Ptolemies when a Greek captain named Hippalus discovered a short-cut from the mouth of the Red Sea to the south of India. The trick was to use the seasonal winds: the south-western monsoon that blows from May to October to get there, and the north-eastern monsoon that blows from November to March to get back. The course was simple, a matter of sticking

to the same latitude (12° N) all the way. The open water stretch from Socotra to the Malabar coast (modern Kerala) probably took no more than three weeks. Apparently, in Augustus' time 120 ships a year were using this route.

Long-distance traffic of this sort could only be sustained if the commodities traded were low bulk and high cost. Silk is the perfect example; India's equivalent was pepper. This originated further east, in Indonesia, as did other spices like cloves and nutmeg. Indian traders brought them across the Bay of Bengal and round the tip of India to Malabar. There, Arab or Greek vessels picked them up and took them to ports on the Egyptian side of the Red Sea for distribution to the Roman world.[2]

1. If Rome was entirely parasitic, Italy had its commercially positive side – most of the west Mediterranean wrecks of this period are of vessels carrying Italian wine to Gaul. There is probably some bias in this sample because French and Italian sub-aqua clubs are most active on the Riviera coasts, but there is no doubt that the trade was significant. The ships engaged in it seem to have varied from 15-metre tramps, displacing 25 tons and carrying 500 25-litre amphorae, to larger vessels of around a 125-ton burden, with a carrying capacity of 2–3,000 amphorae.

2. This map also shows the expansion of the literate world since the fifth century BC when this topic was last addressed. The most obvious advance is in the west where the Romans have brought the Latin alphabet to Spain, Gaul and the Danube lands. As a result the various Iberian scripts have been abandoned, as indeed have the competing Italian alphabets – Lepontic, Venetic, Etruscan and Oscan. There have also been big advances eastward. Central Asia became literate with the opening of the silk road: it eventually produced a Kharosthi-based alphabet of its own, Sogdian. The non-alphabetic writing systems were fading fast. The Cypriote syllabary had gone out of use in the third century BC, as had the Persian and Elamite versions of cuneiform. Babylonian cuneiform was on its last legs: the latest tablet known is dated AD 75. Egyptian hieroglyphic survived and even managed to bud off a new variant, Meroitic, used in the Kingdom of Kush from the third century BC.

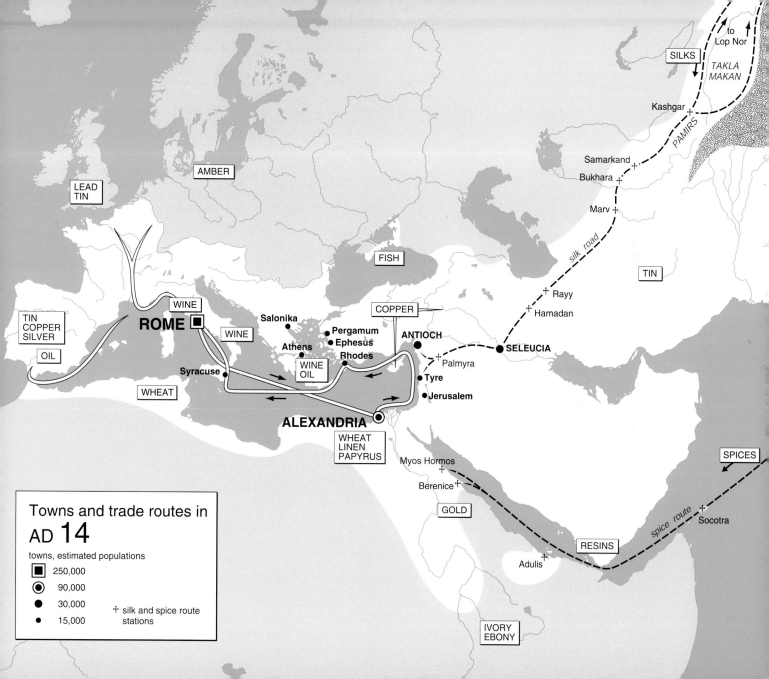

SILKS

to Lop Nor

TAKLA MAKAN

Kashgar

PAMIRS

Samarkand

Bukhara

Marv

silk road

TIN

Rayy

Hamadan

SELEUCIA

AMBER

LEAD TIN

FISH

WINE

ROME

WINE

Salonika

Pergamum

Athens

Ephesus

Rhodes

COPPER

ANTIOCH

Palmyra

TIN COPPER SILVER

OIL

WINE OIL

Tyre

Jerusalem

Syracuse

WHEAT

ALEXANDRIA

WHEAT LINEN PAPYRUS

SPICES

Myos Hormos

Berenice

GOLD

RESINS

spice route

Socotra

Adulis

## Towns and trade routes in AD **14**

towns, estimated populations

■ 250,000

◉ 90,000

● 30,000

• 15,000

✝ silk and spice route stations

IVORY EBONY

The governmental machinery created by Augustus continued to function smoothly during the reign of his astringent step-son, Tiberius (14–37), and even the antics of Gaius Caligula (37–41) who dismissed the whole system as so much claptrap surrounding an autocratic power that he, in contrast, nakedly paraded, did little to disturb the Empire outside of Rome. On Caligula's assassination, the Praetorians selected his uncle, the elderly Claudius; the Senate's acquiescence in this choice marks the absorption of the Republican tradition by the Imperial.

Claudius (41–54) showed unexpected initiative. The pacification of Spain and Dalmatia had proceeded to the point where a legion could be withdrawn from each; two further legions were raised. Four legions would, it was (correctly) calculated, suffice for the conquest of Britain, a safe project sanctified by the memory of the deified Julius. The southern third of the country was rapidly overrun (43–47); the halt called at this stage was prolonged throughout the reign of Claudius' step-son Nero by the revolt of Boadicea (61).

Nero had other troubles too, particularly in the East. First there was a ten-year war with Parthia over Armenia,[1] then in 66 the Jews, who had never reconciled themselves to Roman rule, rose in bitter revolt. These imbroglios are often quoted as reasons for Nero's loss of popularity, as are a fire and near-famine in Rome itself, but it is difficult to believe that his reign would have been longer if it had been more fortunate. His position required of him little more than the appearance of gravity, yet this was a role that Nero, the self-declared actor, was never able to sustain. When the Romans had only just accustomed themselves to the sight of a palace in Rome, Nero cleared a quarter of the city to create the setting for a country house. The ease of the pastoral life was delightfully heightened by the thought of the sweaty bustle outside, but few Romans appreciated the conceit. The end came in 68, when the governor of Spain proclaimed the Emperor unworthy and marched on Rome. Beside the Praetorians, Nero had two newly raised legions in Italy (one intended for use against Parthia, one raised to meet the current emergency); he was unable to interest either in his survival and the last of the Julio-Claudians died by his own shaky hand. The usurper was soon replaced by the Praetorians' candidate, and he, in his turn, by the commander of the Rhine legions, but the final say was with the legions of the East. At the end of 69 – the 'year of the four emperors' – they fought their way into Rome on behalf of Vespasian, the general in charge of the suppression of the Jewish revolt.

Vespasian's immediate task was the restoration of order, particularly on the Rhine where German auxiliaries had taken advantage of the civil war – and the absence in Italy of many elements of the legionary garrison – to mount a formidable challenge to Roman rule. Within a year Vespasian had matters under control and a reconstructed Rhine army was back in position along the left bank of the river. At the same time his son Titus took Jerusalem, effectively ending the Jewish war.[2]

The normal business of the empire could now resume. In Britain the legions moved forward again, completing the conquest of England and Wales by 75. Elsewhere the changes were administrative rather than military. The number of client kingdoms had been further reduced since Augustus' day: Cappadocia had been annexed by Tiberius, Mauretania by Caligula, Thrace by Claudius and Pontus by Nero. Vespasian all but completed the process by absorbing Emesa and Commagene. One small principality remained, ruled by Herod's great-grandson Agrippa II: the southern half of Ituraea had been folded into this, the northern half into the province of Syria. There were now thirty-six provinces, guarded by twenty-eight legions.[3]

Outside the Empire there are few changes to note. The Sarmatian tribes of south Russia have shifted westward, with the Alans moving into the Caucasus and the Jazyges, as end men, being pushed off to the Hungarian steppe. Further east the clan of Kushan has established a paramountcy over the other four tribes that constitute the Yuezhi nation. The Suren kingdom has evolved into an 'Indo-Parthian' state centred on the Punjab.

Nowadays the date of this map is remembered less for the death of Vespasian and the accession of Titus than for the eruption of Vesuvius, of which Pliny the Younger has left us such a vivid description. In two days in August the ash and lava flows, which were spewed forth by the hitherto quiescent volcano, overwhelmed the towns of Pompeii and Herculaneum, along with many of the luxury villas lining this part of the Bay of Naples. Thousands died, thousands more were dispossessed. Yet, as Goethe remarked, few tragedies have given so much pleasure to later generations. To walk through the excavated streets of Pompeii, to see where an ordinary Roman bought his bread, his wine and oil, to visit his and his friends' houses, the eating-places where they met and the workshops where their household goods were made, is to have a unique experience. The walls still bear the slogans of the last elections, along with lovers' scribblings and losers' curses. And, out of the corner of your eye, you can see the same peaceful-looking mountain.

1. This ended in compromise (63), a scion of the Parthian royal house being recognized as King of Armenia, but under Roman suzerainty.

2. After the fall of Jerusalem the Jews were reduced to three strong-points: the last of them, Masada, fell in 73.

3. On top of the two legions raised for the invasion of Britain and the two added by Nero, two more were created during the year of the four emperors. The next year Vespasian broke up five legions of the demoralized Rhine army, forming two new legions from the remnants. The end result was an increase of three on the Augustan establishment of twenty-five.

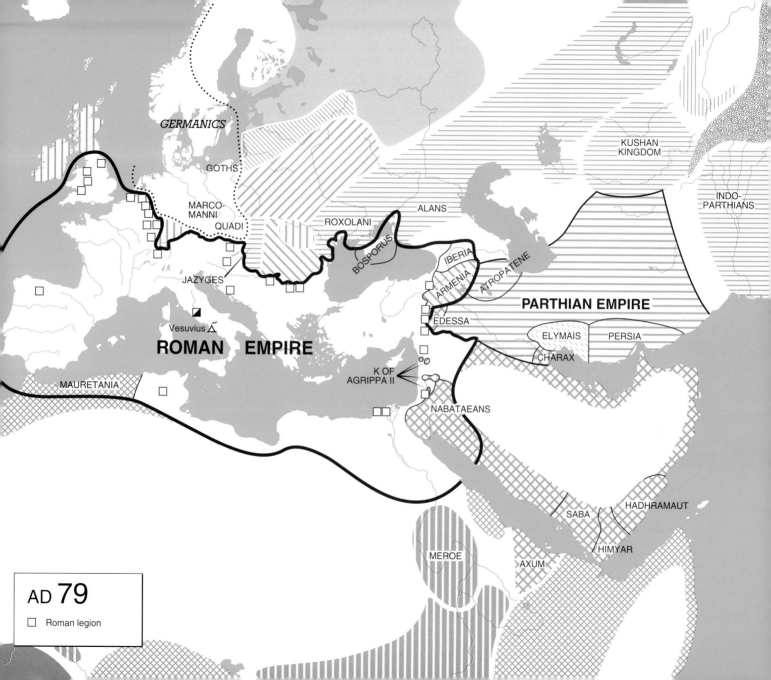

GERMANICS

GOTHS

MARCO-
MANNI

QUADI

JAZYGES

ROXOLANI

ALANS

BOSPORUS

IBERIA

ARMENIA

ATROPATENE

KUSHAN
KINGDOM

INDO-
PARTHIANS

PARTHIAN EMPIRE

EDESSA

ELYMAIS

PERSIA

CHARAX

Vesuvius △

**ROMAN    EMPIRE**

K OF
AGRIPPA II

MAURETANIA

NABATAEANS

SABA

HADHRAMAUT

HIMYAR

MEROE

AXUM

AD 79

☐  Roman legion

The Flavian dynasty founded by Vespasian lasted till 98, when the second of his two sons was assassinated. The elder, Titus, the conqueror of Jerusalem, had died after reigning only two years: the younger, Domitian, always less well regarded, became increasingly paranoid as time went on, terrorizing the Senate quite unnecessarily and eventually provoking the conspiracy he feared. To replace Domitian the Senators chose the upright, but very old, Nerva: to placate the soldiery the childless Nerva adopted Trajan,[1] an experienced and popular general.

Domitian (81–96) made two additions to the Empire, lowland Scotland and, more significantly, the triangle of land between the upper Rhine and the upper Danube. His main military concern, however, was the defence of the lower Danube, where the Dacians were proving troublesome. He didn't manage to solve this problem, and it was left to Trajan (98–117) to do so. The new emperor massed ten legions for an offensive that completely crushed the Dacians: he then turned their land into Rome's first and only trans-Danubian province (105). The next year Nabataea was transformed into the province of Arabia. And Trajan wasn't finished by any means. In 114–5 he led the Roman army eastward to conquer first Armenia, then Mesopotamia. The greatest of the soldier emperors stood in Charax, thinking aloud of Alexander, but it was not to be: he was at the end of his career, not the beginning, and the next year he died. Hadrian (117–38), his ward and successor, immediately pulled back to the Euphrates, abandoning Mesopotamia and allowing Armenia to revert to its traditional status as a client kingdom. The wall in Britain, with its corollary the abandonment of southern Scotland, signalled the change in policy. There were to be no more conquests: the Empire, in Hadrian's view, was already quite big enough.

Domitian raised one new legion, but also lost one in his Dacian war. Trajan raised two, bringing the total to thirty. Hadrian lost one in the final messianic Jewish revolt of Simon-bar-Kochba (132–5), and another drops out of the army list around this time, though no one knows exactly how or when. But if this map's total of twenty-eight is the same as the last, the distribution is significantly different: there are four fewer legions on the Rhine and four more on the Danube – a result of the forward policy in Dacia.

In the eastern half of the map, the change to note is the Kushan expansion into India. This resulted in the creation of a formidable empire corresponding to modern Pakistan, but still including the old Yuezhi territories in Bactria, Transoxiana, and the Tarim. The most famous of the Kushan sovereigns is Kanishka, a convert to Buddhism: his dates are uncertain but fall within the period 120–60.

1. The first Emperor to have been born outside Italy, Trajan came from a Roman colonial family resident in Spain.

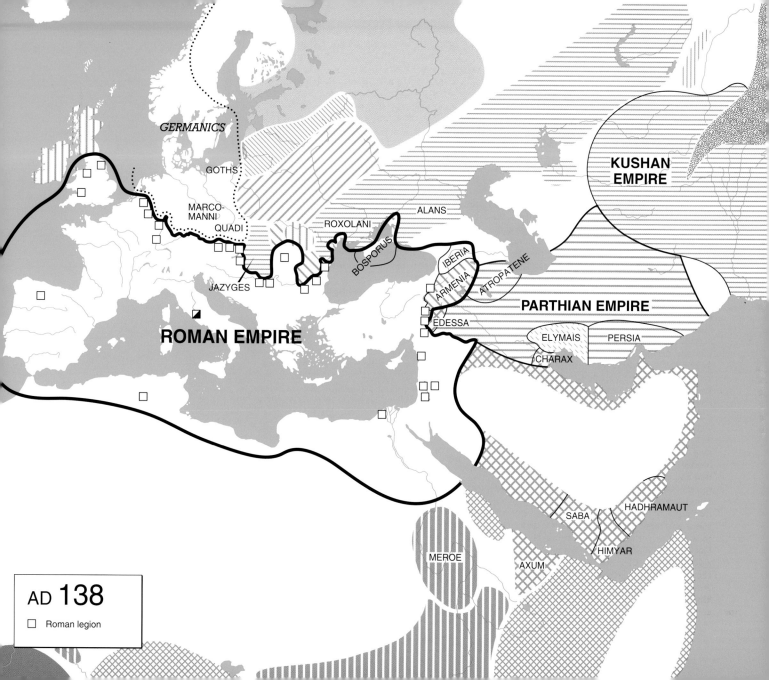

GERMANICS

GOTHS

MARCO-
MANNI
QUADI

ROXOLANI

ALANS

JAZYGES

BOSPORUS

IBERIA

ARMENIA

ATROPATENE

KUSHAN
EMPIRE

ROMAN EMPIRE

EDESSA

PARTHIAN EMPIRE

ELYMAIS

PERSIA

CHARAX

HADHRAMAUT

SABA

HIMYAR

MEROE

AXUM

AD 138

☐ Roman legion

The defensive policy to which Hadrian returned continued in operation throughout the second century AD, a period generally considered the golden age of the Roman Empire. It was certainly one during which the Pax Romana was less troubled by enemies within and without than it had been before, or was to be after. The succession passed smoothly from Hadrian to Antoninus Pius (138–61) to Marcus Aurelius (161–80), each chosen by his predecessor for proven efficiency and probity. Marcus then spoilt the sequence by bequeathing the purple to his foolish son Commodus, whose assassination provoked a civil war similar to that at Nero's death. The British, Danubian and eastern armies each proclaimed their candidates; not surprisingly it was the choice of the biggest battalions, the Danubian commander Septimius Severus, whose cause prevailed. He ruled from 193 to 211; the Empire then passed through an increasingly alarming series of his relatives, the last of whom was assassinated in 235.

Maintaining the Hadrianic frontier was not a very taxing business: Marcus Aurelius fought a war with the Marcomanni, which had its tense moments (167–70), but in general the Roman army had the situation well in hand. Particularly helpful was the decline of the Parthian empire, which fought two wars with Rome during these years and lost both of them (162–6 and 197–9). As a result the Romans were able to annex the northern third of Mesopotamia.[1]

Two developments clouded the end of this period. One was the overthrow of the Parthian monarchy – and its subordinate sub-kingdoms – by the Persian king Ardashir (c. 225). The Sasanid dynasty Ardashir founded revived the pride and energies of the Iranian people and he and his successors made no secret of the fact that they intended to use this new-found sense of purpose to re-create the glories – and frontiers – of the Achaemenids. However, Ardashir was at a strategic disadvantage vis-à-vis the Romans because the Armenian kings, being of Parthian blood, naturally allied themselves with the Romans against a man they saw as a usurper. Perhaps because of this the first Sasanid attempt on Roman Mesopotamia failed to win any ground. The new kingdom did much better in the east where it put an end to the Kushan Empire and took over most of its territories this side of the Indus. Bahrain, on the southern side of the Persian gulf, was also brought under Sasanid control.

The other area where the situation was changing to Rome's disadvantage was the lower Danube region. Starting in the late second century the Goths had begun to move south-east from the Baltic littoral toward the Black Sea steppe. By the beginning of the third century they were in possession of the lands between the lower Danube and the Dnieper, and were pressing the Roxolani back towards the Don. Not far behind the Goths were the Vandals, who settled the province of Silesia around this time, and from there expanded south, across the Carpathians, displacing the Jazyges from the upper Theiss. These new 'East German' nations were confident, aggressive and growing rapidly, making them potentially much more threatening enemies than the Sarmatian tribes that the Romans had been dealing with before.

By 230 the legion total had risen to thirty-three. Marcus had raised two for his war against the Marcomanni and they remained on the upper Danube at its end. Septimius Severus raised three for his Parthian war and left two in the new province of (northern) Mesopotamia. The third he kept near Rome as a reminder to the Praetorians to behave.

---

1. This area included the Arab Kingdom of Edessa, a Parthian client state with a history going back to the late second century BC. The Romans let it be for a while, then incorporated it in their new province of (Upper) Mesopotamia (213).

Another advance was Antoninus Pius' reoccupation of lowland Scotland, marked by the construction of a new wall at the level of the Clyde (143). This was only manned for ten years, and Hadrian's wall remained the effective frontier thereafter. Later emperors, most notably Septimius Severus, campaigned north of it, and may have entertained other ideas. After all, Britain was an island, and if you could get to the end of it the military problems it posed would be greatly eased. But the logistics were impossible: Scotland was too thinly inhabited to support any sort of garrison, and a forward policy could never be sustained for more than a few years.

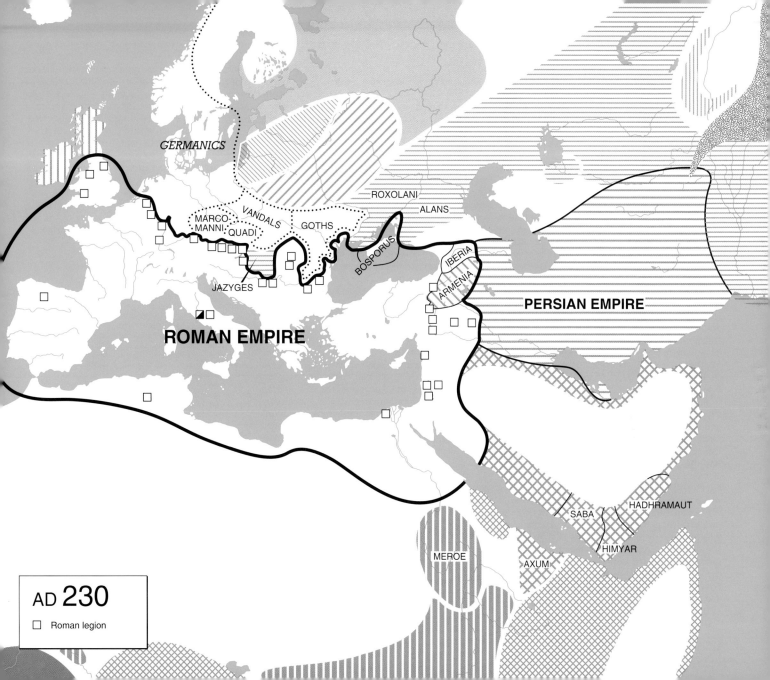

GERMANICS

ROXOLANI

ALANS

VANDALS

MARCO-
MANNI     QUADI     GOTHS

JAZYGES

BOSPORUS

IBERIA

ARMENIA

**PERSIAN EMPIRE**

**ROMAN EMPIRE**

MEROE

AXUM

SABA     HADHRAMAUT

HIMYAR

AD **230**

☐  Roman legion

The Roman Empire's top jobs were the preserve of the Senatorial aristocracy. Ability mattered – only those who had proved their competence in a defined series of civil and military appointments could expect a significant posting – but family was what got you on to the ladder in the first place. This meant that when new emperors were needed the choice was restricted to men from Rome's upper crust. At least that was the way things were until 235 when the Rhine legions followed their murder of the final Severan by the proclamation of Maximin, a Thracian soldier of obscure birth and exclusively military experience. To this the Senators could not agree, and, after an eyeball-to-eyeball confrontation they managed to face the soldiers down. The subsequent run of emperors – Decius, Gallus, Valerian and Gallienus – were all generals and gentlemen. Their many misfortunes finally destroyed the prestige of the Augustan system, leaving military rule as the only alternative.

Before the army could take over it had to go through the fire itself. Its basic structures had barely changed in 300 years, a situation that contrasted ominously with the advances in cavalry equipment and tactics made by the Iranians, and communicated by them to the Goths. The consequence was a catastrophic set of defeats beginning in 251 when the Goths invaded the Balkans and overwhelmed an army commanded by Decius, the first emperor ever to be killed by barbarians. Five years later, the Rhine frontier collapsed and Gaul was overrun by the Franks and Alemanni (new confederations formed by the merger of smaller, less formidable tribes). By this time the Goths were not only reaching deep into the Balkans, some of the more venturesome elements among them had taken to the sea and were busy torching the coastal towns of Anatolia. Still worse was to come on the eastern front, where the Persians had broken through and put Antioch to the sack (252). In 260 Emperor Valerian attempted to stop the rot, only to be captured by Shah Sapor and paraded in his train. At this nadir of Imperial fortune, Valerian's son Gallienus held the centre of the Empire; Britain, Gaul and Spain recognized Postumus, an Emperor created by the Rhine army, and the East a third, Macrianus. Gallienus disposed of the latter and deputed the East to the Sheikh of Palmyra, Odenathus, who, using his own troops, drove back the Persian forces. The Gothic invasion of 268 was broken by Gallienus himself. But then the Palmyrenes seceded, taking most of the eastern provinces with them. Things seemed as bad as ever.

In fact the army was on the mend. The peasantry of Illyria provided it with the tough recruits it needed, and officers risen from the ranks gave it vigorous leadership. The next stage saw these new men becoming emperors. The reign of Aurelian (270–75) proved a turning point. By overthrowing the Gallic and Palmyrene sub-empires he restored the outline of the Empire (bar Dacia and the Rhine-Danube angle, which were formally abandoned[1]). Others in the Illyrian sequence (Claudius II, Probus, Aurelian, Carus, Diocletian and Maximian) re-established barbarian respect for Roman arms. The most important of them is Diocletian (284–305), who translated the helter-skelter reforms and extemporizations of the crisis years into a new system of government, the Tetrarchy ('rule of four').

Diocletian saw that it was no longer possible for one man to run the empire. The troops, who got extra money every time an Emperor was proclaimed, were used to setting up a new one at the drop of a hat: the only way to stop them was to have an Emperor already in charge. So, a year after his accession, Diocletian made a co-emperor, Maximian, to whom he delegated the West and, in 293, he appointed two junior emperors ('Caesars' as opposed to 'Augusti') who undertook the more pressing military tasks. Caesar Constantius fought on the Rhine and, in 296, re-conquered Britain (in revolt since 287); Caesar Galerius was employed first on the Danube then, after 297, against Persia. The triumphant conclusion of the Persian war gave Rome her most favourable Mesopotamian frontier to date.

Diocletian also reformed the administration and the army. The number of provinces was doubled (from under fifty to more than a hundred) to create taxation units of standard size. The army was split into two separate forces, a garrison army committed to the forward defence of the frontiers, and a field force that could be used offensively or, in the event of a barbarian breakthrough, deployed to deal with the threat. Each of the frontier provinces was given a pair of legions, but these were of much smaller size than the legions of old – around 1,000 men as against 5,000 – the 50 per cent increase in the number of individual legions (from thirty-three to fifty) actually represented a 60 per cent fall in manpower. The difference was only partly made up by the tetrarch's field armies (headquarters at Trier (Constantius), Milan (Maximian), Nicomedia (Diocletian) and Antioch (Galerius)), which were unlikely to have averaged more than 15,000 apiece. The fact that the defence budget had risen considerably – and there is little doubt that it had – is to be explained by the much higher proportion of cavalry in the auxiliaries. As the Roman army had finally recognized, the nature of war had changed: cavalry units were now as important as legions.

1. Dacia was occupied by a Gothic tribe, the Gepids, who soon acquired an identity of their own. At the same time the main body of Goths divided into Ostrogoths (East Goths) and Visigoths (West). The Ostrogoths expanded eastward as far as the Don, eliminating or absorbing the Roxolani: they also extinguished the Greek settlements on the estuaries of the Dniester and Dnieper that have been a feature of the map since the sixth century BC. Other changes of note among the barbarians are the division of the Vandals into Asding and Siling branches, the appearance of the Burgundians on the Main and the disappearance of the Bastarnae who took refuge within the Empire. The Saxons started raiding Britain in the 280s.

As a result of the extra information provided by these various comings and goings, we can finally complete the tribal patchwork for the Germanic area. For the caveats on this see p. 119.

In Egypt Diocletian withdrew the frontier to the first cataract: in Transjordan he pulled back to a much shorter and more heavily defended line, something that suggests that the local bedouin – Saraceni in the terminology of the time – were becoming a problem.

In Arabia the Himyarites unified the Yemen (c. 290, though Hadhramawt was only retained till 319).

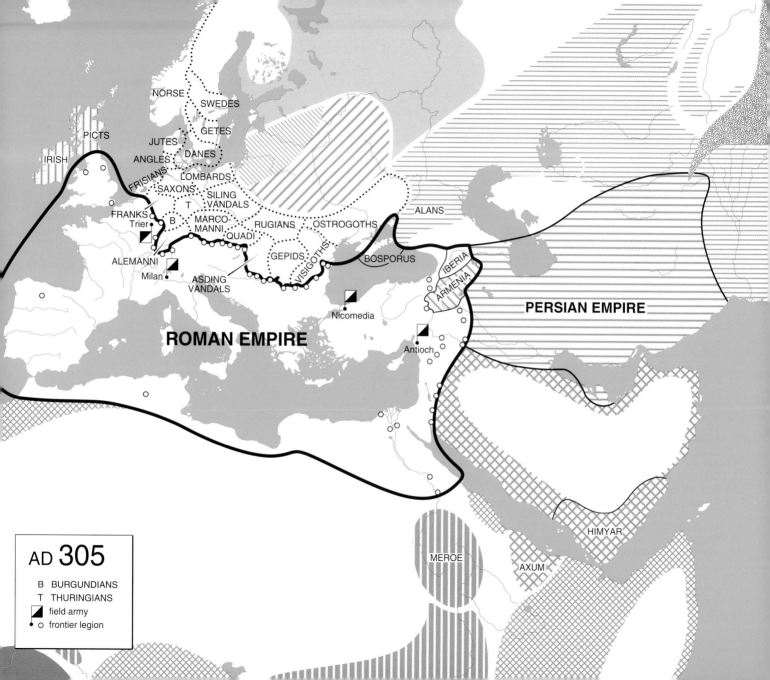

NORSE

SWEDES

GETES

JUTES

PICTS

IRISH

DANES

ANGLES

FRISIANS

LOMBARDS

SAXONS

SILING
VANDALS

T

FRANKS

Trier

B

MARCO-
MANNI

RUGIANS

OSTROGOTHS

ALANS

QUADI

ALEMANNI

GEPIDS

Milan

ASDING
VANDALS

VISIGOTHS

BOSPORUS

IBERIA

ARMENIA

**PERSIAN EMPIRE**

**ROMAN EMPIRE**

Nicomedia

Antioch

MEROE

HIMYAR

AXUM

AD 305

B  BURGUNDIANS
T  THURINGIANS
▰ field army
• ○ frontier legion

In 305 Diocletian and Maximian abdicated and Galerius and Constantius became the new Augusti. At the same time two new Caesars were appointed. This was the way Diocletian had intended the tetrarchical system to work, but it only did so when he was there to turn the crank. The next year, when Constantius died, his troops didn't consult anyone before proclaiming his son Constantine emperor. Later that same year Maxentius, the son of Maximian, seized power in Italy. Diocletian had divided the imperial responsibility; now self-declared Augusti divided the Empire. Once rivalry replaced partnership the threat of civil war was ever present, the more so as Constantine had no intention of remaining content with his initial stake (Britain, Gaul and Spain). In 312 he invaded Italy and, in a battle at the Milvian bridge on the outskirts of Rome, overthrew Maxentius. Eleven years later he took over the East too.

If Constantine the Great earned his epithet on the battlefield, he ensured its perpetuation by his patronage of the Christian Church. This is a topic we will return to in the closing text and map: here we only need to note it as an example of his instinctive feel for the tide of history, for going with the flow rather than, as had been Diocletian's habit, against it. For example, Diocletian had taken great pride in his restoration of the empire's frontier defences, providing garrisons that mimicked the traditional roster of legions and auxiliary cohorts. Constantine saw that this whole concept was obsolete: the field armies were the ones that had saved the empire and they were all that was needed. So he built the field armies up and let the garrison army run down.[1] Another example of his sharper wits is his choice of a seat for the government of the eastern half of the empire. Diocletian seems to have picked Nicomedia simply because that is where he had originally been proclaimed emperor. Constantine saw that Byzantium was a far better site and made it his 'New Rome'. First as Constantinople, then as Istanbul, it was to become one of the world's great cities.

Constantine died in 337, leaving the empire divided between his three surviving sons. After a certain amount of pushing and shoving it was reunited by the middle one, Constantius II, who, finding the responsibility more than he could easily handle, brought in his nephew Julian as Caesar (355). Julian's first task was to restore order in Gaul where the Franks and Alemanni had been making free with the borderlands. He did a reasonable job, pushing the Alemanni back over the upper Rhine and making a treaty with the Franks which allowed them to settle Belgium on condition that they paid lip-service to Roman authority and assumed responsibility for the defence of the lower reaches of the river. If it attracted little attention at the time this was an arrangement pregnant with meaning for the future. Constantius then ordered Julian to send his best regiments east where trouble was brewing with the Persians. The troops weren't prepared to go, though, somewhat illogically, they were prepared to back Julian in a bid to become sole emperor. Once acclaimed Julian had no choice but to try his luck: fortunately the senior emperor died before the conflict became too serious (361). Julian continued his march eastward with the intention of taking up the quarrel with the Persians.

Beyond the Roman frontiers the major event is the arrival of the Huns. A Turkish people, the Huns had spread westward from their original homeland on the slopes of the Altai, reaching the Jaxartes c. 340 and the Volga c. 350. In the 350s the eastern group, the White Huns, conquered Transoxiana and Bactria, depriving the Persian Empire of these provinces and putting an end to any pretensions the Persians may have had as regards Khwarizm and north India. The western group didn't make a comparable impact at this stage, but they will have established contact with the Alans and Ostrogoths by the 360s. This decade marked the Ostrogoths' high point. Under the leadership of King Ermanarich, they held sway – in legend at least – not only on the Pontic steppe, but also over a long tail of territory reaching back to their point of departure on the Baltic coast. The Bosporan kingdom, for centuries a sleepy Roman protectorate, had disappeared into the maw of this Ostrogothic empire in 336.

In the silent north, changes that have been in the making for centuries are now reaching completion. The most important is the expansion of the Slavs at the expense of the Balts and Finns, a migration that has created the heartland of the future Russian state. Another is the movement of the Finns into their present-day homeland, putting the squeeze on the Lapps. The Lapps were to hold on to their identity, but not their language, so if this atlas was to go on for much longer they would end up getting shaded as Finns. An isolated group that did better as regards language, and has been specially resurrected for this map, is to be found at its right-hand border. What the political status of the Brahui people was at this time is unknown – there is no connected history of the Indian subcontinent to turn to – but as they are still there today they must have been there in the fourth century, and they deserve a moment in the spotlight for (a) surviving; and (b) providing us with confirmation of the link between Elamite and Dravidian.[2]

In the south the Kingdom of Meroe collapsed following a devastating raid by the Axumites (c. 350).

---

[1]. Constantine disbanded the Praetorian Guard, which didn't really fit into the new model army. Despite this the number of separate field army commands steadily increased reaching seven (probably) by the date of this map and nine (by the addition of detachments in Britain and Spain) by the end of the century. Every frontier wanted its fire brigade.

[2]. The map also provides an *ave atque vale* for the Irish and Picts, who first make their mark with a combined raid on Roman Britain in 367.

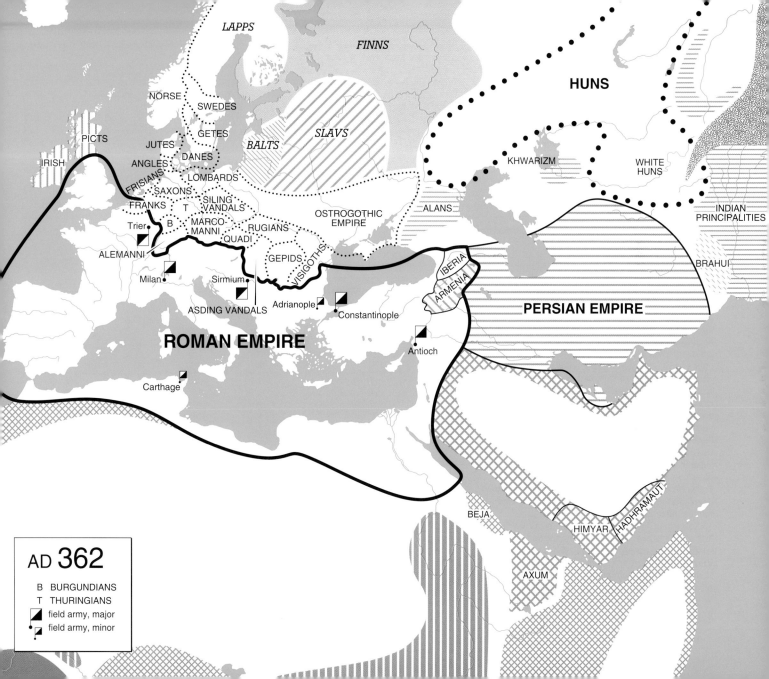

LAPPS
FINNS
HUNS
NORSE
SWEDES
GETES
JUTES
BALTS
SLAVS
DANES
ANGLES
KHWARIZM
WHITE
HUNS
FRISIANS
LOMBARDS
SAXONS
INDIAN
PRINCIPALITIES
FRANKS
SILING
VANDALS
ALANS
T
OSTROGOTHIC
EMPIRE
Trier
MARCO-
MANNI
RUGIANS
B
BRAHUI
QUADI
ALEMANNI
PERSIAN EMPIRE
GEPIDS
VISIGOTHS
Milan
IBERIA
Sirmium
ARMENIA
ASDING VANDALS
Adrianople
Constantinople
Antioch
ROMAN EMPIRE
Carthage
BEJA
HADHRAMAUT
HIMYAR
AXUM

AD 362

B   BURGUNDIANS
T   THURINGIANS
◥   field army, major
◣   field army, minor

It is nearly 800 years since we last looked at our area's population and, as might be expected, numbers have gone up considerably in the interim. The total in 415 BC was around 40 million: now it is about 65 million, a rise of 60 per cent. Europe is the star performer, notching up an above average increase: Asia and North Africa have under-performed by a balancing amount. More significant than this continental arithmetic, however, is the political distribution. The Roman Empire contains well over half the area's population – 39 million out of 65 million – a higher proportion than any state before or since.[1]

How did the Romans do it? There is nothing particularly special about their method of government: it was a variant of the usual king–council–assembly system, in which the king had been replaced by a pair of annually elected consuls. But the Romans did have an unusual attitude towards citizenship. In most Mediterranean communities this was easy to lose and difficult to get: departing colonists, for example, automatically lost the citizenship of the parent community, becoming exclusively citizens of the colony; conversely, resident aliens almost never gained citizenship no matter how long the period of their residence. Roman practice was the opposite of this. Colonists retained their Roman citizenship and were regarded as fully functional members of the Roman state. Loyal allies had citizenship conferred on them *en masse*. More extraordinarily, freed slaves automatically became citizens, even being entitled, if resident in Rome, to the same hand-outs as their free-born brethren. Because of this liberal attitude, the number of people with a stake in the republic kept pace with the expansion of its boundaries. The process continued under the Empire, culminating in AD 212 when the Emperor Caracalla, Septimius Severus' son, made all free men Roman citizens.

This expansion of the citizen body meant that Rome always had the military manpower to meet its commitments. By the time of Augustus there were 4 million Roman citizens, which, if we assume that a million of them were males of military age, means that a 15 per cent call-up would be sufficient to sustain the army's twenty-six legions. Of course, by this time the army was no longer the representa-tive cross-section of the community it had been in the days when Rome's power was still in the making. The yeoman farmer who had taken his shield and spear down from the wall and seen off Pyrrhus and Hannibal could hardly be expected to do duty in far-off countries and fight in campaigns lasting years. His place had been taken by professional soldiers recruited from those who were too poor to have shields and spears, let alone farms. Marius made the change-over at the end of the second century BC, providing the arms and promising that farms would follow in due course, when the time came for discharge.

The Marian reform created a division of interest between the citizens who were soldiers and the citizens who were not. This was apparent even in the Empire's early days when theoretically the only important distinction was between Roman and non-Roman.[2] As citizenship became the norm the polarization between serving soldiers and the rest became more obvious. Equally obvious was the relative importance of the two groups to the Emperors. 'Pay the soldiers and f*** the rest' are said to have been Septimius Severus' last words to Caracalla. The only trouble was that there was no longer enough money to pay the soldiers the sums they were demanding.

1. The peak percentage was reached in the second century AD when the Roman Empire possibly had as much as 66 per cent of the area's population (46 out of 70 million). Subsequently numbers started to decline, with the Empire suffering disproportionate loss. The reasons for the downturn are obscure: it could have been disease-driven – there was an outbreak of plague in 167–170 that may have marked the beginning of a new cycle of epidemics, much as the Black Death of 1346–50 did in medieval Europe. The remarkable thing about the slide was the length of time it lasted: it wasn't till the seventh century that the population graph finally bottomed out.

The drop in population clearly added to the problems experienced by the later Roman Empire: defence had to be supported from a smaller economic base, while untilled lands were an added attraction for footloose barbarians. But the empire had such a huge numerical advantage over its adversaries that demographic contraction can hardly have been a major factor in its fall.

2. The turbulence of the legions under the early Empire is not quite so reprehensible as it seems at first sight. The legionaries were, after all, Roman citizens, entitled to a vote in the assembly. The fact that they were stuck out on the frontier didn't mean that they shouldn't have a say in how they were ruled and by whom. But that said, their behaviour quickly degenerated into organized blackmail: the custom was for each emperor to make a cash payment on his proclamation, so the more emperors there were the better. The culmination of this practice was a famous auction of the empire in 193 in which the Praetorians solicited competitive bids from two rival Senators.

Population in
AD 362

250,000
125,000

areas averaging 10 or
more persons per km²
left unshaded

The Romans never developed a proper banking system; the government simply kept its surplus money in a drawer and hoped that, over all, good years would cover bad. If outgoings exceeded the cash coming in – around 37,500 talents per annum in the mid-second century – there were only two possible courses of action. One was to soak the rich by accusing them of treason and confiscating and selling their estates. The other was to debase the silver coins used to pay the military (three-quarters of the government's outgoings). In the first 150 years of the Empire's existence, the coinage was only debased once, by Nero, and relatively mildly, by 16 per cent. After AD 150 the story was very different: the silver content fell by a third in the remaining years of the second century, by another third in the opening twenty-five years of the next century, and to near enough zero in the 250s as a desperate exchequer tried to persuade the soldiers to accept silver-washed coins as the genuine article. Inevitably, prices inflated in line with the fall in silver content: the soldiers' repeated demands for more pay had ended up making their pay all but worthless.

Diocletian went about restoring order in his usual bull-headed way, publishing a list of maximum prices for all goods and services and threatening dire penalties for anyone caught exceeding the official charges. The only effect was to destroy the last vestiges of the money economy. It was left to Constantine to get the show back on the road by creating a new gold-based currency. This quickly gained public acceptance because:

(1) Constantine (and his successors) kept the gold content steady; and

(2) everyone could see this was so because you can't debase gold coins without altering their colour.

The gold came from the myriad temple treasures of the old religions, no longer sacrosanct now that Constantine, and an increasing proportion of his subjects, had seen the light.

Constantine also tidied up the empire's metropolitan arrangements. He saved money in Rome by disbanding the Praetorian Guard, and by transferring 80,000 of the city's 200,000 wheat rations to Constantinople. This will have meant the end of wheat shipments from Egypt to Rome, reinforcing the trend towards distinct, economically self-sufficient Western and Eastern Empires.[1]

How did the sum of these two economies compare with the single economy of earlier days? Probably not too well. We know that land was going out of cultivation, which means that the agricultural base – and the population dependent on it – was in decline. It seems that commerce was too. The number of shipwrecks that date to the period AD 150–300 is only half that for the two equivalent earlier periods (150 BC–AD 1 and AD 1–150). Though the figures may be unduly influenced by the collapse of Italian wine exports to Gaul, something that happened in the course of the second century AD as the Gallic vineyards reached maturity, there is little doubt about the trend. The basic trouble with the ancient economy was the ease with which demand could be satisfied locally. There was an unstoppable secular shift to self-sufficiency both on the macro-economic scale (as with the wine trade) and on the micro-economic level (as exemplified by the tendency of the rich to retire to their estates and eat, drink and wear what their estates produced). The social values of the Mediterranean world were in retreat.

The literate world has not grown significantly since the last time it was outlined, in AD 14. The Germans have developed an alphabet of their own, the runic 'futhark', but found so little use for it that they cannot be classed as more than protoliterate: runes, like the later Celtic ogham, seem to have been valued as much for their magical power as for any information they might carry. Within the literate area, however, there have been important changes, most of them secondary to the success of Christianity. Demand for vernacular bibles meant the creation of new alphabets for Armenian and Georgian: both used the Greek script as a model. The same can be said of the 'Coptic' script developed for the Egyptian version of the scriptures: this quickly became the civil standard too and as a result, both hieroglyphic and demotic passed out of use in the course of the third century.[2] The Axumites, who already had a consonantal alphabet of South Arabian type when they were converted, used the occasion to improve it by the addition of vowels. The most important development in this part of the world, however, was the appearance of the Arabic script, based on an earlier, Aramaic-derived type used by the Nabataeans.

1. Other changes in the urban roster worth noting are the decline of Alexandria and the dwindling of Athens and Rhodes down to levels too low to justify a place on the map. Jerusalem has been replaced by Caesarea, and, outside the Empire, Seleucia by Ctesiphon. The success story is Carthage, which was refounded by Augustus and soon recovered its old position as the metropolis of Africa (in the Roman sense, meaning present-day Tunisia).

As regards internationally traded commodities, the change to note is the falling off in the traffic in Arabian resins as the pagan temples, heavy users of incense, went into decline.

2. Hieroglyphic and demotic lingered on at the Temple of Isis at the first cataract, where the Beja still came to worship the old gods: the last hieroglyphic inscription there is dated 394, the last demotic 452. Meroitic disappeared with the collapse of the Kingdom.

SILKS

AMBER

LEAD
TIN

Milan

WINE

TIN
COPPER
SILVER

OIL

**ROME**

**CARTHAGE**

WHEAT
OIL

WHEAT

**CONSTANTINOPLE**
Salonika

WINE
OIL

Smyrna
Ephesus

FISH

COPPER

**ANTIOCH**

silk road

TIN

Ctesiphon

SPICES

Tyre
Caesarea

**ALEXANDRIA**

WHEAT
LINEN
PAPYRUS

SPICES

GOLD

spice route

RESINS

IVORY
EBONY

Towns and trade routes in
AD **362**

towns, estimated populations

■   125,000
◉   60,000
●   30,000
•   15,000

Jesus of Nazareth was probably born a year or two before Herod the Great died – the date favoured by most scholars is 6 BC.[1] Nothing is known of his adult life until the fifteenth year of Tiberius' reign (AD 27/8) when he travelled to the Jordan to be baptized by John the Baptist. After this, he began to preach his gospel on the shores of the Sea of Galilee, where he built up a following among the local fishermen. Meanwhile, John the Baptist's criticism of Herod Antipas, particularly of his marriage, which was irregular under Jewish law, led to his imprisonment and execution. Jesus doesn't seem to have had any trouble with Antipas, but when he decided to go to Jerusalem for Passover, he left the jurisdiction of the king and entered the area of direct Roman rule. The Romans were notoriously jumpy about Jewish dissidents: Jesus had only been in the city two days when he was arrested, found guilty of preaching sedition, and crucified by order of Pontius Pilate, Prefect of Judaea. The whole story from baptism to crucifixion was probably over in six months.

It was, of course, only the first chapter. The core of the Christian community was kept in being by the apostles under the leadership of St Peter, while the gospel Jesus had preached to the Jews was taken to the gentiles by St Paul. St Paul's energy transformed what could have been no more than a minor Jewish sect into a potential world religion, and, as far as the Roman Empire is concerned, this potential was soon realized. The Christian message was one that people wanted to hear: it softened some of the many cruelties of the Roman system; it encouraged respect for the individual, no matter how insignificant and, above all, it gave purpose and comfort to lives that were short and harsh. As a product, it was clearly superior to the mix of smoke, spells and incantations offered by the pagan temples. But what made victory absolutely certain was Christianity's organization. Pagan religion was essentially local: with the possible exception of the brain-dead Imperial cult, the question of central regulation never arose. The Christian church, on the other hand, was an ordered and disciplined body from the start: it soon commanded an administrative network that rivalled that of the state. In fact it was a near-enough exact copy of the empire's civil administration, with a bishop in every community, reporting to a senior bishop (a metropolitan, or, as we would say, an archbishop) in the provincial capital.

How did the state react to its new rival? Up to the third century it pretended not to notice. The exception, Nero's persecution, was confined to Rome and amounted to little more than an attempt to find scapegoats for the fire that devastated the city in 64. His successors generally turned a blind eye to the Christians' eccentricities: the fact that they wouldn't offer sacrifice to the Emperor's image hardly mattered if no one asked them to. Then, in the 250s, the government suddenly realized just how strong and challenging the new religion had become. The emperors Decius and Valerian committed themselves to cutting Christianity off at the knees and, if the humiliating manner in which they were overthrown brought their policies into disrepute, the renewed assault on the church made by Diocletian and Galerius in 303 was backed by the immense authority they had won as saviours of the Roman world. However, not all the tetrarchs agreed on the wisdom of the persecution: Constantius made it clear that he had no quarrel with the Christians, and his son Constantine actually promoted the church.

Constantine's personal beliefs are hard to fathom: even after the battle of the Milvian Bridge, at which he is said to have ordered his soldiers to place the Christians' chi-rho logo on their shields, he continued to proclaim his devotion to Sol Invictus, the invincible Sun. However, for all practical purposes, he reigned as a Christian monarch. He liberated the eastern church from its time of trial; he transferred much of the wealth of the pagan temples to the new religion, and personally sponsored a vast programme of church building (the original St Peter's in Rome and the Church of the Holy Sepulchre in Jerusalem are examples of his patronage); he even stepped into the murky waters of theological controversy, calling a council of the church at Nicaea in 325 in an effort to get the bishops to agree on a definitive statement of their faith. On his deathbed he accepted baptism, leaving it for others to argue whether this was his last public act, or his first private one.

Now officially established, even cosseted, the Church still had its problems. One, as already remarked, was theological: disagreements about the nature of the Trinity, often of a hair-splitting nature that seem totally meaningless today, tore Christian communities apart, causing riots, even bloodshed. Another was hierarchical: was the ultimate authority collegiate, i.e. exercised by the senior bishops in council, or was the church to keep to the imperial model and have a supreme pontiff? The Bishops of Rome – the popes of the future – had no doubt as to the answer. Rome might have lost its capital status in the secular scheme of things but its congregation had been founded by St Peter himself, the rock on whom Jesus had said he would build his church. Its bishop had to be the final arbiter on all matters of faith. This claim was generally accepted in the west and in the diocese of Salonika, but the eastern bishops weren't so sure. All the senior ones expected to have a say in how the church was run, and the top two, the bishops of Antioch and Alexandria, regarded themselves as effectively the equals of Rome: they recognized Rome's seniority, but not its authority. Another still undecided question was the position of the Emperor. Constantine trod gently, but Constantius II made it clear that his was to be the casting vote, even in matters of faith. When Liberius, Bishop of Rome at the date of this map, opposed one of his rulings, the Emperor slapped him down hard, forcing him to toe the imperial line and subsequently to share his office with a more co-operative colleague, Felix II. Constantinian patronage was not without its downside.

Nonetheless, despite searing disputes and frequent anathemas, the work of the church went ahead. Each generation, more of the inhabitants of the Empire were converted and a religion that had been a minority choice when Constantine took power (guesses are of the order of 15 per cent in the east and 5 per cent in the west) gradually became the faith of the majority. The pull exerted by the old superstitions weakened with each decade: the temple precincts emptied as the churches filled. It is true that at the date of this map – inappropriately for our thesis – the Empire had officially reverted to paganism under the last of the Constantinians, Julian the Apostate, but Julian's attempt to puff up the dying fires of the ancient cults had no lasting success. After his short reign (360–63) the Empire

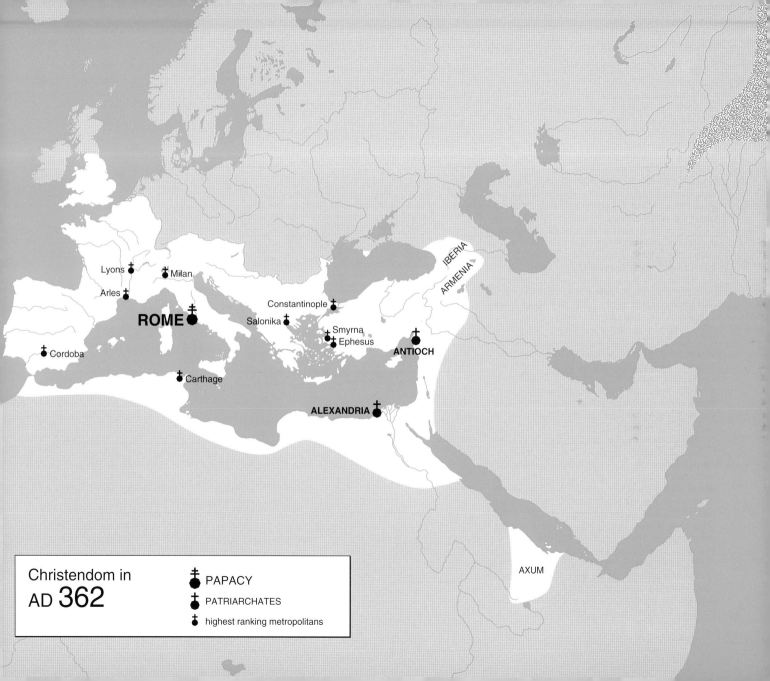

Lyons

Milan

Arles

ROME

Cordoba

Carthage

Salonika

Constantinople

Smyrna
Ephesus

ANTIOCH

ALEXANDRIA

IBERIA

ARMENIA

AXUM

Christendom in
AD 362

✟ PAPACY

✟ PATRIARCHATES

✟ highest ranking metropolitans

immediately became Christian again, this time for good.[2]

This brings us to the boundary between classical and medieval worlds. The distinction between the two is genuine, not just a matter of chopping history up into convenient lengths for pedagogues and publishers, and that the changeover occurred during the last phase of the Roman Empire, when there was a paradigm shift in social forms, attitudes and beliefs, is generally accepted. But if no one doubts the validity of the division, the question remains as to where we draw the line, especially when we take into account the fact that the process itself took generations. Many historians favour a position within Constantine's reign, taking an event such as the battle of the Milvian bridge (312), the foundation of Constantinople (326) or its official dedication (330), or the Emperor's deathbed conversion (337), all landmarks in the creation of Christendom. Others look to the next century, to the sack of Rome by the Goths (410), or the deposition of the last western Roman Emperor, the aptly named Romulus Augustulus, by his German army commander Odoacer (476). Only then was the fate of the Roman order finally sealed. But there is a lot to be said for the intervening period, for the era between the early fourth century remodelling of the Empire by Constantine and the fifth century collapse of the West. This is not just a matter of arithmetical compromise, but of taking the two trends – the rising star of Christendom and the slow decline of the pagan world – and looking for the cross-over point. On this analysis the obvious contender is 362, the mid-point of Julian's reign. In retrospect it is easy enough to see that the cults Julian attempted to rejuvenate were dead already, but at the time, when the temples of old Rome were still as much a part of its life as its new churches, who can have been so sure of the outcome? The pagan establishment must have seemed very strong: classical learning still dominated the education of the rich and powerful, and if the legionary was now as likely to be a Christian as not, the influx of barbarian auxiliaries diluted the gain. We know now that the future belonged to the counts, the bishops and the barbarians, not the senators, the old priesthood and the traditional supporters of the Roman state, but to contemporary eyes, for one last moment, all will have seemed to stand equally tall. Few will have realized that the centre could not hold.

1. The calculation underlying the Christian era's AD 1 was made in AD 531 by the Roman abbot Dionysius Exiguus. Previous to this the Church had used an 'era of Martyrs' based on the accession date of Diocletian (the Coptic Church still does).

2. The map is an attempt to illustrate an ecclesiastical hierarchy that was in reality still evolving. There were no problems about the top of the pyramid: the exceptional status of the bishops of Rome, Alexandria and Antioch had been formally recognized at Nicaea, where they and they alone had received the ennobling title of Patriarch. Equally, there was no problem about the pyramid's base, the metropolitans and the run-of-the-mill bishoprics under them (not shown). The question that was still unanswered was whether the highest-ranking metropolitans constituted an administrative level between the Roman patriarchate and the ordinary metropolitans. An equivalent rank existed in the Roman bureaucracy as reorganized by Diocletian, but the Roman pontiffs never took to the idea. Circumstances might force them to recognize the right of Carthage and Salonika to speak for the African and Macedonian churches but they never allowed Cordoba, Arles and Lyons similar status as regards Spain and southern and northern Gaul, nor Milan to speak for northern Italy. Further east the problem was eventually solved – to Rome's disadvantage – by the Council of Chalcedon's recognition of Constantinople and Jerusalem as Patriarchates (451). The end result was that Rome was able to deal directly with its West European metropolitans, but had to accept intermediaries as regards Africa and the East. The more disciplined nature of Western Christendom has its roots in this distinction.

Another point to note on this map is the adoption of Christianity by the Kingdoms of Armenia (314), Iberia and Axum (both in the period 325–50).

# Appendices

The first Roman provinces were prizes of the Punic wars, Sicily (1) and Sardinia (2) of the First, Near and Far Spain (3 and 4) of the Second, and Africa (5) of the Third. Eastward expansion began with Macedonia (6), taken over in the same year that Carthage fell, followed shortly after by the Kingdom of Pergamum, which became the province of Asia (7). By 100 BC the addition of a slice of Transalpine Gaul, Gallia Narbonnensis (8), and a stretch of south Anatolian coast somewhat misleadingly termed Cilicia (9) meant that Rome was in direct control of much of the Mediterranean littoral.[1]

The last years of the Republic brought important new additions to this provincial roster. Cyrene (10) and Bithynia (12) were bequeathed by their rulers, Syria (13) was conquered by Pompey (who also added Pontus to Bithynia), and the rest of Gaul (14) and Numidia (15) by Caesar. Nearer home, Cisalpine Gaul (11) provided a solution to the complex administrative situation that had developed in the Po Valley: subsequently this area was so successfully Romanized that it could be annexed to Italy after a mere forty year life (82–42 BC). Its abolition brought the provincial total back from fifteen to fourteen.

Augustus almost doubled this figure. Some of the new creations were made by splitting up existing provinces that he thought over-large, most notably Caesar's Gaul into three (Gallia Belgica, Gallia Lugdunensis, and Aquitaine, 14 a–c) and Far Spain into Baetica (4a) and Lusitania (4b). Augustus also separated Achaea (6b) from Macedonia. However, the majority of additions to the list reflect Augustus' programmes of annexation in the East and military advance in Europe: Egypt (16), Galatia (17), Cyprus (18) and Judaea (23) in the former case, and Raetia (19), Noricum (20), the Maritime Alps (21), Moesia (22), Dalmatia (24) and Pannonia (25) in the latter. Subtracting the two provinces he abolished – Numidia (added to Africa) and Cilicia (divided between its neighbours) – the total at his death works out at twenty-six.

By the end of the first century AD the Empire had gained another eleven provinces. Upper and Lower Germany (14d and e) were organized by Tiberius to mark the division between the military zone along the left bank of the Rhine and the civil-ian interior of Gaul. Cappadocia (26), Mauretania-Tangier (27) and Mauretania-Caesarea (28) were created from client kingdoms. Claudius annexed Thrace (31), conquered Britain (29) and organized the province of Lycia and Pamphylia (30), which represents a revival of the Cilician province of Republican times. Nero's contribution was the Cottian Alps (32). Vespasian set up a new Cilicia (13b), this time in the correct geographical location. Domitian divided Moesia into Upper and Lower provinces (22a and b).

The second century began with Trajan's annexation of Dacia (33) and Arabia (34); thereafter it was mostly a matter of more sub-divisions. Trajan split Pannonia into Upper and Lower halves (25a and b), Hadrian split Dacia into three (33a, b and c) but all three parts were put under one governor again by Marcus Aurelius.[2] Subsequently, Epirus (6c) was separated from Achaea, and Corsica (2b) from Sardinia. At some time, another mini-province appeared in the form of the Pennine Alps (35). The century ended with Septimius Severus adding Mesopotamia (36), splitting Phoenicia (13c) off from Syria and dividing Britain into Upper and Lower provinces (29a and b). The sole addition in the early third century, at which point this survey ends, is the revival of Numidia (37).

1. Because the term *provincia* meant 'command', the names of the provinces sometimes referred not to the area under Roman control (as would be the case with province in our sense of the word), but to the area of military responsibility. Thus the provinces of Upper and Lower Germany were military commands responsible for keeping the Germans in check, not part of Germany, just as the (much later) Count of the Saxon Shore was charged with the defence of the east coast of Britain against marauding Saxons, not the administration of Lower Saxony. The Republican province of Cilicia was named for this command function, the Imperial province embraced the territory

2. Hadrian also renamed Judaea 'Syria Palestina', presumably to underline the fact that Rome saw no special role for the area's Jewish population.

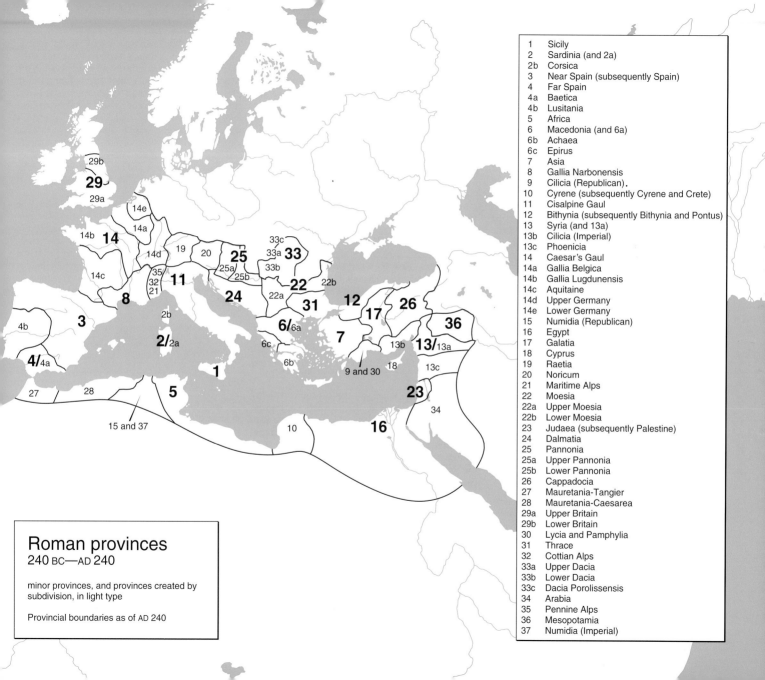

| | |
|---|---|
| 1 | Sicily |
| 2 | Sardinia (and 2a) |
| 2b | Corsica |
| 3 | Near Spain (subsequently Spain) |
| 4 | Far Spain |
| 4a | Baetica |
| 4b | Lusitania |
| 5 | Africa |
| 6 | Macedonia (and 6a) |
| 6b | Achaea |
| 6c | Epirus |
| 7 | Asia |
| 8 | Gallia Narbonensis |
| 9 | Cilicia (Republican). |
| 10 | Cyrene (subsequently Cyrene and Crete) |
| 11 | Cisalpine Gaul |
| 12 | Bithynia (subsequently Bithynia and Pontus) |
| 13 | Syria (and 13a) |
| 13b | Cilicia (Imperial) |
| 13c | Phoenicia |
| 14 | Caesar's Gaul |
| 14a | Gallia Belgica |
| 14b | Gallia Lugdunensis |
| 14c | Aquitaine |
| 14d | Upper Germany |
| 14e | Lower Germany |
| 15 | Numidia (Republican) |
| 16 | Egypt |
| 17 | Galatia |
| 18 | Cyprus |
| 19 | Raetia |
| 20 | Noricum |
| 21 | Maritime Alps |
| 22 | Moesia |
| 22a | Upper Moesia |
| 22b | Lower Moesia |
| 23 | Judaea (subsequently Palestine) |
| 24 | Dalmatia |
| 25 | Pannonia |
| 25a | Upper Pannonia |
| 25b | Lower Pannonia |
| 26 | Cappadocia |
| 27 | Mauretania-Tangier |
| 28 | Mauretania-Caesarea |
| 29a | Upper Britain |
| 29b | Lower Britain |
| 30 | Lycia and Pamphylia |
| 31 | Thrace |
| 32 | Cottian Alps |
| 33a | Upper Dacia |
| 33b | Lower Dacia |
| 33c | Dacia Porolissensis |
| 34 | Arabia |
| 35 | Pennine Alps |
| 36 | Mesopotamia |
| 37 | Numidia (Imperial) |

# Roman provinces
## 240 BC—AD 240

minor provinces, and provinces created by
subdivision, in light type

Provincial boundaries as of AD 240

### Introduction: Fig. 2

Using a modern map to indicate the areas Ptolemy knew about credits him with rather more geographical knowledge than he had. His coastlines are often very approximate – his North African coast, for example, runs in a straight line from east to west – and sometimes plain wrong – Scotland is bent at right angles to England, so that its northern end is pointing at Denmark. In India he gets the Indus and Ganges valleys roughly right, but squares off the subcontinent below them: the area that belongs to south India is given instead to an over-large Sri Lanka. On the other hand he has a surprisingly good grasp of the 'Golden Chersonese', his term for the Malay Peninsula. His two worst topological mistakes are to make an island out of the small bit of Sweden that he is aware of, and a single sea out of the Aral and Caspian. The most significant error, however, is in the grid. Ptolemy had no way of measuring longitude, and consistently overestimated east-west distances. As a result his Eurasian landmass is spread over 180°, where the true width of the part he was concerned with is only 130°. This miscalculation provided the grow-bag for Columbus's 'Big Idea'.

### 40,000 BC

The outline of the ice-cap is based on the line it reached at the time of the last Wurm maximum in 18,000 BC. The map assumes that the penultimate peak of 40,000 BC, which was certainly of similar magnitude, produced an ice-cap of the same general appearance.

The list of sites where Neanderthal remains have been found is independent of the date of the map, and includes all specimens known for the period 100,000–30,000 BC. My thanks to Chris Stringer of the Natural History Museum for running his eye over this. Earlier material is not fully Neanderthal, merely suggestive of Neanderthal origins: the terminal date is supported by radiocarbon determinations of 28,000–29,000 BP, obtained from sites 3, 23 and 31.

Recently, sufficient DNA has been obtained from sites 19 and 31 to make it quite certain that (a) Neanderthal man was a distinct species; and (b) there is no trace of his lineage in modern Europeans.

The BP ('before the present') baseline is AD 1950, the year radiocarbon dating became an accepted tool, but radiocarbon dates, alas, do not translate arithmetically into dates AD or BC; formulae have to be applied to get the 'true' BP date or, to be more exact, the range within which the true date is likely to fall. As the formulae have evolved over the years it's often unclear whether dates quoted for any particular site are fully up to date ('corrected') or not.

Moreover, though the corrections needed for BP dates are reasonably well established for dates later than 12,000 BP (because they have been checked against tree-ring and varve counts), they are shaky for earlier periods. As things stand all one can say is that a reasonable guess at a BC date for the Neanderthal determinations would be 31–32,000 BC.

In this context it is perhaps worth noting that a growing number of Ice Age specialists hold that the long-accepted date of 18,000 BC for the last Wurm maximum is 2,000 years too young.

### 2750 BC

Many accounts contrast the invading (Indo-European) Hittites with the native (Caucasian) Hattites. Etymologically this is nonsense: the two words are simply variant spellings taken from the same root, Hatti, meaning central Anatolia. But though it's not used here, the dichotomy is useful: the Hattites retained their identity throughout the period of Hittite rule, and made significant contributions to the culture of the Hittite Empire.

### Literacy in 2250 BC

The contemporary Mesopotamian and Elamite writing systems are cuneiform and Linear Elamite: the examples chosen are taken from a temple dedication of Gudea, ruler of Lagash, and an inscription of the Elamite King Puzur-Inshushinak, both dating from around 2100 BC.

The proto-Sumerian and proto-Elamite inscriptions belong to a much earlier period than the map – the thirty-first century BC as opposed to the twenty-third – and are included purely for interest. The proto-Sumerian tablet is a straightforward tally: the top left compartment has a drawing of a wheat stalk accompanied by nine circular depressions indicating that this was the number of bushels of wheat received or disbursed. The proto-Elamite tablet employs a similar system, with incised symbols for the categories and blunt depressions for the units, though in this case what is being dispensed is less clear.

The Egyptian hieroglyphs are taken from the kiosk of Sesostris I at Karnak, dated to the late twentieth century BC. Because the appearance of the glyphs remained the same throughout the 3,000-year history of the script, the same example is used on both this map and the next in the literacy sequence. Hieratic, on the other hand, did evolve, as can be seen by comparing this specimen (from a sixth-dynasty archive of c. 2300 BC) with the equivalent on the map for 1275 BC (from a scroll of Ramesses III, of the same period as the map).

The Indus Valley glyphs are copied from seal impressions.

### 1575 BC

The map follows the standard reconstruction of the Aegean situation for this date which has the Greeks in full possession of their peninsula, and the Minoans still holding Crete and the Aegean islands. The Minoans are also thought to have held Miletus on the Anatolian mainland (Linear A inscriptions have been found there), though probably under the suzerainty of Arzawa, the Luvian kingdom that dominated this end of Anatolia.

### Literacy in 670 BC

The example in the true alphabet box is part of a Greek inscription from Thera: that in the consonantal alphabet box is taken from the Hebrew inscription in the Siloam tunnel, Jerusalem; both date to c. 700 BC.

### Towns and trade routes in 670 BC

I've put in an 'amber route' on this map because it's something archaeologists lobby strongly for, but I'm doubtful about its validity. A route implies that individual merchants moved the length of it: my guess is that amber passed from hand to hand, and that there wasn't anyone making journeys from Baltic to Mediterranean and back again. Of course you could say that the track simply represents the route by which amber reached the Mediterranean, but in that case it isn't comparable to the other routes shown on the map and doesn't deserve a place alongside them.

### 515 BC

The Carthaginians, it is worth pointing out, didn't actually occupy the North African coast in the continuous way the new border implies. There were few stations between Tangier and Tunisia, and none in Tripolitania outside its central third. Nonetheless, they did regard themselves as owners of the whole stretch and acted promptly to expel any intruders.

### Population in 415 BC

Where the text talks of a total population of 40 million, the symbols on the map add up to 43.5 million. The difference is due to the 2.75 million outside our area of concern (0.75 in sub-Saharan Africa and 2.0 in the Indian subcontinent).

The population database used throughout the atlas is taken from McEvedy and Jones *Atlas of World Population History* (Penguin Books, Harmondsworth, 1978).

### 218–216 BC

The frontier given to Rome represents its area of authority. The extension along the Mediterranean coast of France to the Ebro in Spain was not directly administered; within it Massilia was technically an ally, not a subordinate. The same is true of Syracuse

within Sicily, though in this case the rest of the island was under a Roman governor.

Syracuse's independence ended with its capture in 211 BC: the Massiliotes retained their theoretical freedom until 47 BC when they had to choose between Pompey and Caesar, and chose wrong.

### AD 14

The distribution of the legions is reliable as regards the province, but not as regards the individual camps, which are only known in about half the cases. For example, no one knows where the three Spanish legions were quartered at this time, though it is generally agreed to have been within the area conquered by Augustus.

Augustus fixed Egypt's southern border, which had been oscillating between the first and second cataracts for centuries, at Hierasykaminos, 70 miles (115 km) upstream from the first.

### AD 79

The legion total could be twenty-eight or twenty-nine, depending on whether you think *5 Alaudae* was still in existence or not. There's no evidence for it after AD 70, but some believe that it survived Vespasian's reordering of the army, and was only finally dismembered in one of the Domitian's or Trajan's Dacian wars.

### AD 138

This time it's *9 Hispana* whose existence is uncertain. It is last documented in the 120s, at Nijmegen. It could have perished shortly after, in some unrecorded incident, or it could have survived long enough to be the legion that Dio Cassius says was lost in Cappadocia in AD 161.

### AD 305

It seems clear that Diocletian planned to give each province on the Rhine, Danube and Eastern fronts a garrison of two legions. The map assumes that,

except in the case of Pontus, he achieved this aim. In fact there is no documentary support for a second legion in either Sequania or Raetia, and the evidence as regards Osrhoene is ambiguous. On the other hand, it is possible that Pontus did have a second legion, maybe garrisoning Colchis.

The positions of most of the German tribes shown on the map are secure, but there are some dodgy items. Norse is a purely geographical term: it is unlikely that the patriotisms of people living in the area extended beyond their own particular fjords. Swedes and Getes are documented as far back as the first and second centuries AD respectively, but Danes and Angles not till the mid sixth century, and the Jutes not till the early eighth. However, the Jutes are reasonably located in Jutland and according to Bede, they were there in the mid fifth century, so they probably were in the fourth century too. Some philologists equate Jute and Gete, in which case the Jutes are simply a branch of the Getes who acquired a separate identity while the intervening Danes developed into a distinct race of islanders. The Saxons, Frisians, Franks and Alemanni pose no problems, but the Burgundians are only certainly located on the Rhine in AD 413: however, as they were raiding Raetia in AD 278, they must have been neighbours of the Alemanni by this date. The Thuringians and Rugians first come up in the fifth century when they formed part of Attila's empire. There is no reason to believe the Thuringians were ever anywhere else than Thuringia, but the Rugians are a problem: the usual view is that they originated somewhere near Rugen, off the Pomeranian coast and slowly drifted south to Moravia. I put them in north of the Carpathians because there is a vacant slot there, but it is perhaps more probable that they were sharing Silesia with the Siling Vandals.

### Population in AD 362

Where the text talks of a total population of 65 million, the symbols on the map add up to 69 million. The difference is due to the 4.25 million outside our area of concern (1.25 in sub-Saharan Africa and 3.0 in the Indian subcontinent).

The initial, bold-face entries are locations. Most of them refer to the two index maps, for example the bold-face entry for Alexandria, **A:d6**, means that it is to be found on index map **A** in square **d6**: and the entry for Argos, **B inset**, means that it is to be found on the small map set inside index map **B**. Entries beginning **RP** refer to the map of Roman Provinces on p.116. The rest are references to the maps in the Atlas itself, for example **map 74** (meaning 74 BC), or **map 2250t** (meaning the map of that date that deals with towns and trade routes). All dates are BC unless AD is specified.

Geographical locations are not given for countries either ancient (Assyria, Persia) or modern (Germany, Iraq), but they are given for regions (Anatolia, Lycia, Tripolitania) and for the mountains, rivers and other physical features mentioned in the text.

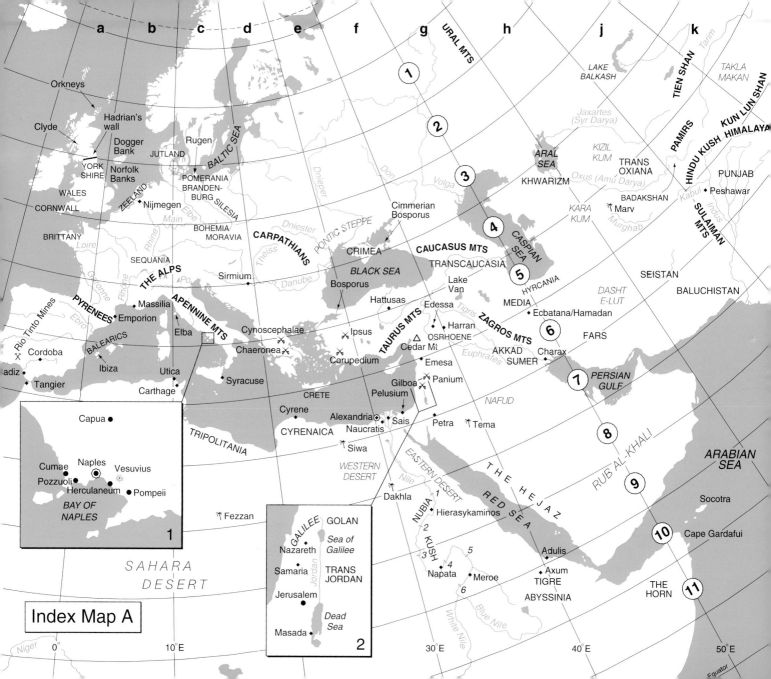

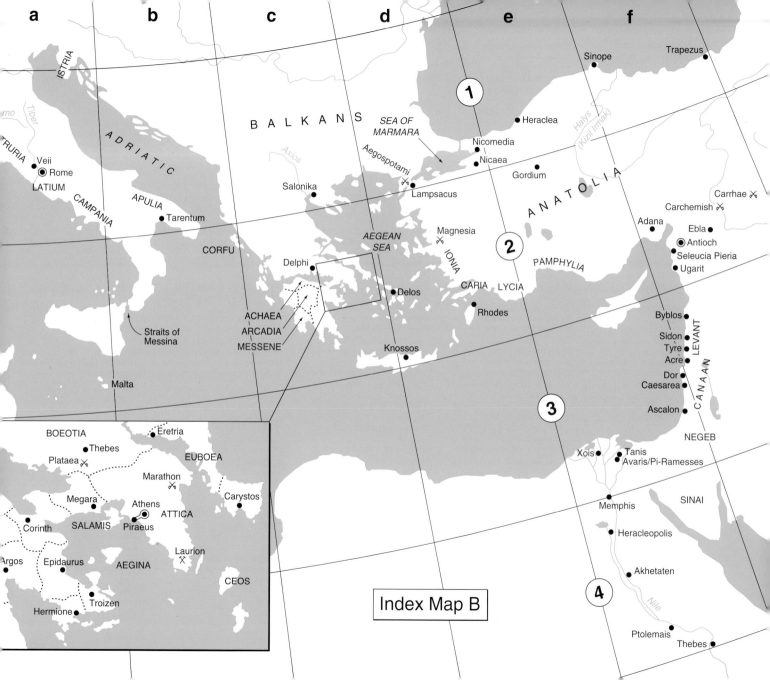

**a**  **b**  **c**  **d**  **e**  **f**

ISTRIA

BALKANS

ADRIATIC

ETRURIA
Veii
Rome
LATIUM
Arno
Tiber

CAMPANIA

APULIA

Tarentum

CORFU

Straits of
Messina

Malta

① 

SEA OF
MARMARA

Aegospotami

Salonika

Axios

Delphi

AEGEAN
SEA

ACHAEA
ARCADIA
MESSENE

Sinope

Trapezus

Heraclea

Nicomedia
Nicaea

Gordium

Lampsacus

Magnesia

② 

Delos

CARIA    LYCIA

Rhodes

Knossos

Halys
(Kizil Irmak)

ANATOLIA

IONIA

PAMPHYLIA

Carrhae

Carchemish

Adana

Ebla
Antioch
Seleucia Pieria
Ugarit

Byblos
Sidon
Tyre
Acre
Dor
Caesarea

Ascalon

③ 

LEVANT

CANAAN

NEGEB

BOEOTIA

Eretria

Thebes

Plataea

EUBOEA

Marathon

Megara

Carystos

Athens
ATTICA
Piraeus

Corinth

SALAMIS

Laurion

Argos

Epidaurus

AEGINA

CEOS

Troizen

Hermione

**Index Map B**

Xois

Tanis
Avaris/Pi-Ramesses

Memphis

SINAI

Heracleopolis

Akhetaten

④ 

Nile

Ptolemais

Thebes